The Canadian Small and Medium-sized Enterprise

Situation and Challenges

The Canadian Small and Medium-sized Enterprise

Situation and Challenges

by

Gérald d'Amboise

The Institute for Research on Public Policy
L'Institut de recherches politiques

Printed in Canada

Legal Deposit First Quarter
Bibliothèque nationale du Québec

Canadian Cataloguing in Publication Data

Amboise, Gérald d'

The Canadian small and medium-sized enterprise

Translation of: La PME canadienne.
Prefatory material in English and French.
Includes bibliographical references.
ISBN 0-88645-121-3

1. Small business—Canada—Management.   2. Small
business—Canada.   I. Institute for Research on
Public Policy.   II. Title.

HD2346.C2D3413 1991   658.02'2'0971   C91-097522-1

Cover: Joanne Ouellet

Camera-ready copy and publication management by
PDS Research Publishing Services Ltd.
P.O. Box 3296
Halifax, Nova Scotia B3J 3H7

Published by
The Institute for Research on Public Policy
P.O. Box 3670-S
Halifax, Nova Scotia B3J 3K6

TABLE OF CONTENTS

LIST OF TABLES

FOREWORD

Never before has small and medium-sized business been praised so much as in the last few years. Not only is its importance to the Canadian economy explicitly recognized, but also every effort is being made to project it further still, into roles that are particularly demanding in terms of its development. Long considered to be on the periphery of social dynamics, small and medium-sized business has gradually become, for some, in the wake of "small is beautiful," a sort of panacea for the numerous problems created by giant organizations and industries.

One may wonder why such an about-face has taken place. The many studies made of the subject have taught us, and have actually demonstrated, that small and medium-sized firms have played a specific role in the socio-economic structure and cannot easily be replaced by other production units. Without going into details concerning the main research done on this type of business, certain important conclusions are worth recalling.

On the economic level, in fact, we have been witness to a real revolution in Canada over the last 10 years; from 1978 to the present day the number of enterprises has risen from 600,000 to 900,000, an increase of 50 per cent. Between 1978 and 1987, 93 per cent of the net number of private sector jobs were created in this country by enterprises employing fewer than 100 people; more than three-quarters of these jobs, moreover, are to be found in firms that didn't even exist before 1978.

On the social level, small business has a stabilizing effect on major disturbances such as economic crises, market reversals, factory closings, the exhaustion of certain natural resources and so on. However, the most important socio-economic influence of small business is still felt through its regional, and especially its local, presence. Because of its origins, its adaptive capacities, its great flexibility and its size, this type of firm is the ideal instrument for regional development. It is able to use the know-how and the resources of its milieu, develop them, energize them and above all integrate them into the already existing infra-structure.

The moderating role played by small and medium-sized business in the major issues of the day has not always been very well understood. For instance, for any given investment in the area of research and development, it is about 20 times more innovative than the large enterprise. It makes use of technology which, while up-to-date, calls for a larger number of workers, re-quires more modest investments, is more energy-efficient and causes less pollution and, above all, allows the enterprise to main-tain a better control and a greater technological self-sufficiency.

The more human dimension of the small business favours the development of each person's capacities, stimulates creativity and the entrepreneurial spirit and constitutes at the same time fertile ground for the creation of new enterprises. In a more and more global market, this type of firm provides a possible substitute for imports and a launching pad for local inventions. These aspects, along with various others, are presented and developed in Gérald d'Amboise's work. The French edition, published in 1989, was the first of its kind in Canada. It has been revised and updated, so that this edition, in English, can be read and used by a larger number of people interested in the Canadian SME in this country and else-where.

This volume is not meant to replace or complement manuals on the management of small and medium-sized businesses or works of popularization or description. The author clearly shows that these firms are neither miniature versions of large businesses nor improvised units. The approach taken here brings out the particular characteristics of small and medium-sized businesses, their dynamics and, above all, their requirements on the management level. Management must be based on criteria of rationality and logic which in turn lead to the application of good judgment and controlled intuition. From this angle we can see better why this type of firm is so difficult to run.

There was a need for this kind of work for the further development of the discipline; it was only right that its main sponsor be the Research Program on Small and Medium-Sized Businesses of the Institute for Research on Public Policy, and that its author be the Program's first director. This is a long-awaited volume and it will be of great use to the heads of small and medium-sized businesses themselves, who can glean judicious advice on management and strategy from its pages. Specialists and interested parties from government will have at their disposal here a body of knowledge which will allow them to establish a support policy and programs of aid for the development of such businesses. Since their management has become a discipline in its own right, researchers, professors and students in the area will thus have access to a well-elaborated report on the state of the situation, along with paths to explore for many years to come. Its references and diverse, exhaustive documentary sources make it an all-purpose work which is easily accessible and of significance for all of Canada.

Rod Dobell
President
The Institute for Research on Public Policy

January 1991

AVANT-PROPOS

On n'a jamais fait autant l'éloge de la PME que depuis quelques années. Non seulement on reconnaît explicitement son importance dans l'économie canadienne, mais on cherche par tous les moyens à la projeter encore plus loin dans des rôles particulièrement exigeants pour son évolution. Longtemps considérée comme marginale dans la dynamique sociale, la PME est graduellement devenue pour plusieurs, dans les sillons du «small is beautiful», une sorte de panacée aux nombreux problèmes créés par le gigantisme organisationnel et industriel.

On peut encore se demander pourquoi un tel revirement de la situation. Les nombreuses études sur le sujet nous ont appris et même démontré que les PME jouaient un rôle précis dans la structure socio-économique et étaient difficilement remplaçables par d'autres unités de production. Sans entrer dans les détails des principales recherches sur les PME, on peut cependant en rappeler les grandes constatations.

Sur le plan économique, en fait, on assiste depuis une dizaine d'années au Canada à une véritable révolution ; de 1978 à aujourd'hui, le nombre d'entreprises est passé de 600 000 à 900 000, ce qui représente une augmentation de 50 pour cent. Entre 1978 et 1987, 93 pour cent du nombre net d'emplois dans le secteur privé ont été créés au pays par des entreprises employant moins de 100 personnes ; plus des trois quarts de ces emplois se retrouvent, par ailleurs, dans des entreprises qui n'existaient même pas avant 1978.

Au niveau social, la PME a un effet stabilisateur sur les grands mouvements comme les crises économiques, les retournements de marché, les fermetures d'usines, l'épuisement de certaines ressources naturelles, etc. Cependant, la dominante socio-économique de la PME, c'est encore sa présence régionale et surtout locale. À cause de ses origines, de sa capacité d'adaptation, de sa grande flexibilité et de sa taille, la PME est l'instrument idéal de développement régional. La PME est en mesure d'utiliser le savoir-faire et les ressources du milieu, les développer, les dynamiser et surtout les intégrer à l'infrastructure existante.

Dans les grandes questions d'actualité, on ne réalise pas toujours très bien le rôle modérateur de la PME. Par exemple, pour un investissement donné en recherche et développement, la PME est environ 20 fois plus innovatrice que la grande entreprise. Elle utilise généralement des technologies qui, tout en étant modernes, font appel à une proportion plus grande de travailleurs, exigent des investissements plus modestes, sont moins énergivores et polluantes et, surtout, permettent à l'entreprise un meilleur contrôle et une plus grande autosuffisance technologique.

La dimension plus humaine de la PME favorise le développement des capacités de chacun, stimule la créativité et l'entrepreneuriat et constitue du même coup un terrain fertile pour la création de nouvelles entreprises. Dans un marché de plus en plus globalisant, la PME est un substitut possible aux importations et une rampe de lancement pour les inventions locales. Ces aspects, ainsi que plusieurs autres, sont présentés et développés dans cet ouvrage de Gérald d'Amboise. La version française de ce livre, publiée en 1989, était la première du genre au Canada. Elle a été révisée et mise à jour, et la présente version anglaise peut maintenant être lue et utilisée par un plus grand nombre de personnes qui s'intéressent aux PME, au Canada et ailleurs.

Ce volume n'est ni un substitut ni un complément aux manuels sur la gestion des PME ou aux ouvrages de vulgarisation ou de description. L'auteur montre clairement que les PME ne sont pas des miniatures des grandes entreprises et encore moins des unités improvisées. L'approche privilégiée ici fait ressortir les caractéristiques particulières des PME, leur dynamique et surtout leurs exigences sur le plan de la gestion. Celle-ci doit reposer sur des critères de rationnalité et de logique qui feront intervenir le bon jugement et l'intuition contrôlée. C'est dans cette perspective que l'on comprendra mieux pourquoi une PME est si difficile à gérer.

Un tel ouvrage s'imposait dans le développement de la discipline ; il était donc normal que le principal commanditaire en soit le Programme de recherche sur la PME de l'Institut de recherches politiques, sous la plume de son premier directeur. Le volume était attendu et sera d'une grande utilité pour les dirigeants de PME eux-mêmes qui pourront y puiser de judicieux conseils de gestion et de stratégie. Les spécialistes et intervenants gouvernementaux disposeront ici d'un corpus de connaissances leur permettant d'établir une politique de soutien et des programmes d'aide au développement des PME. La gestion de la PME étant devenue une discipline en soi, les chercheurs, professeurs et étudiants du domaine auront ainsi accès à un état de la situation bien élaboré et à des pistes à explorer pour plusieurs années à venir. Les références et les sources documentaires diversifiées et exhaustives en font un ouvrage d'utilisation générale, d'accès facile et de portée pancanadienne.

Rod Dobell
Président
L'Institut de recherches politiques

Janvier 1991

SUMMARY

Today the role of small and medium-sized businesses is recognized everywhere. These firms make an important economic contribution to Canada. They increase the chances of success for all kinds of individual and collective initiatives. Finally, they ensure the development and maintenance of an economic and social fabric which promotes positive change in all walks of life.

This work introduces the many facets of the Canadian small and medium-sized business. Many parts of it are based on syntheses of empirical research carried out among heads of small businesses in Canada. The author's inspiration also comes from his personal experiences as a researcher and while he was associated with the activities of a number of small businesses; this makes his comments on their situation and the challenges they have to face even more concrete and pertinent.

In the first chapter, the author asks the usual question: what is a small or medium-sized business? He clarifies the criteria used to define this entity in many countries. He offers a practical definition in a Canadian context. After presenting the general context of their operations in Canada, the second chapter offers a quantity of statistical data concerning the importance of their role in our economy. Some niches that are appropriate for small and medium-sized businesses are also pointed out. The third chapter deals with the central figure at the heart of small and medium-sized businesses. From the many published studies of the heads of such firms, both specific and general profiles emerge.

Next comes a discussion of the necessary distinctions to be made between the terms entrepreneur and manager. The major advantages and problems peculiar to small and medium-sized businesses in Canada are given detailed analysis in Chapter 4. Some requirements for success are examined in this chapter, taking into account both the particular difficulties that these businesses often face and the advantages that they nonetheless usually enjoy.

The objective of the last chapter is to sensitize the reader concerning what is being done about getting to know these businesses better—and about making them better known. The author gives us a glimpse of various aspects in the area of research on the subject that have been emphasized up to now. He brings out certain needs which should be met, and recalls the contribution made by several organizations that have been dedicated to promoting the interests of Canadian small businesses for a number of years, whether in the area of research or training, or actually representing them.

This book is for all those who are interested in small and medium-sized business. Students and teachers will find information that is useful to their understanding of the business milieu. Specialists in the area of development will be able to use the book as an instrument for reflection and inspiration. In reading it, heads of firms will discover an opportunity for broadening their managerial approach.

Each chapter ends with practical proposals. Some are likely to lead to more advanced reflection on the subject at hand; others, to concrete action. Anyone who would simply like to be initiated into the fascinating world of small and medium-sized business will certainly find an adequate portrait of our enterprises, and will probably also learn to like them.

ABRÉGÉ

Le rôle des petites et moyennes entreprises est maintenant partout reconnu. Les PME fournissent une contribution économique importante au Canada. Elles favorisent la réalisation d'initiatives individuelles et collectives variées. Enfin, elles assurent le développement et le maintien d'un tissu économique et social propice à l'évolution de nos divers milieux de vie.

Cet ouvrage présente la PME canadienne sous de multiples aspects. Plusieurs de ses parties sont basées sur des synthèses de recherches empiriques effectuées auprès de dirigeants de PME au Canada. L'auteur s'inspire également de ses expériences personnelles comme chercheur ou associé aux activités d'un certain nombre de PME afin de rendre plus concrets et pertinents ses commentaires sur la situation des PME canadiennes et les défis qu'elles doivent affronter.

Au premier chapitre, l'auteur pose la question usuelle : qu'est-ce qu'une PME? Il explicite les critères utilisés dans plusieurs pays pour définir cette réalité. Il propose une définition pratique dans un contexte canadien. Après un exposé sur le contexte général des opérations des PME au Canada, le deuxième chapitre présente une quantité de données statistiques relatives à l'importance du rôle des PME dans notre économie. Quelques niches appropriées aux activités des PME y sont également repérées. Le troisième chapitre porte sur l'âme dirigeante au coeur de la PME. Plusieurs études publiées sur les dirigeants et dirigeantes de PME canadiennes permettent d'en dégager des profils généraux et particuliers.

Suit une discussion sur les distinctions qui s'imposent entre les termes entrepreneur et gestionnaire. Les principaux attraits et problèmes particuliers des petites et moyennes entreprises au Canada sont analysés en détail au quatrième chapitre. Certaines exigences de la réussite y sont examinées, en tenant compte à la fois des difficultés particulières que rencontrent souvent ces entreprises et des atouts dont elles bénéficient néanmoins habituellement.

Le dernier chapitre a pour objet de sensibiliser le lecteur à se qui se fait pour mieux connaître et mieux faire connaître les PME. L'auteur y donne un aperçu des aspects du domaine de la recherche sur les PME, déjà privilégiés jusqu'à ce jour. Il met par la suite en évidence certains besoins de recherche qui méritent d'être comblés. Il rappelle en outre la contribution de quelques organismes véritablement voués aux intérêts des PME canadiennes depuis plusieurs années, sur le plan de la recherche, de la formation ou de la représentation proprement dite.

Ce livre s'adresse à tous ceux qui s'intéressent aux PME. Les étudiants et enseignants y trouveront des informations utiles pour comprendre le milieu des entreprises. Les spécialistes en développement pourront en faire un instrument de réflexion et d'inspiration. Les dirigeants d'entreprises découvriront à sa lecture l'occasion d'approfondir davantage leur gestion.

Chaque chapitre se termine par des propositions pratiques. Quelques-unes sont susceptibles de faire progresser la réflexion sur le sujet ; d'autres inciteront principalement à l'action contrète. Celui/celle qui voudra simplement s'initier au monde fascinant des PME y découvrira certainement un portrait adéquat de nos entreprises, et apprendra probablement aussi à les aimer.

ACKNOWLEDGEMENTS

An author never works alone. The idea for his project is usually generated by a number of people, who encourage him to undertake it. Other people are more directly involved, by helping him in various ways to complete it. I would like to thank all those who stimulated my thought process on our firms and led me to the decision to write this book. However, I want to emphasize more particularly some immediate contributions towards *The Canadian Small and Medium-sized Enterprise: Situation and Challenges*.

My family has been of great encouragement to me throughout the process. Lucile, Jacques and Louise have always accepted my all-too-frequent absences. I am grateful to them for their understanding and for their frequent questions on my progress.

A number of chief executives have allowed me to confront my ideas with their practice over the years, and I thank them for having helped me to formulate realistic propositions for the management of small and medium-sized firms in this book.

Andrée-Anne Côté was of tremendous help in the initial stages of the project by researching, examining and summarizing many documents dealing with Canadian SMEs. I am very grateful to her for the rigour with which she carried out this difficult task.

Thanks also to Christine Gardner, who translated the original text into English and also incorporated the many alterations and updates to the statistical content and examples.

Both the French and English versions of this work would never have been initiated without the financial contribution of the Institute for Research on Public Policy. May they play a part in achieving the Institute's objective of enhancing our knowledge of SMEs in Canada.

Finally, my colleague and frequent co-author, Yvon Gasse, has also played an important role in helping realize my ambition to make the Canadian SME better known. I would like to thank him most sincerely, in particular for his suggestions and constant support.

INTRODUCTION

A country is built by the men and women who make up its population. They promote its growth and prosperity by initiating all kinds of activities. Through them, the country is able to play its part on the world chess-board by contributing, competing, influencing and making the most of the stakes available.

These citizens have needs and ambitions. They produce and consume; they set up working and trading structures. From common points of interest and exchange, organizations and enterprises emerge and institutions develop to support them and provide a framework for their activities.

Natural evolution seems to suggest that occupations come first and structures afterwards, not vice versa. We live in a world where organizations, institutions and superstructures abound. Many of them work for their own benefit; their managers have forgotten their *raison d'être*.

Every small business is an exchange mechanism, a real or symbolic place, more or less structured. However, more than being simply an empty shell, it is an everyday place with a soul and an attitude that brings people together for action. The small business I am talking about here is a social and economic entity with a clear *raison d'être* experienced by its members and quickly sensed by its visitors. It is vital for both its environment and the country as a whole. As long as people want to trade and do business together, they will create forms which allow them to do so. Such forms usually start out small; they could be called small businesses or anything else. But whatever their name, whatever their potential, they will always be very different in lots of ways from big organizations.

Canada has a multitude of enterprises. We could all name a long list. We are their customers, their employees, their partners or simply their observers in some way. The street-corner store we try to encourage, the shopping-centre boutiques and the restaurants we use are all likely to be independent establishments; in other words, small businesses. The firms that manufacture our shoes, build our homes or help us move house are probably medium-sized businesses. Many of the organizations with which we do business on a regular basis are small or medium-sized firms. Often they restrict their operations to a local or regional market and are usually managed by people who live in the area, often by members of the same family. Small and medium-sized firms belong to "ordinary people," people like you and me, our neighbours or friends, people we know. In short, they belong to identifiable groups of middle-class people.

According to official statistics, in 1986 there were almost 900,000 enterprises in Canada. More than 99 per cent had a total revenue of less than $20 million. More than 95 per cent employed less than 50 people, and 99 per cent employed less than 500.[1] Whatever criteria we use to define them, the presence of small and medium-sized firms is unquestionably significant. They provided almost 60 per cent of all private-sector jobs in Canada in 1984; their contribution to the GNP generated by enterprises during the same year is estimated at 54 per cent.[2] While this book is not meant to be a statistical handbook, nevertheless I will be devoting some pages to an assessment of the place occupied by small firms. A detailed analysis of the available data will illustrate more clearly their contribution to many different aspects of the Canadian economy.

Some entrepreneurs choose to limit their growth from the outset, while for others the decision to stay small comes later. They illustrate perfectly the old saying "Small is beautiful." Andrée's chocolate store in Montreal has been satisfying its customers' sweet tooth since 1940. The co-owners have deliberately chosen not to open other branches for fear of losing control of their product quality. The firm provides permanent jobs for six people, and a good living for its founders. Flags Unlimited of Thornton in Ontario is a small business in an apparently saturated market. Nevertheless, the entire Burke family is kept busy selling flags. The managers of the Laurier furniture company near Quebec City have recently drawn up their plans for the coming years. They do not expect to increase the firm's size. They employ 150 people, make good profits and simply do not want to grow, preferring to renew their equipment instead. Stephen Sandler's business makes an extraordinary mustard. Sales reached $2.5 million in 1985. This small Toronto-based firm's products can be found on the shelves of most specialty food stores in Canada and sometimes abroad. The firm is a gold mine for its owner, but despite his ambitions, he will probably increase turnover much more slowly now, even though he could still continue to build up profits.

Other enterprises that started out small have already grown to a respectable size. In 1956, Bonnex was a simple craft workshop turning out metalwork. After merging with other firms, this Laval-based business became Artopex and now has a turnover of $60 million in high-quality office furniture. It has been quoted on the stock market for some years now, and its share value had doubled before the Crash of autumn 1987. Shermag is another example of a firm which has grown very quickly; during a 10-year period it went from five to 800 employees and became a leader in Canada in other furniture market sectors. Both these businesses, along with countless others in this country, are prosperous; they are already well on the way to becoming big firms. A few champion businesses have led the way. The names of McCain Foods, Canam Manac, Bombardier, Cascades, Bata Shoes and DoFasco are known throughout the world today. They are no longer small businesses, but they were once.

Some firms stay small, others do not. Some are small because their owners have chosen to stay that way, others do not have the potential to go any further. Some firms are doomed to fail from the start, but others succeed, whether on a smaller or larger scale. Whatever their individual fate, small and medium-sized firms play an essential role in our society. They form an integral part of the various activities which make up our socio-economic tissue and are often the source of much larger complexes.

The people who create or manage small businesses recently acquired greater status in our industrialized societies. World economies are changing, and with them, industrial structures. Modern ambitions focus on possibilities for initiatives and the quality of life at work. These phenomena have favoured the emergence of small production and service units, and small firms have appeared in greater numbers during the last decades. They are often launched in new market segments, they create jobs and allow entrepreneurial people to fulfil their ambitions. A significant difference in attitudes has become clear: now, their presence and the part they play are acknowledged. Their collective contribution is a considerable one, and today it is finally recognized as such.

In Canada, as elsewhere, the spotlight is on small business. Society has confidence in its potential and wants to support it. Governments, plagued by budgetary difficulties, are withdrawing from many sectors of activity by privatizing their operations. Private firms, small and large, are being invited to improve the management of these resources. A multitude of financial and technical support programs exists for small and medium-sized businesses, and more recent legislation has shown some concern for it. The media try to outdo one another in singing the praises of small business. Entrepreneurship is the way forward of the future; incubators are the new formula for providing a head start. The race is on to discover the secrets of the successful small business. We have the small business chronicle, the entrepreneurship file, the company profile, the program "Venture," and so on. We organize Small Business Weeks, Small Business Exhibitions and countless other similar events. All tastes are catered for; small business is fashionable. All this goes hand-in-hand with the currents of permitted initiative, anti-bureaucracy, ideological alternatives, technology at our service, and may even, perhaps, be linked with our new ecological conscience. Today we value what business people do, but above all we value what *small* business people do. They represent resourcefulness, courage, responsibility towards others and, sometimes, financial success.

This new social attitude in favour of small and medium-sized business can be seen throughout Canada, but especially in Quebec. There, a renewed entrepreneurial state of mind has emerged, encouraged and supported by most public and private authorities.

It coincides with the advent of a new self-confidence largely inspired by the success of Expo '67, the hydroelectric projects in Manicouagan and the growth of champion businesses such as La Laurentienne, Cascades, Bombardier, Provigo and others. The Quebec entrepreneur has never before been backed up by such popular approval. He is committed to all kinds of projects. Family businesses have enjoyed a remarkable boom during the last few years. Business networks have been formed and entrepreneurs' associations created to provide information and services; in short, to move forward together. Small business people now take part in the decisions that concern them; politicians consult them and even listen to them on occasion. These leaders necessarily influence everyone else. Quebecers are integrating the economic variable into their cultural stock of knowledge, efficiently and in concrete terms. Perhaps small business allows this to be done while at the same time respecting emerging collective values.

Entrepreneurs are said to be born and not made. A person is entrepreneurial, or he is not; so goes the saying. However, management skills can be acquired through experience and training. Business education in its many forms has made a valuable contribution in Canada in recent years, and is even more generally available today. Introductory management courses themselves form a flourishing industry. Young people are being made aware of the economic facts of life early on in their studies. Administration is widely taught at university level. In particular, research carried out in the field of small business is as rigorous as that done in the other social sciences. It all goes towards preparing people who have the skills to enter the business world. The economic conditions prevailing in the early 1980s, the reduction in the number of public sector jobs and the limited number of jobs offered by big business have encouraged many college and university graduates to create their own jobs or offer their services to small and medium-sized businesses. For example, some graduates in administration can be found at the head of their own firms, which they founded or bought on their own or in partnership. Others have taken over family businesses. The training they received is clearly useful in helping them to run the firm professionally. The small business phenomenon is more than just popular infatuation; it also provides the chance for new, more educated generations to put their knowledge to work.

Small business differs from big business not only in terms of its reduced size, its restricted range of operations and its generally limited resources, but also from the point of view of its culture. Its characteristics include independence, simplicity and adaptability. It is this culture, above all, which this book aims to examine. More formal and technical considerations must clearly be taken into account, but small business culture remains the focal point of interest. The book seeks to explore and explain small business, illustrate its attractions and its problems, and set out its qualities. The reader may learn to love this type of business—if he does not already. Perhaps he will even want to consider the possibilities it offers him personally.

A corpus of Canadian literature and documentation on the subject of small and medium-sized business now exists, and this book is largely inspired by some such publications. Despite growing interest in the field, there are nevertheless very few large-scale works. Among the better-known contributions, only a small number needs to be listed. In *L'entrepreneurship au Québec*, Jean-Marie Toulouse sets out some aspects of the French-Canadian entrepreneurial fact. Rein Peterson had previously situated small business in the Canadian economy in his book *Small Business, Building a Balanced Economy*. In 1981, Russell Knight published *Small Business Management in Canada*. Knight drew case studies from his experience with Canadian small firms and suggested guidelines for their management. Among Pierre-A. Julien's recent publications is *La PME dans un monde en mutation*, which draws together texts dealing with the role of small business in the face of environmental changes. Two specialized journals deserve to be mentioned here for their contribution towards maintaining a high level of thought on the subject. *La Revue de gestion PMO* and the *Journal of Small Business and Entrepreneurship* provide outlets for research papers on the subject of Canadian small business. Since 1986, two provinces have published highly relevant documentation on their small business economy. The governments of Ontario and Quebec intend to update *The State of the Situation* on a regular basis in future.

This book is clearly different from these publications. The owner-manager's real-life experience plays a more important part. More studies on Canadian small businesses are probably taken into account. A large amount of information has been drawn from the two journals mentioned above, as well as from a number of documents provided by authors themselves from their conference contributions, research reports or other publications.

The real reason for this book is my own affection for the people who have rolled up their sleeves and created their own jobs by doing what they like to do. It is a clear acknowledgement on my part of their contribution to our country's socio-economic dynamism. My main aim in this book is to paint a better picture of the Canadian small business owner-manager, his real-life experience and his firm's context and functioning. By sharing a vision of these facts, a vision based on many studies of Canadian businesses and personal experience of some of them, many readers will, I hope, begin to understand the small business phenomenon.

This book is intended for anyone who is interested in any way in Canadian small and medium-sized business. University professors, researchers and business students will find an overview of the state of small business in Canada. Small business creators and managers will find hints to help them guide their firms. Program designers and civil servants will undoubtedly discover points of interest. Socio-economic development specialists will see examples which may influence their actions abroad. I hope that everyone who reads it will acquire the taste to go further, whether by study or action.

The book is divided into five chapters. An attempt to define small and medium-sized business is followed by a chapter which situates it in the Canadian context. The actors are described, and the usual characteristics of small firms are studied in depth. Finally, the work being done to promote small business is examined. The subject of each chapter is dealt with from different perspectives, and each chapter ends with some practical hints.

The first chapter presents a real challenge: defining small business. An exhaustive review of several definitions in use leads to a proposed definition in a Canadian context. The second chapter discusses the environment of small business operations in Canada and the economic role they play. It contains much data on the place of the small firm in the business or economic world, and suggests some sectors which are particularly favourable to SMEs. The small business manager is the subject of the third chapter. General profiles and some specific profiles are presented, and the distinction between the terms "entrepreneur" and "manager" is brought out through comparisons. The fourth chapter provides a reminder of the attractions of small firms and an understanding of the problems of managing them in Canada. In conclusion, some conditions for achieving success are set out. What is being done to get to know small business better, and to spread the word? This is the subject of the last chapter. The efforts being made to promote Canadian small and medium-sized business are illustrated through an inventory of existing studies and organizations. The book ends on an optimistic note for the future of small business, and emphasizes the need for a renewed management style.

NOTES

[1] See Chapter II, the part which deals with the importance of the role of small business in the Canadian economy, for exact sources.

[2] H.I. Macdonald, "Shaping the Industrial Renaissance," *Journal of Small Business Canada*, vol. 1, no. 4, Spring 1984, p. 5. SMEs represented nearly 30 per cent of revenues in 1986 and 61 per cent of employment in 1987. See Appendices C and E.

CHAPTER 1

WHAT IS AN SME?

In spite of recent awareness of the primordial role played by small and medium-sized business, exactly what it is has never been precisely defined. The term "small and medium-sized business," although commonly used, is nevertheless vague, suggesting mainly the idea of a firm which is not large, without being more specific. Clearly, this is not explicit enough. The phenomenon deserves to be described and understood better than that.

How can small business be defined? What criteria are used to recognize it? How have other countries tackled the problem? These questions form the subject of this first excursion into the field of small and medium-sized business, and the answers are brought together into a tentative practical definition of small and medium-sized business, more particularly in a Canadian context.

SOME POSSIBLE CRITERIA FOR RECOGNIZING SMEs

Take the case of a student who decides to create his own summer job: mowing lawns. He buys the necessary equipment and then recruits regular customers. He even asks his friends for help from time to time. During the summer he earns nearly $10,000 from his contracts. He looks after his customers and has to declare his income. Occasionally he even employs people. But is this really a small business?

In the 1950s, a couple went into the restaurant business. Their excellent food and service attracted customers to all their restaurants. Business improved and, as their children joined the firm, the number of restaurants increased. Today, their holding company controls more than $15 million in business. Is this a typical or representative Canadian small business? Or is it more than one entity, made up of several small units?

A parts manufacturing company is still managed by its three founders—two engineers and a chartered accountant. They have exploited a particular expertise and their accurate work has enabled them to penetrate foreign markets. Their first public stock issue took place in 1990; the company is now quoted on the stock market. Its average revenue is $30 million and it employs more than 1,000 people. The owners have even more good ideas for the future. Is their enterprise still a small business?

Or take the case of the following two firms. The first is managed without fuss. It achieves sales of $5 million without really trying. There are no plans. Everything is mixed up, including the roles. But its survival is guaranteed by its many customers. The other, more or less the same size, is managed by the book: a clear structure, job definitions, annual plans, etc. You would think it was a multinational. Which best fits the idea of a small business? Which type of functioning typifies small firms?

These examples provide a glimpse of some of the kinds of firms to be seen in Canada. In many cases, the reality is even more complex. It is very difficult to establish adequate and definitive categories, and therefore the wide range of definitions and the resulting confusion should come as no surprise. The following pages present a review of current conceptual issues and present a glimpse of the problems encountered.

There is no standard or universal definition of small and medium-sized business; rather, there is a wide range of different definitions and limits which are sometimes difficult to reconcile. Some common definitions are based on a description of specific clienteles. In general, they come from various government ministries which have tried to provide guidelines to help administer the various financial and technical support programs aimed at particular groups of firms.

The main definitions given are based on qualitative and quantitative criteria, and should be used in practice to distinguish small, medium and large enterprises.

Qualitative Aspects

The geographical scale of operations, the degree of independence and the type of management are the main qualitative aspects used to help classify enterprises.

A small business usually operates locally or regionally. Its owners and employees generally come from the same community. Its market share is often limited to the needs of nearby customers. Its negotiating power when buying is relatively weak, as is its influence on the conditions of sale of its products and services. However, in certain circumstances it may have more room to manoeuvre and exercise more influence on a limited market than a big firm; this would be the case, for example, of a small rural manufacturing enterprise which is well-established in its area, or a corner tobacconist who opens on Sundays. But many local firms have also expanded into foreign markets. The geographical scope of its activities is not enough to distinguish a small business from a big one.

The second criterion relates to both the type of ownership and, to a certain extent, the decision-making latitude which results from it. The typical small business is independently owned and operated. This requirement excludes government enterprises, subsidiaries of big businesses and franchises which belong to a large group. However, the question of franchises remains a controversial one. When the franchisee controls all the operations, personally assumes all the risks and benefits from all the profits, his firm clearly belongs to the class of small or medium-sized business. In some cases, decision-making independence can be questioned, even in businesses classified as SMEs. The true small business should not, for example, play the role of captive supplier for a larger organization or satellite company for a single contractor. Independence is a characteristic and indispensable feature of the SME.

The type of management is also a useful differentiating factor. Some medium-sized firms and most large enterprises are professionally managed. On the other hand, the typical small business is usually characterized by personal or direct management.

Professional management requires strategic decisions to be made separately from decisions governing everyday operations. The accent is on task specialization: for example, in the organization structure, the people charged with hierarchical authority can be distinguished from those in a staff role. Administrative responsibilities are also divided up according to the firm's operational functions, which are traditionally production, finance, sales, etc. However, the management of a small or medium-sized business rarely respects these divisions to the letter.

A personal type of management is far more typical of small business. One person or a very small group of people make all the decisions concerning both general orientation and everyday operations. These same people usually own the company and control everything it does. Management is personalized; the enterprise is identified with the individuals. The decision-making process, which often follows the sequence: intuition–decision–action, is simple and quick. Although elements of professional management can be found in some small businesses, in Canada there is a marked correspondence between the small firm's status and the existence of direct and personal management.

The small or medium-sized firm is therefore a business that operates in a relatively restricted environment, seeks great independence and favours a simple structure. P.A. Julien adds that it looks for a stable context in spite of changes in its environment and that it favours an elementary information system which makes internal communication easier and exchanges with its relevant environment more efficient.[1]

More Precise Measures

Economic policy designers, researchers, support program administrators and company managers alike do not rely only on qualitative criteria to identify the particular group of enterprises known commonly as SMEs. They also need to use quantitative criteria.

Quantitative criteria are really measurements of size; they are suggested since they are based on accessible existing data. Table 1 sets out the measurements most commonly used.

Table 1
Measurements of Size of an Enterprise

| | Financial Measurements | |
Concrete Measurements	Flux	Situation
• Number of employees	• Total annual sales	• Assets (total, net, fixed)

• Quantities produced:
  - units
  - volume
  - weight
	• Added value
	
	• Salaries
		• Capital stock
		
		• Owners' equity

		• Working capital

Number of employees and total annual sales are the measurements most frequently used. Every firm knows precisely how many people it employs and its annual sales figures at any given time. This information can often be obtained by consulting official and public documents; chief executives themselves rarely hesitate to supply it. However, categorization based on the number of employees can result in overvaluing the size factor, since small firms usually employ more people than larger ones to produce the same quantity of goods or services. There are other reasons why this criterion alone is not sufficient. Increases within the organization in terms of productivity, for example, mean that some "small" firms may be bigger than they seem. The number of employees is not a so-called homogeneous factor either, giving equal weighting to employees with different qualifications, specializations, levels of pay and productivity.

The annual sales figure may seem to be a more neutral measurement than the number of employees, in that it results from various production factors. However, it does not always give a fair idea of a firm's main production activity, and sometimes does not bring out adequately an organization's level of economic activity because of its sensitivity to short-term fluctuations in demand. Also, when comparisons are made over several years, the adjustment for inflation can cause problems. Likewise, as with the number of employees, a selection based on sales figures would not allow fair comparisons to be made between sectors, since such criteria may vary considerably for a typical firm from one industrial sector to another.

Added value seems to be the best solution. It is directly linked to the firm's economic activities and takes into account the level of internal activities as a result of the implementation of all production factors. Unfortunately it often cannot be used, because it requires data which are more difficult to obtain than is the case for the criteria previously discussed, and because it requires complicated calculation. Estimating certain values can also pose problems.

Other measurements such as quantities produced, salaries, assets, capital and even profits have also occasionally been used to determine an enterprise's size.[2] They are, however, limited in their usefulness, as they only allow comparisons to be made within fairly homogeneous sectors of activity, and they underestimate the place of the smallest units where salaries and capital investments are proportionally lower than in larger organizations. Some advantages and disadvantages of a number of quantitative criteria are summarized in Appendix A. Their rate of use is also indicated to help with assessment.

Quantitative criteria are in themselves practical; they are useful for situating each enterprise in relation to others in the same set, although it is left to users of such criteria to determine the upper and lower limits for each category. The criteria as well as the categories chosen seem relatively arbitrary. The choice of a measurement of size is often guided by the ease of access to the required data. Category boundaries are often fixed without being explicitly justified, or they simply correspond to common use. Ideally both qualitative and quantitative criteria should be taken into account when defining small business and identifying small firms.

The same problem arises wherever small business is studied. The following review of the definitions used in certain countries illustrates various ways of considering the question.

DEFINITIONS OF SME IN CERTAIN COUNTRIES

Theoretically, qualitative considerations are used to define SMEs. In practice, however, precise quantitative criteria are generally resorted to. The following pages summarize common practice in certain countries.[3]

United States

There is no universal definition of small business in the U.S.. According to the *Small Business Act* of 1953: "A small business is independently owned and operated, and is not dominant in its field of operation."[4] This act specified limits on the number of employees and the volume of sales for each of the main sectors of economic activity.[5] The Small Business Administration (SBA) at present uses the number of employees to differentiate small and big firms. It also resorts to several sectoral and size criteria when administering its programs.

There is some consensus on the fact that a small business should be independently owned and of limited importance in its field of activity. However, the country's various bodies propose and use widely differing sizes in their definitions.[6] Despite this, a number of authors agree on the upper limit of 500 employees when discussing the general situation of small business.[7]

The exact number of small firms in the U.S. has never been accurately determined. Some calculations set it at 14 million.[8] According to the Small Business Administration database, small firms represented 42 per cent of the non-agricultural workforce in 1982.[9]

England

Efforts have been made in England to define small business. In 1971 the Committee of Inquiry on Small Firms drew up the Bolton Report where the following points were set out:

> Firstly, in economic terms, a small firm is one that has a relatively small share of its market. Secondly, an essential characteristic of a small firm is that it is managed by its owner or part owners in a personalized way, and not through the medium of a formalized management

structure. Thirdly, it is also independent in the sense
that it does not form part of a larger enterprise and that
the owner-managers should be free from outside control
in taking their principal decisions.[10]

Having thus defined small business in qualitative terms, the
committee inevitably faced problems caused by a definition which
was difficult to apply. They finally arrived at the following solution:

> For practical purposes we are obliged to use a "sta-
> tistical definition" [...] for these statistical and descrip-
> tive purposes of our studies, [we] adopted the 200
> employee upper limit for manufacturing and a series
> [... of] definitions in terms of whatever measures
> appeared appropriate for other trades.[11]

Here, as is usually the case in practice, quantitative criteria
are used to complete qualitative requirements.

In 1979, small firms accounted for 96 per cent of England's
87,000 manufacturing firms. They employed 23 per cent of the
manufacturing workforce and were responsible for 19 per cent of
manufacturing production.[12]

Japan

In Japan, a small business is defined as a firm where the number of
employees or capital do not exceed some precise figures. These
indicators are fixed for each major sector. They differ according to
whether the company in question is a manufacturing, wholesale,
retail or service enterprise.

Appendix B sets out the criteria used by a Japanese
government financial establishment in its regular fund-allocation
activities. In official publications many statistics are supplied according to categories based mainly on the number of employees.[13]

In 1981, the number of small firms in Japan was estimated at
6 million. They employed 81 per cent of the total workforce. In the
manufacturing sector, they represented more than half the value
of shipments; they accounted for 62 per cent of sales in the
wholesale trade and 79 per cent in retail trade.[14]

France

There is no formal definition of small and medium-sized business in France. The term "PME" ("petite et moyenne entreprise") traditionally designates industrial, commercial and service enterprises whose capital stock belongs to a small number of people with independent management powers. Agricultural, financial and non-commercial services enterprises are excluded.

PMI ("petites et moyennes industries"), or small and medium-sized industries, form a sub-group within the overall group PME. This designation is limited to firms which manufacture and market production and consumer goods, or which carry out an industrial sub-contracting activity.[15]

In official texts, firms employing less than 500 people are generally considered to be small businesses. Those employing less than 10 people are usually classified as "craft industries." Equally, the term "small business" is reserved for enterprises with a pre-tax turnover of less than 200 million francs (1980).[16] These figures seem to apply to enterprises in general; no specific sizes are suggested for particular industrial sectors, as is the case in other countries. However, the Confédération générale des petites et moyennes entreprises (General Confederation of Small and Medium-Sized Businesses) recognizes that each profession has its own characteristics. Thus, in a particular profession, a medium-sized business will regularly have 100 people on the payroll, while in another it will employ 200-300 people.[17] Turnover is also used to classify French firms.

Small and medium-sized firms play an important role in the French economy. Numbering 700,000, they account for 57 per cent of jobs and 58 per cent of the total enterprise turnover.[18]

Canada

There are several definitions based on a variety of criteria in Canada, but no single definition of small business has yet been agreed upon.

The Small Business Secretariat defines small business as one "which is independently owned and which does not have management structures characteristic of large developed corporations."[19] It reserves the term "small business" for organizations employing less than 100 people in manufacturing sectors and less than 50 people in other sectors; it does not specify the size of medium businesses.[20] In its statistical publications, however, the secretariat refers to small businesses as those having annual sales of less than $2 million and to medium businesses as those having annual sales of between $2 million and $20 million. Firms are also classified according to the number of employees: a small business will have a maximum of 50 employees, and a medium-sized business between 50 and 499.[21] However, it has not been able to supply a list of small and medium-sized businesses meeting both criteria. Elsewhere, the Bureau de la statistique du Québec defines a small manufacturing business as one which employs between 5 and 199 people and whose added value contribution does not exceed a certain figure.[22]

The Canadian Federation of Independent Business limits its definition of small business to "a firm owned and managed by an independent owner and which does not monopolize its field of activity."[23] Each government program aimed at small business has its own set of admission criteria, usually including asset value, sales or number of employees. A relatively recent summary confirms the variety of criteria effectively used by those in charge of the main programs.[24]

In 1986, 870,000 enterprises had a turnover of less than $20 million in Canada. They accounted for 45.5 per cent of total sales and employed more than 60 per cent of the country's total workforce.[25]

It can be seen that many of the definitions examined here result mainly from attempts to classify manufacturing enterprises. Despite the growing importance of the commercial and service sectors, little effort has been made in Canada to define their parameters. Normally these sectors include all economic units which cannot be described as agricultural, mining or manufacturing. No precise definition of a commercial or service sector small business exists.[26] Despite this, it is generally recognized that to achieve the same turnover, this type of business employs fewer people than a manufacturing enterprise.

In most of the countries mentioned above, the main characteristics of small businesses have been defined in qualitative terms. Agreement has generally been reached on this point. Limited activities, concentrated ownership, decision-making independence and direct management are the recognized characteristics of small and medium-sized businesses. However, concrete identification presents difficulties everywhere, and simple quantitative criteria are usually resorted to. The number of employees is the factor most often used to decide if a firm qualifies as a small business. Sales or equity capital are sometimes used. The limits set on the categories vary widely from one country to another and from one body or program to another, even within the same territorial jurisdiction.

A PRACTICAL DEFINITION IN A CANADIAN CONTEXT

As we have seen, small business can be defined in many ways. This comment is clearly of little use to anyone interested in the subject. Standardization of language and agreement on common size criteria are needed. Even a general agreement on what a small business is would lead to more coherence in discussions and policies. The suggestion set out below is not particularly original; it has, however, the merit of taking into account accepted notions and reconciling common practices in Canada. It is proposed that any firm which fulfils all the following conditions could be designated as an SME:

- managers have decision-making independence; subsidiaries and franchises are excluded;
- the firm has an annual sales figure of less than $20 million and employs less than 500 people;
- it does not dominate its economic sector of activities; its turnover is less than that of market leaders.

This definition covers the usual qualitative considerations and the most important quantitative criteria. The size of the workforce and the sales figure represent a firm's dimensions fairly well. They complement each other, and yet are both applicable at the same time. The number of employees serves as a limit in relation to manpower resources, and the sales figure in relation to the overall results. The specific limits of 500 employees and $20 million in annual sales cover a large proportion of enterprises in most Canadian industrial sectors.

This is a general definition of small business; no particular classification method is proposed to differentiate the major sectors. Such details have often remained purely theoretical in the past, and the use of quantitative limits expressed in both number of employees and sales figures should in practice compensate for particular aspects which cannot always be taken into account.

This general definition has the merit of being simple and easily applicable. Applying it to the enterprises described briefly at the beginning of this chapter results in four of the five being considered as small businesses. Only the parts manufacturing company is excluded, as being too big. It has a dimension, resources and skills which distinguish it from many Canadian enterprises. A small business does not suddenly become medium-sized or big. Its characteristics, like its size, change gradually.

The basic data needed to apply this definition are on the whole easily accessible. Official databases contain information on many businesses. Chief executives can also supply data; it is simply a matter of asking for it. Statistical reports supplied in the past by the Department of Regional Industrial Expansion were based on categories determined by the number of employees and sales figures. The same criteria were occasionally used to supply information for the country's business inventory. Statistics Canada would certainly pave the way by producing intersecting tables of firms according to these two criteria.

Such a wide-ranging definition will not satisfy everyone. No definition can do that. Government program designers will still need to determine categories according to their particular support objectives. Researchers will still have to present their findings according to the most significant groupings. May they all find inspiration in the suggestions put forward here, and, above all, may they also always clearly explain the definitions that they decide to use.

NOTES

1 P.A. Julien, "Qu'est-ce qu'une PME?," *Le Devoir*, cahier spécial, 25 October 1984, p. 11.

2 Although there is usually a strong correlation between most of these size indicators, they are not necessarily interchangeable. See T.H. Nguyen and A. Bellehumeur, "A propos de l'interchangeabilité des

mesures de taille d'entreprise," *Revue d'économie industrielle*, no. 33, 3rd quarter 1985, p. 44-57.

3 The term "small business" is used regularly to denote "small and medium-sized businesses" in English texts. Appendix B gives a general view of the main measurements of size in the countries discussed here.

4 *Small Business Act*, Public Law 85-536 U.S. Government Printing Office, Washington D.C., quoted in R. Peterson, *Small Business: Building a Balanced Economy*. Erin, Porcepic Press Ltd., 1977, p. 58.

5 See L. Hertz, *In Search of a Small Business Definition, An Exploration of the Small Business Definitions of the U.S., Israel and the People's Republic of China*, Washington, D.C., University Press of America, 1982, p. 59-77.

6 A.T. Nappi and J. Vora, "Small Business Eligibility: A Definitional Issue," *Journal of Small Business Management*, vol. 18, no. 4, October 1980, p. 22-27.

7 See U.S. Small Business Administration, *The State of Small Business: A Report of the President*, Washington, D.C., United States Government Printing Office, 1983, p. 28, and 1984, p. 7.

8 H.J. Bocker, "Small Business Today - Canada, South Africa and the United States - A Comparison," *Working Paper Series No. 4982*, Waterloo, Wilfrid Laurier University, School of Business and Economics, 1982, p. 4.

9 U.S. Small Business Administration, 1984, *op. cit.*, p. 9.

10 Bolton Report, *Report of the Committee of Inquiry on Small Firms*, London, Her Majesty's Stationery Office, 1971, p. 1.

11 *Ibid.*, p. 2.

12 M. Binks and J. Coyne, *The Birth of Enterprise, an Analytical and Empirical Study of the Growth of Small Firms*, London, The Institute of Economic Affairs, 1983, p. 27-29.

13 See Small and Medium Enterprise Agency, *Small Business in Japan - 1984*, White Paper on Small and Medium Enterprises in Japan, Tokyo, Ministry of International Trade and Industry, 1984, 97 p.

14 National Finance Corporation, *National Finance Corporation, Its Character and Present State*, Tokyo, National Finance Corporation, 1983, p. 2-3.

15 For a description of the importance of this sub-group, see l'Association pour la promotion et le développement industriel (APRODI), *Les PMI en France aujourd'hui*, Paris, Fondation nationale pour l'enseignement de la gestion des entreprises (FNEGE), 1985, 502 p.

16 See P. Joffre, "Le rôle de la taille ne doit pas être surestimé," *Revue française de gestion*, no. 55, January-February, 1986, p. 73.

17 Association pour l'emploi des cadres, *Les guides fonctions de l'emploi des cadres - Le gestionnaire de PME*, Paris, APEC, Dossiers emploi, 1980, p. 28.

18 Secrétariat d'État à la petite et moyenne industrie, *Les PME face à leur avenir*, Paris, Ministère de l'Industrie, 1980, p. 114.

19 Minister of State (Small Business).

20 *Ibid.*

21 Minister of State (Small Business) . . .

22 This amount was set at 6.2 million dollars for 1982. See Bureau de la statistique du Québec, Statistiques des PME manufacturières au Québec, données détaillées 1980-1981-1982, Québec, Gouvernement du Québec, 1984, p. 11.

23 Canadian Federation of Independent Business, *Guide de gestion de la petite entreprise*, 2nd edition, Projet Éducation PME, Chicoutimi, Université du Québec à Chicoutimi, p. 5.

24 T.H. Nguyen and A. Bellehumeur, "Les mesures de taille d'entreprises canadiennes: une étude théorique et empirique," special document no. 83-115, Research Laboratory, Administrative Sciences Faculty, Université Laval, 1983, p. 21-23.

25 See Chapter II in the section entitled "The Canadian SME: Operational Context and Economic Role," where more complete data are set out.

26 As early as 1977, C. Desjardins suggested a grid incorporating the number of employees and the sales figure to help identify the sizes of enterprises in the commercial and service sectors. However, little came of his suggestion. See C. Desjardins, *La PME au Québec - Situation et problèmes*, Québec, Ministère de l'Industrie et du Commerce, 1977, p. 12.

CHAPTER 2

THE CANADIAN SME: OPERATIONAL CONTEXT AND ECONOMIC ROLE

All firms work within some form of milieu. They are faced with a multidimensional environment made up of a set of situations and conditions, together with a variety of other actors. They play a role in their milieu by obtaining resources in exchange for their own goods and services. The real context of a small firm's activities is made up of actors with complex interests, and a number of situations, resources and constraints that have to be taken into account. While dependent operationally on their environment, small firms nevertheless play an essential role within that environment. The following outline of Canadian environmental conditions likely to influence SME activities clarifies some of the factors that could either promote their survival and growth or lead to their disappearance. Small firms have carved out an important place for themselves, as can be seen from their increasing numbers and considerable contribution to Canadian life. Some general principles concerning the orientation of small and medium-sized business will also be set out.

REAL EVERYDAY CONTEXT
A Juridical Entity in its Milieu

Whatever their size, all firms have a legal status in society. The simple fact of being in business confers rights, but also obligations and responsibilities. The form a firm takes gives it an official place in the commercial and legal world.

Many different legal structures are available to anyone wanting to launch a business. The three most popular are sole proprietorship, partnership or corporation. Each brings with it certain consequences for the small or medium-sized business owner-manager. In the first case—sole proprietorship—the owner assumes full responsibility for everything the firm does. Setting up a partnership is more complex. Two or more people agree to pool resources with the aim of running a business, and need to establish rules to govern their relations. This usually results in a partnership agreement in due form. The partners are jointly responsible in all circumstances.[1]

The most common structure adopted by small or medium-sized firms is the limited company or joint stock company. Applications for federal charters are subject to precise procedures, and regular reports on the firm's business activities must be made to the authorities concerned. As the company is a legal entity, distinct from its shareholders, the shareholders' responsibility is, in principle, limited to their capital outlay. If the directors wish, they can claim private company status, as opposed to public company status, for their enterprise. To do this, a clause is inserted in the deed of incorporation limiting the number of shareholders and the possibilities of transferring shares. Firms wanting to go public should avoid such restrictions or abolish the clause when the time comes. Many SMEs are in fact private companies. The owner-manager is responsible for directing his firm and guiding it on a daily basis through the maze of situations and threats facing it. Part of his responsibility is to ensure that all relevant laws and regulations are respected.

General Economic Environment

Between 1981 and 1983, firms suffered the repercussions of a faltering economy. Small business owner-managers still remember those years. Since then, many SMEs have enjoyed a degree of prosperity. However, again economic conditions are less favourable. Free trade with the United States is now a reality. Major structural changes are on the way in the shape of globalization.

All sectors of activity will undoubtedly be affected one way or another by this opening-up of markets.

In the early 1980s, Canada moved from an inflationary economy to deflation and an unforeseen recession. Many SMEs were seriously shaken; some have not yet been able to pick themselves up. Small firms are highly vulnerable to fluctuations in interest rates, and this has often made them early victims of a recession. In Canada, the weakest, or less well-managed, have disappeared. However, many have adapted to the new economic reality by joining forces with other firms, by revising their general management strategies or by changing their financial structures. From a macro-economic point of view a purge was needed: many small firms needed to rekindle their operations.

Afterwards, economic conditions improved. Western economies in general grew for a number of consecutive years. The average growth rate in industrialized countries, as high as 10 per cent during the last decade, lately fell to a more modest level. At 3.7 per cent, Canada led the field in 1987.[2] Economies seem to have returned to less dazzling, and less hazardous growth rates. At the time of this writing, there are reasons to believe that in real terms the Canadian GDP was even negative for 1990.

In Canada, a period of slower growth is on the way, a situation partly caused by the policy of high interest rates that dampens internal demand after causing a strong rise in the dollar exchange rate and a sharp deterioration in the balance of trade. It was hoped that a recession could be avoided by a less restrictive budgetary policy, advance buying to avoid the GST (goods and services tax) in 1991 and a drop in interest rates. Nevertheless, we are now in a recession, felt more strongly in Canada than in the United States. And with high interest rates,

> ". . . the Canadian dollar will continue to be overvalued . . . The really bad news has not to do with the immediate past and present, but with what happens after this recession . . .
>
> The good news is that capital-spending plans that were already in line with weak profits and a lack of inventory excesses mean that this recession won't be nearly as severe as the last one. But persistently high interest rates will lead to continued restraint by consumers, a

cautious investment and inventory stance, and only a meagre recovery in exports."3

Unemployment in Canada is still very high and the American deficit weighs heavily on capital movements and interest rates. In fact, without the Canadian government's continual interventions, interest rates would be higher still. In the whirlwind of easy and profitable speculation, the "paper dealers" went too far and, in spite of a good performance by North American companies, investors were nervous; stock market prices came tumbling down. Investors are still worried, conscious of the fragility of economic infrastructures and aware that economic risks and international policies can strongly influence the situation.

Canadian small business also faces a new challenge in the shape of increasing competition from newer industrialized countries such as Formosa and Korea, with their lower labour costs, state-of-the-art equipment and modern management methods.

The aging population in Western industrialized countries is also beginning to have an effect. The marked changes in the structure of private and public demand for goods and services resulting from this trend will require considerable capabilities of adaptation on the part of our enterprises.

Despite stock market crises, many Canadian small and medium-sized businesses have continued to invest. However, some owner-managers have had to come to terms with changing public financing conditions. In Quebec, for example, unscrupulous businessmen and brokers realized they could get rich quick at the expense of small savers investing in the stock of companies that were not solid or profitable enough. This somewhat painful experience was a lesson for small businessmen and the investing public alike. Small businessmen learned that product quality and operational efficiency above all were the best guarantees of success both for the enterprise itself and the stakeholders involved.

On several occasions over the last few years, Canadian SMEs have been subject to the sudden changes in attitude of American neo-protectionists who, despite strong demand, tried to restrict access to the American market for dynamic Canadian medium-sized firms by applying stricter standards or imposing quotas or special import duties on their products. The Canadian government wanted to clarify the rules of the game; a negotiated agreement was needed. From its point of view, the American government, grappling with huge commercial deficits, needed to show its other trading partners that it was capable of negotiating mutually profitable agreements. If it could not formalize its trading practices with its most loyal partner, how could it hope to inspire confidence in future discussions with other countries' representatives?

The Free Trade Agreement leaves the door ajar for Canadian firms to gain access to the huge, rich American market, but at the same time it also opens up our markets to American companies: an open invitation to competition. The challenge for all Canadian firms is unprecedented—and also very threatening for weaker companies, whatever their size. Arguments for and against free trade abounded: one sector would benefit, another would not, and in yet another, jobs would be threatened.[4] But, in a nutshell, the agreement was to benefit only dynamic and efficient firms. The wider openings would inevitably attract firms from over the border to set up shop in Canada, and Canadian firms with deficient management and shaky activities in those sectors would simply disappear. They could no longer rely on a relatively weak Canadian dollar, as was the case before. As transactions of goods and financial operations become easier, the economies of the two countries will become more uniform. The gap between the two currencies should dwindle bit by bit. Fortunately for many firms, the gradual application of the agreement will bring a temporary respite. Those who really want to succeed must rapidly prepare for the eventual disappearance of still existing barriers.

Knight[5] surveyed a sample of 100 Canadian high-tech entrepreneurs on their current export experiences and their views on free trade. Some of his observations are informative:

> "The area in which most of the participating firms expressed frustration was the whole area of government activity, primarily on the customs and duties side, rather than in terms of government programs. They said that the tariffs and customs duties were a great frustration, particularly in terms of the paperwork and the time involvement required to pursue export markets."

> "Exporting high technology companies who responded to [the] survey stated that they had relatively few problems with their export sales which the Free Trade

Agreement would change significantly. The elimination of tariffs and customs duties on various products over time, as proposed by the Free Trade Agreement, will mean some of the smaller mechanical problems of dealing with the government bureaucracies involved in customs duties may be eliminated.

"One overwhelming concern that these exporters expressed was that they had, in general, underestimated the effort which it would take to penetrate the U.S. market and the time which it would require from top management in the firm, as well as their marketing departments in general. (. . .) they suggested that every company should evaluate its potential markets in Canada and then consider whether or not the real opportunities for them existed in the U.S."

According to surveys conducted by the Canadian Federation of Independent Business, the Canadian small business community strongly and consistently supported the Canada-U.S. Free Trade Agreement. But now:

"The members are taking a hell of a hit.

. . . the anger is not focused on the free trade agreement . . . But competitiveness is the real issue. The high Canadian dollar is the worst impediment to competitiveness. And the growing burden of taxation is falling very heavily on domestic companies."[6]

A world-scale economic and industrial transformation is taking place. Canadian firms will experience hitherto unknown business conditions as a result of the new agreement. The trade liberalization process has already created a shift in the Canadian entrepreneurial climate.

"It has increased the awareness of small-business managers of the potential of adapting niching strategies in the U.S. market. In contrast, the perceptions of U.S. small business managers are quite different. The Canadian market is perceived as merely a small increment of the U.S. market, which is not worth penetrating so long as there is the possibility of additional geographical expansion in the home market."

"Existing Canadian firms have an advantage over new U.S. entrants; the Canadians know the customer and local culture. Therefore, successful Canadian firms have nothing to fear if they are well-managed and continue a niche strategy. Their knowledge of the local market should be superior to that of U.S. corporations. U.S. service firms cannot rush in like U.S. beer manufacturers who would compete at low cost."[7]

Nevertheless, competition is now closing in on Canadian small and medium-sized service firms as well as on those in resources and manufacturing.

Small firms will need to be more competitive on their own territory, and even more so if they venture south of the border. New trading conditions with Mexico and Europe '92 could also set the level of requirements even higher. Some will be assured of markets because of their cost advantages arising generally from conditions other than economies of scale. Many others will succeed because of the quality and unique aspect of their product or service.[8] A few SME owners are already showing the potential of their businesses.

Main Sectors

Small and medium-sized firms exist in various sectors; many are to be found in manufacturing, wholesale and retail and services. However, conditions and skills needed vary from one sector to another.

A manufacturing establishment converts raw materials into products. This often requires a large capital outlay, and manpower is usually proportionally higher than in small firms in other sectors. The inherent risks in manufacturing activities are normally higher than in commerce or services. Firms must constantly face up to new manufacturing technologies and product innovations. Computers and robots are making their appearance in small firms; they could offer new production possibilities.

Small and medium-sized firms dominate in terms of numbers in the Canadian manufacturing sector. However, big firms are responsible for the major part of annual sales figures, and many small businesses benefit from their presence by acting as subsidiaries or sub-contractors. In many cases this places them in a very vulnerable position. The big firms set the rules of the game, while the small ones are subject to the contingencies of economic reality. Clearly, the manufacturing sector offers a considerable challenge to SMEs entering it, although it also offers unique opportunities. Many medium-sized firms operating in one or other of the most technical sectors in Canada have chosen, for their part, to specialize.[9] Others could imitate them. The most promising sectors are transport equipment, forestry products, the petro-chemical industry, oil and gas.[10] A whole range of business opportunities resulting from important investments in these fields is available to SMEs who are prepared to take advantage of them.

The commercial sector includes both wholesale and retail operations. The wholesale merchant plays an intermediary role. He is situated somewhere in the distribution channel between the product manufacturer and the retailer. Storage, packaging and transport are activities well-suited to smaller organizations. The small firm is naturally close to a particular territory and can adjust quickly to its customers' demands. It will never be short of contracts if it ensures that products are shipped better than the suppliers themselves could do it. Speed and efficient service are comparative advantages that a small firm cannot afford to set aside if it wants to meet the challenge.

Small, and even very small firms, occupy an important place in the retail sector, being responsible for more than 90 per cent of regular operations. The field is characterized by the wide variety of products sold and the smaller number of people employed by most firms, many of which have less than 50 employees, and a good proportion of those have less than 10.[11] Many of them are facing markets that are shrinking at an alarming rate because of new consumer habits and fierce competition for survival among small establishments. Also, for standard consumer goods, supermarkets are threatening many small or medium-sized businesses as a result of the variety they can offer. The drop in the birth rate in many parts of the country and the aging population also affect market structures. The consumer is generally "better equipped, better educated and better protected than ever before by all sorts of organizations, television and radio programs, publications and magazines which flood him with all kinds of information."[12] Will the small tradesman be able to satisfy these new customers? He must give better service than his competitors if he wants to attract them and keep them loyal.

The service sector, for its part, groups together a panoply of activities. It is not precisely defined. Belonging to the tertiary sector, it can be distinguished from commerce by the nature of the exchanges taking place. Services rather than tangible products are transacted. The skills offered by firms to their customers generally belong to individuals who hold recognized professional titles, or who have acquired relevant practical experience. The sector includes professional practices which are really small firms: expert-consultancy firms, brokers, assessors, etc. Most of the professions in these categories are governed by strict rules; an office cannot be opened by just anybody. Also included are firms offering repair and maintenance services, secretarial services, various types of advice, and so on. It is usually fairly easy to set up premises from which to operate; much of this type of business can even be done from home, because sometimes a room or a telephone is all that is necessary. In many cases, start-up requires very little investment. All these points explain why there are so many small firms in the service sector. A certain transformation in the economic structure during the last few decades has meant a proliferation of service enterprises of all kinds. In Canada, as elsewhere, this sector has been the most dynamic in recent years. In Canadian SMEs alone, it provided jobs for 1.4 million people in 1987, compared to 0.9 million in 1978, an increase of 55 per cent in the number of small service business jobs.[13] Although competition is strong in many branches of the sector, there is still room for new SMEs. The knowledge industry has no limits; skill and imagination are the ingredients that will produce a multitude of small firms in the future.

Normally, as an economy develops, activities move from the primary sector to secondary and, finally, tertiary activities. In Canada, the dynamism of the tertiary sector has recently replaced growth in the manufacturing sector.[14] New activities will continue to appear mostly in trade and service sectors. It is plausible that

"Enterprises in the next twenty years (will operate) in an economic landscape highly modified by the irruption of new information and telecommunications means, which are increasingly transforming our societies into electronic information societies."[15]

Only the real entrepreneurs will be able to create their niche.

Financial Markets

Access to financing is vital for the small or medium-sized business. This access clearly depends on the existence of sources of funds that can be put at the firm's disposal. In Canada, institutional and private investors, as well as government bodies, play a leading role. They can supply funds in the form of loans with interest and repayment conditions fixed beforehand. They can also invest directly in a company's stock; the stock certificate will normally give entitlement to profits and sometimes a say in management.

Small firms benefit from strong competition between the various financial institutions. The number of chartered banks, for instance, has increased considerably in recent years. From around 10, there are nearly 80 today. Inter-bank competition has led to the introduction of a range of financing modes, expertise and management services aimed specifically at small firms. Chartered banks are the most popular kind of institution among SME owner-managers, accounting for more than 80 per cent of loans.[16] To this can be added the possibilities of personal and commercial loans offered by the Caisses populaires and other credit institutions, trust services, leasing and so on. The Federal Development Bank also contributes in various ways towards financing many of its small business client projects, which numbered more than 5,000 in 1989.[17] Funds are also easier to obtain, thanks to several government guarantee and financial support programs.

However, share capital is less easily available to small and medium-sized firms. Ontario has its Small Business Development Corporations (SBDCs), and Quebec its Quebec Business Investment Companies (QBICs), not to mention the Fonds de solidarité des travailleurs du Québec (FTQ).[18] The SBDCs seem to have been fairly successful and have created a favourable climate for new initiatives. More and more private risk capital companies exist; they are obviously very selective in choosing the projects in which they are prepared to invest. Only a few small firms venture onto the stock exchange floor. Some did so through a special

Quebec government program that absorbed registration fees. Unfortunately, because of abuses of the system, the Department of Finance abolished the program. In many cases, financial support—allocated more wisely—is urgently needed, as are mechanisms to encourage trading in small firm shares if the formula is to gain real impetus and allow these companies to benefit from public financing.

Often, all the small business owner-manager can do is call on his friends and relations to help him shoulder his organization's risks. In many cases they are willing to pour in their savings because they have confidence in him personally. All too often, however, the owner-manager will try to avoid any financial contribution entailing power-sharing.

The Labour Environment

The success of any organization is a result of team effort. Small firm owner-managers rely on the skills, energy and goodwill of their colleagues. They draw most of the human resources they need from the working milieu, with which they should be reasonably familiar.

In many SMEs, the average age of the workforce is over 45. Few among the large numbers of unemployed young people have the necessary preparation and attitude to be efficient in the short-term in a small business context. In many job sectors, women are playing a more important role. Part-time and shared jobs are better suited to the lifestyle sought by some workers. If workers are dreaming of "made-to-measure" jobs, perhaps small business can provide them.[19]

Middle-aged employees want job security, reasonable pay and financial security when they retire.[20] Young people are looking for worthwhile work, career possibilities and a good income. Many employees want to be on management committees; they are sometimes interested in becoming co-owners, sharing risks and profits.[21] Can Canadian small firms satisfy these needs? Can they channel all this energy and ambition?

Unions are rarely present in the SME workforce. Nevertheless, the owner-manager has to deal with a social atmosphere where industrial relations are in crisis. In Quebec, for example, labour legislation has undergone many changes during recent years. New and increasing numbers of standards govern personnel management methods in every possible situation. Collective relations are regulated by law, generating huge and complex collective agreements.[22] Legislation has become extremely complex, and neither side is satisfied. Unions point out certain obstacles to their presence among the SME workforce: owner-managers, worried by government requirements, want the balance of power to be re-established, the development of a small business negotiating model and even a return to individual employer-employee relations.[23]

Some SME owner-managers have learnt to live with a union presence in their firms. A few even credit it with more efficient personnel management. But most are afraid of what would happen if their employees joined a union. Few small business workers see advantages to union membership, and no strong move in that direction is anticipated in the short-term. However, SME owner-managers must constantly remember that they are responsible for the working conditions of their closest colleagues.

The Government

Canada has three levels of government, each with its own areas of jurisdiction and prerogatives, precisely defined in some cases, less complete in others. Clearly, the SME owner-manager benefits from the whole legal and political infrastructure provided by the various government authorities, but he must also pick his way through the advantages and disadvantages of all kinds of laws, programs and rules.

The amount of legislation affecting small firms, the complexity and intransigence of taxation structures, the duplication of information to be provided on all sorts of forms, the multitude of standards applied indiscriminately and the overly-bureaucratic behaviour of some organizations are undoubtedly negatively perceived by most businessmen. According to the Canadian Federation of Independent Businesses, government paperwork and regulations constitute one of the main worries in business today.

Many government bodies, however, offer substantial advantages to small firms. Supply and Services Canada, for example, invites tenders for jobs and supplies. The Government of Quebec keeps a file of suppliers of goods and services called NASIS (National Automated Sourcing Information System) which ensures that small firms get their share of government consultancy and works contracts. The Ontario government has a similar system.

From another point of view, SMEs are in competition with the various governments, sometimes for getting supplies but, more often, for finding qualified personnel. Wages, working conditions, job security and pension plans have all too often tempted good employees to choose a civil service position rather than a job in a small firm. All SMEs, whether in an urban or rural environment, have to face this problem. In an urban context, at least they have a bigger manpower reservoir to draw from, but rural small firms often have to offer conditions beyond their means if they want to recruit and keep good people.[24]

Federal and provincial authorities are beginning to show an interest in small business. In recent years, confidence in their economic and social role has increased, and there is a growing acceptance that the contribution made by entrepreneurs should be recognized and the role of SMEs in Canadian society should be appreciated more fully. Small business now benefits from a favourable public attitude and a multitude of specifically designed support programs offering technical and financial support to SME owner-managers to help them do their job and invest in the property and equipment they need to succeed.[25] In fact, so many programs exist that confusion sometimes arises. But owner-managers should not need more than a basic grasp of what is offered. It is the job of the civil servant advisers to understand the nature of small business needs and direct applications to the right place.

Big Firms

Whatever definition is used, a lot of small and medium-sized firms exist. However, big firms, while fewer in number, are responsible for a much larger proportion of all commercial operations carried out by Canadian businesses. SMEs therefore operate in a socio-economic environment strongly influenced by big firms. Inevitably, they affect the economic and industrial infrastructure of all the country's major cities, and determine the degree of vitality in all mono-industrial regions.

The presence of a big firm leads to a variety of activities in the surrounding milieu. It has to build premises, manufacture parts, maintain equipment, buy supplies, use services or seek professional advice. An organization covering a wide geographical area opens the door to extensive business networks with which dynamic SMEs can familiarize themselves. Big firms generally have considerable resources at their disposal; they have funds, expertise and research laboratories that can support work entrusted to smaller firms. Many Canadian SMEs exist because of nearby sources of contracts; for example, aerospace equipment manufacturing workshops in the Montreal area work almost exclusively as sub-contractors for big firms such as Pratt & Whitney and Canadair.

In other cases, a big firm is just another competitor for SMEs. Its greater means impress potential customers. Its buying power places it in a favourable position in negotiations with suppliers. The working conditions it offers often means that it can lure the best employees. SME owner-managers must be both vigilant and resourceful to survive. The Association of Canadian Manufacturers, the metropolitan Chambers of Commerce and the Conseil du patronat du Québec give priority to the points of view expressed by big firm representatives, and are, in fact, key elements of many political decisions. Until recently, SMEs had no spokesman at all. Today, their voice is heard increasingly through the intermediary of bodies such as the Canadian Federation of Independent Businesses and the Groupement québécois d'entreprises.

Public decision makers have always entrusted the determining roles to big firms, both state and privately owned, as far as exploiting resources, carrying out large projects or administering key economic sectors is concerned. Naturally, this will continue to be the case in the future. The unfortunate effects of the action of some multinational firms are still clear in some countries. The multinationals are often criticized for their bureaucracy and their indifference to the environment. In some cases, the very presence of big firms is now being questioned. The concepts of *corporate entrepreneurship* or *intrapreneurship* are now with us.[26] A few big organizations are interested in experimenting with them. It may be that initiatives like this will create a much more important role for small firms in the Canadian economy during the next few years. Attitudes will probably focus more on entrepreneurship, and more humane firms will gain favour, but small business owner-managers will still have to carve out their place in the sun in a world marked by the power of big firms.

In conclusion, examining the environment means, for a firm, taking a close look at the future to pick out the most significant eventualities. The various aspects of the operational context of SMEs set out previously reveal a dynamic, or even turbulent, general environment. This leads us to expect that there will be lots of room for initiatives by small business owner-managers, and plenty of challenges too. Trends and directions that will continue in the future are already clear in every aspect of this operating framework. Such trends, sometimes called "heavy" trends, will certainly demand reflection and particular effort from the people in charge of the destiny of small and medium-sized firms.

Only rarely will a small firm never have been faced with technological change. Whatever its sector of activity, equipment and working methods have certainly been dramatically affected by recent new technologies. Computer-assisted design and manufacturing are progressing non-stop, office automation and information systems are transforming the workplace and interconnecting communication methods are bringing correspondents closer together all the time. Many small firms will have to change the way they operate. The competitive advantages sought after by small firms now depend on using the latest technology. However, all these new resources impose heavy responsibilities on small business owner-managers. They have to train their staff and prepare the organization to accept the new tools. Will they be able to be selective enough in choosing their technology, and flexible enough in using it?

The social demands on firms have also changed in recent years. They are now expected to be more socially responsible. SMEs certainly do not have the same wide-ranging obligations as big firms in cleaning up the environment, but they do have to do their share. Whatever their size, these days all firms should be able to justify their presence in their milieu. Individual SMEs cause few problems in this respect, generally responding to obvious needs. But owner-managers must show concern for the environment. Will they listen to what the community has to say?

Small and medium-sized firms play an essential role in society by fostering the pursuit of individual initiatives and the satisfaction of many sometimes very specific needs. They contribute enormously to the country's economic activities and provide jobs for countless people. The Canadian socio-economic environment offers small organizations many possibilities, and, consequently, owner-managers often face difficult choices.

The classic entry barriers faced by those coming into a field already occupied by other firms are generally economies of scale, cost advantages or the unique aspects of products produced by the enterprises in place.[27] To succeed, newcomers must count on strategies such as reduction of the basic costs of the product or service, lower prices, superior product quality, concentrating efforts on a little-developed market segment, introducing a commercial innovation or using their existing distribution channels.[28] Owner-managers should be able to assess future operational contexts and judge their capacities before venturing into a new business field. They should set up strategies that take into account their organization's means.

It has long been said that a society's economic and industrial fabric is woven mainly by large organizations. They exploit its most profitable gaps and leave aside the fields and markets that seem to have less to offer. These are the fields and markets that are available to firms with less resources.[29] Often, big firms do not produce a particular product because the market segments involved are of no interest to them. Small firms can usually take advantage of this to become established. Dynamic owner-managers will always keep a close eye on the business environment.

SMEs are known to be vulnerable and subject to the hazards of an environment which is sometimes turbulent. An enterprise that stays where it is and is content with stable activities is less prepared to absorb the shocks generated by events and situations. Despite their relative lack of resources, SMEs are usually well able to adapt and react quickly to new needs and challenges. Owner-managers should be able to use this strength to ensure that their firms hold competitive positions. Freer trade with a vast neighbouring market offers a unique opportunity for many Canadian small firms. Some already have the necessary skills to take advantage of it.

Like all firms, SMEs work in a universe governed by personal interests and competition. However, in the past owner-managers have not always realized that their firms also form part of a network where members' interests are interdependent. Manufacturers look for conscientious suppliers; bankers want their commercial customers to succeed; consumers stay loyal to an efficient convenience store. Interest does not exist only in the usual sense of the word; everyone can benefit from the others' progress. Perhaps small business owner-managers should get to know the range of their immediate network.[30] Perhaps they could increase the advantages it offers and get more out of it.

THE IMPORTANCE OF THE ROLE OF SMEs IN THE CANADIAN ECONOMY

In the preceding pages, we have already seen the growing recognition of the role played by SMEs. This new position can be explained both by better knowledge of the nature and activities of SMEs, and by the lessons drawn from the economic fluctuations of the early 1980s.

A new awareness of the role of SMEs in our economy is a first step towards appreciating their importance. The following pages give an insight into the place occupied by SMEs in the Canadian economy, in the form of a quantitative assessment of their role from several points of view. How many are there? In which sectors do they operate? What proportion of receipts and jobs do they represent in the country as a whole? What are the recent trends in these figures? These are questions that may be asked by anyone interested in his country's economy.

The Number of Firms: The Predominance of SMEs

There are many small and medium-sized firms in Canada. Whatever the definition used, they make up a significant percentage of existing firms.[31] Table 2 shows the number of Canadian firms in 1986 according to size.

In 1986, there were 823,067 firms with a turnover of less than $2 million—i.e., small businesses. A total of 48,414 firms had a turnover between $2 million and $20 million—i.e., medium-sized businesses. Thus, 871,481 firms in all could be considered to be SMEs, if we accept the demarcation of $20-million turnover. Nearly 94 per cent of all Canadian firms were small and 5.5 per cent medium-sized. SMEs therefore made up more than 99.4 per cent of all Canadian firms—a figure that may surprise some people. However, it is a fact confirmed regularly, to within a few hundredths, by various statistics published during the last few years.[32] Moreover, small and medium-sized firms can be found in every sphere of economic activity, where they consistently represent more than 97 per cent of all firms.

Table 2
Total Number and Percentage of Businesses
by Revenue Category
Canada, 1986

Revenue Category (x $1000)	Total Number of Businesses	Percentage of businesses
10 - 99	466,291	53.2
100 - 1,999	356,776	40.7
2,000 - 19,999	48,414	5.5
20,000 +	5,110	0.6
Total	876,591	100.0

Source: Statistics Canada, *Small Business in Canada: A Statistical Profile,* 1984-1986, Cat. 61-231, April 1989, Ottawa.

The 871,481 SMEs that existed in 1986 were divided among economic sectors as shown in Table 3.

The majority of SMEs are to be found in the tertiary sector, mostly in personal or other services. Manufacturing firms account for only 6.8 per cent of the total number. An examination of the primary data gives a better idea of the composition of this particular sector. The proportionally restricted number of very small firms has a strong influence on the percentage shown. However, there are almost as many medium-sized firms as in the wholesale and retail sectors. It should be remembered that the manufacturing sector accounts for the majority of big firms in Canada.

Table 3
Distribution of SMEs by Industry Group
Canada, 1986

Industry Group	Number of SMEs	Percentage SMEs
Services	215,999	24.8
Retail Trade	201,563	23.1
Construction	159,480	18.3
Transportation, Communication, Utilities	85,037	9.8
Wholesale Trade	65,962	7.6
Real Estate, Insurance	61,923	7.1
Manufacturing	59,166	6.8
Forestry	15,855	1.8
Mining	6,496	0.7
Total	871,481	100.0

Source: Statistics Canada, *Small Business in Canada: A Statistical Profile*, 1984-1986, Cat. 61-231, April 1989, Ottawa.

The statistics published on the subject do not show the distribution of small firms by province. However, Appendix D sets out this information based on the number of employee categories for each province. The geographical distribution is shown for 1987. Proportions for businesses with less than 500 employees are shown in Appendix I. The provinces of Ontario (33.2 per cent) and Quebec (24.8 per cent) account for 58 per cent of all businesses with less than 500 employees, and the other provinces follow more or less in order of population.[33]

Business Revenue: The Relative Contribution of SMEs

Because of their numbers in Canada, small firms are responsible for a large part of commercial operations. However, their contribution is proportionally slightly lower than that made by the country's big firms. Table 4 sets out the contribution in 1986 made by each group of firms by revenue.

A total of 16.6 per cent of revenues is generated by firms with less than $2 million annual turnover. Nearly 29 per cent is generated by firms identified as medium-sized. In all, SMEs account for 45.5 per cent of all commercial operations in Canada. For their part, the 5,110 big firms produced $556 billion of business, i.e., more than 54 per cent of all operations in 1986.

Table 4
Total Revenues of Businesses
by Revenue Category
Canada, 1986

Revenue Category (x $1,000)	Revenues (x $1,000)	Percentage of Revenues
10 - 99	18,612,084	1.8
100 - 1,999	151,411,832	14.8
2,000 - 19,999	294,714,816	28.9
20,000 +	556,678,317	54.5
Total	1,021,417,049	100.0

Source: Statistics Canada, *Small Business in Canada: A Statistical Profile,* 1984-1986, Cat. 61-231, April 1989, Ottawa.

As previously indicated, small firms exist in all sectors. Their activities, both considerable and varied, generate 45.5 per cent of total revenue. However, their contribution varies from one sector to another, as may be seen from Table 5.

Clearly, SMEs play an important part in many branches of the tertiary sector, their favourite sector. They are also very active in the construction sector, where they are responsible for 80 per cent of the value of all work done, and in the forestry sector, where they account for 86 per cent of all revenue. Twenty-two forestry firms alone generated more than $20 million in 1986. This sector is undoubtedly ruled by small and medium-sized firms. On the other hand, despite their small number, big mining firms are responsible for more than 80 per cent of the total value of work carried out in mines in Canada. The turnover of the 6,000 or so SMEs in this sector is obviously more modest. The transportation and communications sector also contains some large firms with considerable revenues; small firms, which are nonetheless numerous, account for only 25 per cent of the total. In the manufacturing sector, big firms represent 2.7 per cent of the total number of enterprises, but account for nearly 73 per cent of revenues. In this sector, a large proportion of small firms do not achieve the $2-million turnover mark. The role played by SMEs in manufacturing is undeniably an important one in maintaining a variety of resource conversion activities, but the economic role of big firms is nevertheless vital.

Table 5
Proportion of Revenues Produced by SMEs
by Industry Group
Canada, 1986

Industry Group	Percentage of Revenues Produced by SMEs
Forestry	86.0
Construction	80.3
Real Estate, Insurance	78.2
Services	76.3
Retail Trade	61.8
Wholesale Trade	47.6
Manufacturing	26.5
Transportation, Communication, Utilities	24.9
Mining	18.6

Source: Statistics Canada, *Small Business in Canada: A Statistical Profile*, 1984-1986, Cat. 61-231, April 1989, Ottawa.

Jobs in SMEs: A Substantial Proportion

If the figure of 500 employees is accepted as the dividing line between small and big firms, then we can say that in 1987, 61.7 per cent of all private sector employees in Canada worked in SMEs. Table 6 sets out employment figures for each of the three categories.

Table 6
Number and Percentage of Employees
by Number of Employees Category
Canada, 1987

Number of Employees Category	Number of Employees '000s	Percentage of Employees
<50	3,156.2	37.6
50 - 499	2,023.4	24.1
Total SME	5,179.6	61.7
500 +	3,215.1	38.3
Total	8,394.7	100.0

Source: *Employment Dynamics, by Major Industry Group, Canada and Provinces 1986-1987.* Small Business and Special Surveys, Statistics Canada, June 1989, Ottawa.

Note: It is important to underline that all data concerning employees is based on average labour units and that the following groups have been intentionally excluded from the count: Education, Health and Welfare Services, Religious Organizations and all Government entities.

Appendix E shows that SMEs provide jobs for many people in all industries especially, in order of importance, in services, manufacturing and retail. SMEs also provide more jobs than their bigger counterparts in six economic sectors: farming-fishing-hunting, construction, wholesale trade, retail trade, services, and manufacturing. As may be seen from Table 7, small firms also account for a respectable proportion of the number of jobs in all other sectors.

Table 7
Proportion of Employment Created by SMEs
by Industry Group
Canada, 1987

Industry Group	Percentage of Employment Created by SMEs
Farming, Fishing, Hunting	97.6
Construction	92.3
Wholesale Trade	81.1
Services	76.9
Retail Trade	63.0
Manufacturing	50.1
Finance, Real Estate, Insurance	44.8
Mining	41.0
Transportation, Communication, Utilities	33.4
All Groups	61.7

Source: *Employment Dynamics, By Major Industry Groups, Canada and Provinces 1986-1987.* Small Business and Special Surveys, Statistics Canada, June 1989, Ottawa.

More than 40 per cent of the total SME workforce is employed by SMEs in Ontario, while Quebec SMEs account for 25 per cent. The proportion is clearly less for the other provinces, in the same order as for the number of small firms. The information contained in Appendix D also reveals other facts. In all provinces, small firms employ many more people than big firms. This is perhaps not surprising, given the general percentage in favour of SMEs. However, the proportionate difference is greater in some provinces. In Ontario, for instance, there are 41 per cent more jobs in small firms than in big ones. In Quebec, the difference is more than 90 per cent, while in Saskatchewan, there are 2.2 times as many jobs in SMEs as in big firms, and in Prince Edward Island, five times as many. SMEs have created a greater proportion of jobs in these three provinces than anywhere else. Saskatchewan, Prince Edward Island and the Northwest Territories seem proportionally much more dependent on small business activities than the other provinces. The nature of their principal resources explains this situation to a large extent.

Development of the Situation of SMEs

The number of SMEs increased in Canada by more than 99,180 during the short period between 1984 and 1986, an increase of 12.8 per cent. The service sector has continued to be the largest contributor. The total revenue of SMEs jumped by 53.2 per cent, or nearly $161 billion, in 1986, as shown in Appendix F. The largest revenue increases occurred in the wholesale trade and construction sectors. Table 8 sets out the development of the situation of SMEs in each industry group.

Table 8
Evolution of SME Figures
Variations in Numbers and Revenues
by Industry Group
Canada, from 1984 to 1986

Industry Group	Variation (%)	
	Number	Revenues
Services	15.7	34.6
Retail Trade	8.5	49.2
Construction	13.7	62.8
Transportation, Communication, Utilities	9.4	46.5
Wholesale Trade	12.7	67.2
Real Estate, Insurance	21.8	33.6
Manufacturing	9.6	58.0
Forestry	27.5	46.5
Mining	3.1	30.3
All Groups	12.8	53.2

Source: Statistics Canada, *Small Business in Canada: A Statistical Profile, 1984-1986*, Cat. 61-231, April 1989, Ottawa.

While many new small firms have appeared in a few sectors, five sectors in particular have provided especially fertile ground during the period in question. The forestry sector seems, proportionally, to be the main generator of SMEs. Total revenues for SMEs increased most in the wholesale and construction sectors. Numbers increased much less in the mining sector than elsewhere, and revenues lagged behind too. However, on average, it seems possible that small and medium-sized mining firms are bringing in more revenue than before.

In every group, the positive variation in revenue has been much greater than in the number of businesses. It is therefore easy to conclude that the small business sector is becoming more dynamic. The average revenue per SME has effectively increased.

A more detailed analysis of each group would be needed to reach a better understanding of the various factors that have influenced the situation. Factors such as increased productivity, market aggressiveness or improved economic conditions could all explain some of the performances.

As can be seen in Appendix G, the overall SME population did not change in the period between 1984 to 1986. SMEs continued to represent more than 99 per cent of all business entities.

The proportion of revenues generated by SMEs has, however, increased considerably. They contributed 45.5 per cent in 1986, up from only 38.8 per cent in 1984. This could be seen as a remarkable step forward by small and medium-sized firms in Canada.

The groups mainly responsible for the upsurge in the level of SME contributions are mining, manufacturing, wholesale, transportation/communication/utilities and construction (see Appendix H). As mentioned earlier, however, a deeper analysis would be needed to understand the conditions that have promoted the role of smaller firms in these fields. It would also be necessary to analyze in more depth the recent behaviour of the various categories of firms within the sectors to reach a firmer conclusion. The variations between 1984 and 1986 serve simply to draw our attention, but the period studied is too short for significant trends to emerge. In addition, the lack of uniformity in the methods used to identify and classify firms excludes the possibility of analyzing the figures over a longer period.

More SMEs have always existed in Ontario and Quebec than in any other province. Based on ALUs, Appendix I shows that, in absolute figures, the number of SMEs continued to increase more in these two provinces than elsewhere during the period between

1978 and 1987.[34] The number of existing firms in a particular environment undoubtedly influences the arrival of new ones.

Newfoundland, Saskatchewan and Prince Edward Island experienced important proportionate increases in the number of SMEs over the same 10-year period. This could indicate that new firms are not created only in stronger economies. It is worth mentioning here that studies have shown that even in difficult economic periods, small firms are created at a significant rate.[35]

For their part, jobs in small firms as a whole increased by 32.9 per cent during the period between 1978 and 1987. Since employment statistics in Canada are compiled using more stable methods, the variations can be examined over a longer period than the number of SMEs and their revenues. Table 9, prepared using data from Appendix J, illustrates the changes relating to employment in each sector between 1978 and 1987.

Table 9
Evolution of SME Figures
Variations in Number of Employees
by Industry Group
Canada, from 1978 to 1987

Industry Group	Variation of Number of Employees in SME (%)
Manufacturing	15.7
Services	53.4
Retail Trade	40.8
Transportation, Communication, Utilities	18.7
Finance, Real Estate, Insurance	37.0
Wholesale Trade	18.0
Construction	26.8
Mining	41.9
Farming, Fishing, Hunting	56.4
All Groups	32.9

Source: *Employment Dynamics, by Major Industry Groups, Canada and Provinces,* Small Business and Special Surveys, Statistics Canada, June 1989, Ottawa.

During the period 1978 to 1984, employment increased considerably, particularly in farming, services, mining operations and the retail trade.[36] No sector saw a reduction in the number of employees between 1978 and 1987. The smallest rates of increase appear to be in the transportation, wholesale trade and manufacturing sectors. In the case of manufacturing, this could be partly explained by the transfer of a certain number of SMEs to the big firm category, or by the technological adaptations made by some of them. We should keep in mind that between 1984 and 1986, the number of SMEs increased by 9.6 per cent, while their revenues increased by 58 per cent.[37] These possibilities could easily be verified by a study on the evolution of jobs in firms of all sizes.

As can be seen in Appendix K, the proportion of jobs in SMEs increased by 6 per cent between 1978 and 1987. This means that SMEs play an increasingly important role compared to big firms as far as job offers are concerned.[38] This situation is the same in all economic sectors, with the exception of a slight decrease in the wholesale trade sector, and tends to suggest a widespread rather than a purely sectoral phenomenon.[39] The largest relative increase was in the mining, transportation/communications/utilities and farming sectors.[40] The share of SME revenues in the first two sectors, for instance, increased significantly from 1984 to 1986.

The most important variations in employment in SMEs appeared in Yukon and Ontario. A more detailed analysis may reveal the dynamics in Yukon. All other provinces have seen their SME employment increase reasonably.

In summary, the growing importance of small and medium-sized firms in Canada must be recognized.[41] Their number is growing constantly, and their revenues as a whole are increasing at a greater rate than ever before. SMEs constantly account for more than 99.4 per cent of all firms in this country. They consistently generate approximately 40 per cent of the overall revenue of Canadian business. Their share of revenues increased from 38 per cent to 45 per cent in the period 1984-1986. They seem more resistant to difficult economic conditions and recover more quickly than larger firms. A large proportion are located in Ontario and Quebec, and in these two provinces both the number of small firms and their revenue are increasing at a constant rate.

Small and medium-sized firms account for more than 60 per cent of all jobs in Canadian firms, and the number of such jobs has increased by 32.9 per cent in recent years. In terms of jobs, small firms occupied a more important place in nearly every sector in 1987 than was the case in 1978. The services sector has made a particularly notable contribution to the total increase in the number of people employed by SMEs, and retail trade and manufacturing have also done their share in this respect. However, in the period between 1978 and 1987, the most striking difference in the proportion of employment occurred in the mining sector.

These findings are interesting in themselves as far as job creation is concerned. However, it should be remembered that small and medium-sized firms are generally less well-equipped technologically speaking than bigger firms. Ontario and Quebec inevitably experience the greatest increase in the number of small business jobs,[42] but other less privileged provinces also record high rates of increase in the number of jobs available thanks to their SMEs. Through small firms, progress seems to be possible elsewhere than in economically stronger areas.

A number of estimates concerning other aspects of the role played by SMEs in the Canadian economy can be added to these statistical data. It has been estimated that SMEs contribute directly or indirectly to more than 16 per cent of Canadian exports.[43] Almost 50 per cent of firms participating actively in research and development activities are SMEs; their annual turnover does not exceed $10 million.[44] The exceptional contribution made by some small firms in some industries in terms of general innovation is also recognized.[45] Research has shown that from a sample of 43 manufacturing firms in Quebec specializing in research and development, 42 per cent of the innovations came from independent firms with fewer than 200 employees.[46]

The above account is more than enough to give a fair idea of the role played by SMEs in the Canadian economy. It is not my intention to present an exhaustive analysis of existing statistical data on SMEs; this book is meant to concentrate above all on the qualitative aspects of the state of Canadian small and medium-sized firms. I would have enjoyed working with long series of easily comparable annual data, and would also have been interested in having complete data up to 1989. But this was not the case. Anyone who has tried to obtain valid statistics on small business will undoubtedly have met with disappointment—as I did when working on this book. However, the analysis presented here paints an excellent picture of the scope of the small business phenomenon and its relatively recent behaviour according to some clearly significant variables.

The reader will have noticed that three main sources of data have been used to compile the various tables used to illustrate the discussion. In all three cases the basis upon which they were prepared was sufficiently uniform from one year to another. The figures allow a fairly precise interpretation to be made of the way the situation has developed. However, special attention should be paid to the notes so that the information can be completed and compared with other available data. The most striking trends in the place of small business in the economy emerge from the work done here. As new official statistics appear, the reader can add them to those listed in this chapter and check the trends.

As I have said, it has always been difficult to obtain satisfactory data on small business in Canada. The same can be said of many other countries. For a long time, Statistics Canada analysts did not break down their data in terms of enterprise size; economists and statisticians have always hesitated to consider SMEs as economic units belonging to distinct categories. However, remarkable efforts are now being made to correct these omissions.[47]

It is worth singling out the renewed efforts being made by Statistics Canada, with the help of specialized analysis teams, to supply more complete statistics. Perhaps uniform statistics on all Canadian small businesses will eventually be available on a regular basis. However, Statistics Canada should not concern itself with defining small business, but should instead concentrate on the job—difficult enough already—of gathering and presenting well broken-down statistics on size categories determined according to the usual indicators. Researchers would be left to group the data together according to their particular interests. Let us also hope that in future both federal and provincial publications will be based on the same data—perhaps activities could be coordinated to achieve this.

SMEs play a vital role in Canadian society. The figures set out in this chapter clearly illustrate their wide-ranging contribution.[48] Their human, community and social functions can never be quantified in this way, and as a rule are only briefly and generally mentioned. However, these aspects are vital for our society, and many pages will be devoted to them in the following chapters.

NICHES TO BE CHOSEN

Small and medium-sized firms are everywhere. The opportunities to fulfil given needs are tremendous, and those with the necessary entrepreneurial spirit know how to go about discovering them—or even creating them.

When writing this book I often took refuge in the university library. There, I was fairly sure to find the peace and quiet I needed to speed up production of the manuscript. However, I did not expect to come across real-life examples of small business in action there! Just as I was writing the section on fertile ground for small firms, some striking examples appeared around me. The firm in charge of maintenance had chosen that particular day to change the fluorescent tubes on the floor where I was working, and the employee assigned to the job spent some time in the building. "It costs too much—the guys don't get on with it," he told me, explaining why the university had sub-contracted the job. When I arrived at the library, I almost fell over the bucket and brushes belonging to another employee from the same firm who was carrying out regular maintenance. In a room set back from the main area, a very small firm was doing some renovation work before classes began. Through the window that day I saw at least two young guides go past, probably students who were showing foreign visitors around the campus. All these people had discovered a niche, and knew how to exploit it, probably better than other organizations could have done it. But what are these niches, the popular ones that will probably lead to success? How does a small businessman choose his sector? Everything that was happening around me began to make me think.

So Many Possible Niches . . .

Small and medium-sized firms do not have many resources. Clearly, they do not have the same market scope as big firms. Their assets, however, mean that they can carve out a place in various sectors, and some of them succeed brilliantly.

In the manufacturing field, SMEs have always been present in furniture, shoes, clothing, mechanical parts, and so on. They are now beginning to appear in the plastics industry, fibreglass boats, protective equipment, adapted wheelchairs, high-class furniture, customized electronic components, software, computer-controlled steam-generating systems, freeze-dried foods, and so on. Promising areas seem to be agricultural machinery, transportation equipment parts, automatic machinery, portable micro-computers, waste recycling, haute couture, exclusive clothing, sports clothing, biotechnology, prepared gourmet meals, etc.

Canadian small firms already export a respectable amount of products such as timber, vehicle parts, transportation equipment, wrapping paper, fur garments, etc. If they had appropriate strategies, more firms could also succeed in interesting markets such as airplane parts, handling equipment, safety equipment, office equipment, telecommunications and sound equipment, stylish off-the-rack clothing, etc. Small firms have succeeded, particularly on the export market, with unique and specialized products for well-defined target customers. The same formula should hold good for the future.

Restoration, maintenance and repair services, travel agencies, photographic studios and driving schools are all areas that are easily accessible to anyone who wants to go into business. There are few entry barriers. Other sectors demand more expertise, such as cable television, the sale of complex telephone systems, rewinding electric engines, setting up a new circus, laboratory analysis, etc. Daring adventures in new ways of doing things have often been very successful. Many people have heard of—and perhaps have seen—the Cirque du Soleil, created in 1985. Worlds away from the traditional circus, the Cirque has been heralded as a refreshing "reinvention" of the circus idea breathing new life into a tired industry.[49] Three former Air Canada stewards designed and built a flotation tank for relaxation. They opened facilities in Halifax and Toronto. Their clients are business executives and corporations that take stress management seriously. The owners expect their sales to top $2 million in 1989.[50]

Fields in which success may be possible in the future include storage, transportation, high-class clothing design, products and services for the elderly, "well-being," that is, natural foods, health centres, etc., and various home services. Some small firms are already doing profitable business in the field of services to the elderly. Hilda Stevens started up a home care firm in Halifax in 1980 with $5,000. She increased revenues from $30,000 in the first year to $188,000 in 1988. She says: "We've grown in spite of ourselves. I won't say it's been through great management or promotion programs—it's been need, that's all."[51] Montreal's Lawrence Services fill the gap for elderly clients who want more assistance than the province provides and who have the means to pay for it.[52] Other firms even provide banking, accounting and paperwork services specifically designed for this market segment.

Firms that are able to assure a high-quality service will be able to consider the export market. High-income people will turn increasingly towards small firms that can simplify their lives in some way, by making it easier to buy everyday consumer goods, leaving them more time for work or leisure. They will be ready to pay the price needed to ensure quality, a restaurant meal or one prepared at home, child care, the organization of entertainment, and so on.[53]

Industrial and economic structures change to take account of new materials and new technologies. They are increasingly affected by the "growth of the information and knowledge industries and their associated services, but also by activities linked to new cultural fashions." The western world is moving "from an industrial society towards an information society."[54] The generation, processing and circulation of information are becoming important and will open up opportunities for a host of small firms. Expert services, consultancy firms and professional practices are often small businesses, but of a particular kind. Professional skills are needed to start them up, but once that is done, they usually provide their owners with a good living. The knowledge industry will inevitably develop in all its branches. People with the right training will be able to think about setting up their own firms, alone or with colleagues. Once again, to be successful they will have to offer the latest, the quickest and the most personal service.

Paths for Future Success

A typical portrait of a highly resistant firm in Quebec after the crisis of 1981-82 revealed that many survivors were in the food and drink, transportation equipment, clothing and metal products sectors; in other words, in sectors that were comparatively little affected from an economic point of view.[55] Specific internal characteristics were also found in those firms that had survived this period.

During times of important structural and economic change, SMEs can play a vital part in a country's economy. In most industrialized countries, small firms provide jobs for much of the workforce and have provided fertile ground during the last decade for job creation. Small firms have been more and more innovative and have taken advantage of their flexibility to enter specialized and restricted markets. Some particular fields, however, seem to favour success.

> SMEs are best suited to operating in markets or industry sectors which are relatively small (requiring small production runs), fragmented and producing goods or services which are highly specialized. In manufacturing, the use of robotics and related production technologies (e.g., programmable automation systems) has the potential to assist SMEs further to manufacture goods in small production runs and SMEs will therefore have more opportunities to produce efficiently and prosper in markets perhaps dominated by larger firms. In the services sector the information revolution is already facilitating the profitable growth of small firms. In the areas of word processing, accounting and stock control for example, personal computers and the various software packages have greatly assisted small firms. The expected downward trend in the cost of information technology products can only be expected to further assist SMEs, and small specialist firms with very high levels of technological skill are likely to prosper. For example, firms specializing in computer software systems possess rare skills, work on a limited number of software products and are sufficiently competitive to ensure their survival against the large computer hardware manufacturers.

> SMEs are not only expected to prosper in high technology fields but in some mature industries SMEs

do extremely well. For example, the small specialist knitwear producers of Northern Italy. Such SMEs, because of their high quality speciality products, are able to compete comfortably with imports from developing countries.

There are, as well, important cautions in assessing the potential role of SMEs. In some important sectors of the economy, in particular in capital-intensive industries and in industries characterized by a high rate of technological change, which lessens the life of processing equipment, the role of SMEs will necessarily be modest.

New technologies will undoubtedly offer possibilities for highly innovative SMEs, which are flexible, adaptable and quick to react to market opportunities. However, awareness and willingness of SMEs to involve themselves in the application of new technological opportunities is rather low and very often managerial skills required to make the transition from traditional to new technologies, has to be regarded as an important bottleneck.[56]

The considerations are clear; and anyone interested in setting up a small firm should take them into account when choosing his field of activity.

The weaknesses of medium-sized firms, as far as foreign markets are concerned, are often mentioned. However, the advantages of the size factor are usually left aside, despite the fact that they are particularly marked in the new, more open context of modern international business. The following advantages in particular are worth mentioning:

The reduced size of small firms and their lighter commitments mean that they can more quickly seize the opportunities offered by markets with shorter and shorter life-cycles.[57]

Even though technological advances offer some niches, many small firms favour adaptation to markets and local needs.[58]

The informal structures of SMEs fit more easily into policies of inter-company cooperation which require either a combining of resources or a complementarity of means divided unequally among partners. In this respect, small firms appear to have a distinct advantage over big ones as far as participative and contractual international development is concerned. This advantage becomes even more determining when the enterprise is dealing with foreign SMEs.[59]

Canadian exports are increasing, and many small firms are actively contributing to the increase. The huge American market constitutes the main outlet. It is an important and accessible market for medium-sized Canadian firms, and the Free Trade Agreement opens it up even more. According to K.G. Hardy, the factors which lead to the success of Canadian SMEs on the American market are:

- they export specialized products that are differentiated by their technological characteristics and possible uses;

- owner-managers recognize the limits of the Canadian market in time; the firm already has a good share of the market or needs to go into mass production;

- the firm throws itself wholeheartedly into the project and is ready to invest the required resources in terms of both time and money;

- exports make up a sizable part of the firm's total business; if it lost the market it would be in trouble;

- all owner-managers consider presence at trade fairs as essential for developing new markets and finding new distribution channels;

- owner-managers perceive American distribution methods as being different from Canadian methods. They are more inclined to do business with representatives or manufacturers' agents in the U.S.;

- many firms find it advantageous to deliver their goods f.o.b. in an American town, thus reducing customer apprehension associated with buying a foreign product;

- firms must be able to take care of small details—for example, a poor trademark identification could block the product at Customs;

- government export support programs are considered useful, and businessmen would like to see them maintained.[60]

Many activity sectors are favourable for small firms, although some present a greater challenge than others. Certain

SMEs choose to follow in the wake of big firms as satellite sub-contractors. A number of arrangements are possible with larger firms; a list of the most usual appears in Appendix N. Others innovate and develop slots in the interstices left by big business. New small firms take on their bigger competitors directly, their product rather than the price being the factor that attracts their customers. It is already commonly accepted that:

> The enterprises which succeed best are those able to find new, very specialized and original products, goods or services, thus placing themselves in a very narrow slot in a semi-monopolistic position (. . .) A small firm's strength is precisely its ability to market products which it alone—or almost alone—produces (. . .) This kind of strategy has allowed, and still allows more and more SMEs to establish themselves on important consumer markets, in that the consumer is demanding increasingly individual and diversified products. The idea of the small firm as a simple sub-contractor no longer corresponds to small business dynamics.[61]

A small firm's future success seems to rest largely on its ability to target a well-defined sectoral field. Specificity, quality and flexibility will guarantee customer loyalty far better than product price. This could turn out to be the most effective export strategy, too. However, SMEs need to learn to live in less stable environments. Those which grow will be the ones that can create slots, question them, recycle themselves, change things—in a word, evolve.

A good product and a receptive market are not enough to guarantee success. More is needed. All the authors previously quoted have emphasized this, and others regularly mention it.[62] The pairing of a product with an appropriate market, which can take into account the firm's strengths, is absolutely essential. Without it, the firm will find survival difficult. Appropriateness is needed, and the challenge of assuring it is constant, whether it is a case of starting up or expanding old or new slots. How can small firms best achieve this?

Choice: A Non-Stop Process

The head of an SME always keeps his firm in mind. He thinks about solving its problems; he dreams about its future. If competition or changes in market conditions threaten it, if surpluses have to be invested, he already has ideas. Other people around him probably have very good ideas too. But his decision should not be based on intuition alone. He has to move forward, but the risk should be calculated more precisely. His thought process should cover all the following points:

- *Seeking information.* What opportunities exist? What new markets are available? What does the future hold? Where will business possibilities be?

  This information exists, but it must be sought from various sources. Imagination is also needed. Appendices O and P describe sources of information available.

- *Assessing attractions.* What are the main possibilities worth?
  - Which sectors are growing? Which is the most promising? Which seems to be the most attractive to each owner-manager, and which would be best for the firm?
  - Is it feasible to launch a business? Are present resources adequate? Can we count on an external contribution?

  The number of strategically important areas can be reduced by comparing their characteristics. In doing this, heads of small firms will be able to identify the most interesting sector for his firm.

- *Determining the factors leading to success.* What will future requirements be?
  - What elements will guarantee tomorrow's success in a particular field of activity? What strategies should be the most effective?
  - Does the firm already possess the necessary strengths? Should new strategies be developed?

  The owner-manager should discuss all these aspects. He must do some research and confront ideas. He should respect a certain order in his thought process. However, the following elements will already have provided him with food for thought. There comes a point when a decision has to be made between putting the question aside or pursuing it. The personal hopes and dreams of the person concerned often encourage him to continue.

- *Preparing strategies.* How can a competitive edge be ensured?
    - What main strategy must be developed? Differentiation, segmentation, cost benefits or specialization?
    - How can the firm's present strategic strengths be respected? What resources will be devoted to doing so?

- *Appreciating the human skills needed.* What new skills should be acquired?
    - What technical skills need to be brought in from outside? What new managers will need to be recruited?
    - Will a training program be organized? Will the firm pay training expenses?

- *Estimating the necessary investments.* Will they be profitable?
    - How much will have to be invested in the project? What will equipment, organizational layout and new human resources cost? How far can the enterprise go?
    - What extra revenue is expected? What would be the normal return on investment? Can this be envisaged? What other criteria can be used to justify the decision?

The last three points may perhaps seem to go beyond the bounds of the question of choosing a niche. In practice, though, they belong in the overall process and go hand-in-hand with any important decision. A wise owner-manager will want to translate the eventual results of his decisions into concrete figures. Only then will he make his final decision; he will choose to attack a new market only if he believes he will make a profit by doing so. Later, he can make more precise plans, estimates in hand. He can make the commitments he needs to go into action. However, he will have taken care to slip some contingency plans into his desk drawer, in case the unforeseen happens. Those with first-class management skills will also begin preparing both the organization and the personnel as early as possible for the coming changes.

Few SME owner-managers would want to have to follow a more structured procedure than the one proposed here when choosing their firm's broad orientation. Few would want to carry out an annual revision, as many business planning authors suggest. For the SME owner-manager, the natural process is a non-stop one. He continually thinks about his firm, and sets the process in motion according to the circumstances or ideas which come to mind, rather than just once a year. He agrees to give it a more official nature only if he finds the time and if he is well supported by his personnel. We should not try to paralyze him by imposing rigid planning procedures, but rather try to help him develop a strategic view of his firm.

NOTES

[1] These legal forms of enterprise are described in P.A. Fortin, *Devenez entrepreneur, Pour un Québec plus entrepreneurial*, Québec, Les Presses de l'Université Laval, 1986, p. 170-176.

[2] Various analysts have produced reviews of 1987. See the Caisse de dépôt et placement du Québec, *Cycles et tendances*, Montréal, December 1987, 54p; R. Bourdeau, "Survol économique de l'année 1987 - Dossier," *Finance*, 21 December 1987. For 1988, the PNB increased to 5 per cent, the price index to 4 per cent and unemployment to 7.8 per cent. See Caisse de dépôt et de placement du Québec, *Cycles et tendances*, Montréal, December 1989, p. 21.

[3] G. Vasic, "A short recession and a weak recovery," *Canadian Business*, Vol. 64, No. 1, January 1991, pp. 26-27.

[4] For a summary of the agreement signed on 10 December 1987, see "Accord de libre-échange entre le Canada et les États-Unis," *Le Devoir*, supplement, 18 December 1987.

See also for comments Y. Bourget, "Un accord sur le libre-échange Canada-U.S. propulserait le TSE 300 à 3500 points," *Les Affaires*, 29 June 1985, p. 24; D. McDermott, "Le libre-échange ferait perdre des milliers d'emplois," *Le Soleil*, 2 July 1985, C.-2; Canadian Federation of Independent Business, "CFIB will help SMEs to make the transition. On the whole, SMEs will benefit from free trade," *Mandate*, no. 134, November 1987, p. 1, 4. For an analysis of various sectors, see also C.A. Carrier, Y. Gasse, "Le libre-échange entre le Canada et les États-Unis: Les implications pour l'entreprise." Conference Proceedings, Institute for Research on Public Policy, Québec, 3 March 1988.

[5] R.M. Knight, "Exports as a determinant of success for Canadian high-technology entrepreneurs." Working paper no. 89-06, National Centre for Management Research and Development, University of Western Ontario, 1989, p. 9.

6 See C. Swift, "Small Business and the Canada-United States Free Trade Agreement," *Journal of Small Business and Entrepreneurship*, Vol. 5, No. 6, Summer 1988, p. 5-12. See also the recent comments of CFIB President in D. Best, "Free Trade Reconsidered," *Canadian Business*, Vol. 64, No. 1, January 1991, pp. 36-41.

7 A.M. Rugman, "The impact of Free Trade on small business in Canada," *Journal of Small Business and Entrepreneurship*, Vol. 6, No. 3, Spring 1989, pp. 52-54.

8 See cases in D. Best, "Free Trade Reconsidered," *Canadian Business*, Vol. 64, No. 1, January 1991, pp. 36-41.

9 The most technical sectors are: electrical equipment, chemicals, machine construction, transport equipment, petrol products and charcoal burners. See G.P. Steed, *Les entreprises émergentes: pour jouer gagnant*. Ottawa, Canada Science Council, document no. 48, 1982, p. 58.

10 A. Hains, "Augmentation de 40 pour cent des investissements manufacturiers au Canada en 1985," *Les Affaires*, 29 June 1985, p. 5. See also, by the same author, "Le libre-échange est la voie de l'avenir," *Les Affaires*, 15 June 1985, p. 5, and "1988 - les analystes se font rassurants," *Le Devoir économique*, vol. 3, no. 8, December 1987; P. Dubuisson, "Boom des investissements des entreprises canadiennes," *Les Affaires*, 14 May 1988, p. 5; R.M. Knight, "Opportunities for Entrepreneurs under Free Trade," *Journal of Small Business and Entrepreneurship*, Vol. 5, No. 5, Summer 1988, p. 13-25.

11 Manpower statistics for 1980 are presented in Minister of State (Small Business), "Statistical Profile of Small Businesses in Canada, 1983," Ottawa, Government of Canada, 1984, p. 31 (unpublished text). See also: Ministry of Industry, Science and Technology, *Small Business in Canada, Growing to Meet Tomorrow*, a report by the Entrepreneurship and Small Business Office, Ottawa, 1989, p. 5.

12 S. Blanchard, "Le marché forcera les commerçants à miser sur la personnalisation et l'excellence," *Le Devoir économique*, 18 January 1985, p. 79.

13 See Appendix K for the number of jobs in firms in various activity sectors.

14 Le groupe québécoise de prospective, *Le futur du Québec au conditionnel*, Chicoutimi, Gaëtan Morin, 1982, p. 93; J. Saint-Pierre and J.M. Suret, "Note sur les déterminants de l'importance relative des PME," *Revue de gestion des petites et moyennes organisations*, *P.M.O.* Vol. 1, No. 6, 1986, p. 49-50.

15 Le groupe québécois de prospective, *op. cit.*, p. 109. Our translation.

16 See L. Wynant, J. Hatch and M.J. Grant. *Chartered Bank Financing of Small Business in Canada*. London, University of Western Ontario, School of Business Administration, 1982, p. 13.

[17] In the fiscal year 1989, the FBDB's Lending Division authorized 5,130 loans and guarantees to small and medium-sized businesses for amounts totalling $926.7 million. See FBDB, *Serving Canada's Small and Medium-Sized Businesses*, Annual Report 1989, Federal Business Development Bank, Montreal, 1989, p. 4.

[18] L. Pépin, "Lancées dans le dernier budget Duhaime, comment fonctionneront les S.P.E.Q.," *Les Affaires*, 18 May 1985, p. 8.

[19] D. Lavoie, "Le plein emploi - partagé?," Conference of students in industrial relations, Laval University, *Le Journal du travail*, April 1985; "Le temps de travail partagé - L'État, les entreprises et les salariés doivent s'impliquer," *Le Journal du travail*, Vol. 7, No. 2, March 1985, p. 14.

[20] See M. Côté, "Le vieillissement: actif ou passif? Comment arrêter d'opposer jeunesse et vieillesse?," *Gestion 2001*, Montréal, Chenelière et Stanké, Les Presses H.E.C., 1983, p. 111-128.

[21] Some examples may be found in: National Productivity Institute, "Le partage des gains de productivité: oui ou non?" and F. Vernet, "La participation à la gestion et l'information comptable," *Productividées*, N.P.I., April-May 1985, Vol. 6, No. 1, p. 5, 8.

[22] See N. Moussa, "XV Conference on Industrial Relations, H.E.C.: Impacts des normes du travail sur la gestion des ressources humaines et sur les rapports collectifs," *Le Journal du travail*, Vol. 7, No. 1, February 1985, p. 6, 7.

[23] A. Fortin, "La réforme doit favoriser l'humanisation des relations de travail et la survie des PME," Beaudry Commission Hearings, *Le Journal du travail*, Vol. 6, No. 10, December 1984, p. 6.

[24] Many situations experienced by regional SMEs in Quebec are set out in D. Béliveau, G. d'Amboise and J.R.B. Ritchie, "La PME québécoise en régions périphériques: Un défi à relever," *Revue Commerce*, June 1978, p. 36-48.

[25] See the list in the *Handbook of Grants and Subsidies - Federal and Provinces*, Canada Research and Publication Center, Montreal, 1986 (regular updating).

[26] See R.A. Burgelman, "Designs for Corporate Entrepreneurship in Established Firms," in G. Carroll and D. Vogel, *Strategy and Organization - A West Coast Perspective*, Toronto, Pittman, 1984, p. 145-157.

[27] See R.W. Kao, "Entry Barriers and New Venture Strategies," *Journal of Small Business*, Vol. I, No. 2, Autumn 1983, p. 37-42.

[28] See especially M.E. Porter, *Choix stratégiques et concurrence, techniques d'analyse des secteurs et de la concurrence dans l'industrie*, Paris, Economica, 1982, p. 382.

29 For a discussion of the interstice theory in economics, see J.W. McGuire, "The Small Business Enterprise in Economics and Organization Theory," *Journal of Contemporary Business*, Vol. V, No. 2, Spring 1976, p. 115-138.

30 Encouraging initiatives are described in J.C. Dauphin, "La Croisade des chefs mailleurs," *Revue Commerce*, Vol. 88, No. 5, May 1986, p. 112-120; L.K. Mytelka, *L'économie politique du regroupement stratégique d'entreprises*, Ottawa, Investment Canada, 2987; J. Hubbard, "Banding Together for a Common Cause, Networks Help Small Companies Compete with Multi-Nationals," *The Financial Post*, special report, 27 May 1987, p. 19.

31 The reader may consult Appendices C to M for more detailed figures relating to the tables in this chapter. For more details on the situation and contribution of small firms, see Ministry of Industry, Science and Technology, *Small Business in Canada, Growing to Meet Tomorrow*, A report by the Entrepreneurship and Small Business Office, Ottawa, 1989.

32 Published figures on SMEs are often based on the number of establishments rather than the number of enterprises. Statistics Canada set the number of establishments belonging to the category of SME in 1985 at 928,107. See Ministère de l'Industrie et du Commerce, *Les PME au Québec, État de la situation 1986*, Québec, Gouvernement du Québec, 1986, Table 2.10, p. 31.

33 The number of SME establishments in 1985 was: Ontario, 305,081 (36.6), Québec 222,836 (23.7). See Ministère de l'Industrie et du Commerce, *Les PME au Québec, État de la situation 1986*, Québec, Gouvernement du Québec, 1986, Table 2.10, p. 31.

34 ALU: Average Labor Units as a measure of existing businesses. See notes to Appendix D for details.

35 See for instance P.A. Julien, "La dynamique des PME face à la crise structurelle entre 1975 et 1982 dans la région Mauricie-Bois Francs et ailleurs," compte rendu de la 3e Conférence canadienne, Conseil international de la Petite Entreprise, Toronto, May 1984, p. 41-47.

36 See for comparison G. d'Amboise, *La PME canadienne: situation et défis*, Institut de recherches politiques, Presses de l'Université Laval, Québec, 1989, Table 9, p. 58.

37 See Table 8.

38 While SMEs registered a positive net variation of 1,282,000 jobs, the workforce of firms with more than 500 employees grew by only 113,000. The increase in the number of employees was most marked in the category of firms with fewer than 50 employees. See Appendix L. Between 1978 and 1987, firms with fewer than 100 employees in manufacturing and fewer than 50 in all other sectors accounted for an astonishing 93 per cent of total net new private sector jobs created in Canada. Particularly striking is the fact that more than 50 per cent of

jobs created between 1978 and 1987 were in firms having fewer than 5 employees. It is equally impressive that total employment in these very small firms rose by almost 167 per cent during the same period. Taken from Ministry of Industry, Science and Technology, *Small Business in Canada, Growing to Meet Tomorrow*, A report by the Entrepreneurship and Small Business Office, Ottawa, 1989, p. 6.

39   The farming, forestry and fishing group remains the most favourable for SMEs; 90 per cent of total jobs in this group were in SMEs in 1978, and 97 per cent in 1987. It should be remembered that forestry operations alone (farming and fishing being excluded) occupy the same position in respect of revenues generated by SMEs. See Appendix K and Table 5.

40   Small firms, specifically those in the service and retail sectors, are largely responsible for the growth in the number of new Canadian firms and in new jobs in the last 10 years. Very little has happened in the manufacturing sector according to conclusions of a study by R.M. Knight in "Business growth and job creation in Canada 1978-1986," *Journal of Small Business and Entrepreneurship*, Vol. 6, No. 1, Fall 1988, p. 29-39.

41   The revenue level of firms was used as a criterion for establishing size when determining all the statistics reproduced in Tables 2 to 5 and Table 8. Where the number of people employed is used to determine size, official reports indicate the existence of 545,222 small or medium-sized ALUs in 1978 and 804,362 in 1987. See Appendix M for a breakdown of the figures in Canadian firms.

42   The following publication gives a convincing account of the role of SMEs in Quebec: Ministère de la Main-d'oeuvre et de la Sécurité du revenu, *La PME au Québec: une manifestation de dynamisme économique*, Québec, Gouvernement du Québec, 1988, 66 p.

43   On an estimated $119 billion in revenues from exports of goods and services, the added value of small firms is thought to be 8.4 per cent, and of medium-sized firms (between $2 million and $20 million turnover), 8.3 per cent. This is an assessment of the global direct or indirect contribution made by SMEs to the value of exports. See *Statistiques relatives aux petites entreprises*, Ottawa, Federal Business Development Bank, 1987, p. 15.

44   U.K. Ranga Chand, "Pressure on Research & Development," *The Canadian Business Review*, Winter 1980, p. 42-47. More recently, in 1987, 67 per cent of the firms performing commercial R&D in Canada had fewer than 50 employees and more than 75 per cent had fewer than 100. About 12 per cent of all private sector R&D spending in Canada was attributable to firms with fewer than 50 employees, and 17 per cent to firms with fewer than 100. See Ministry of Industry, Science and Technology, *Small Business in Canada, Growing to Meet Tomorrow, op. cit.*, p. 7.

45   These are the scientific and professional equipment, plastic product manufacturing, industrial organic chemistry and mechanical

construction sectors. C. De Bresson, "Have Canadians Failed to Innovate? The Brown Thesis Revisited," *H.S.T.C. Bulletin-Journal of the Canadian Science and Technology Historical Association*, Vol. VI, No. 1, January 1982, p. 10-23.

46 A. Bellehumeur and T.H. Nguyen, "Processus d'innovation technologique dans les entreprises manufacturières au Québec," working paper 89, Research Laboratory, Administrative Science Faculty, Laval University, 1988.

47 Congratulations are due to the Quebec and Ontario governments for their recent publications on small business: *The State of Small Business, Annual Report on Small Business in Ontario*, Toronto, Government of Ontario, 1986, 127 p., 1987, 164 p. and 1988, 185 p.; *Les PME au Québec, État de la situation*, Rapport du ministre délégué aux PME, Québec, Gouvernement du Québec, 1986, 170 p., 1987, 320 p. and 1988, 141 p. Two other sources of data on Canadian SMEs are also available: *La base de données longitudinales de Dun et Bradstreet*. It contains information on a wide range of firms from a micro-economic point of view in most sectors of the economy. Data were also drawn from *Job Creation in Canada 1974-1982*, Ottawa, Government of Canada, 1985, 92 p., and from the Canadian Federation of Independent Business Database, which contains various information on members and their firms. A *Profile of Small and Medium-Sized Business in Canada*, was based on the data of the Canadian Federation of Independent Business Membership, Toronto, CFIB, 1983, 36 p.

48 The growth of the sector has been maintained. More recent statistics reveal that "the number of Canadian SMEs has risen by 42 per cent between 1978 and 1986 (. . .) Presently there are more than 840,000 small firms (. . .) Of the 1,267,000 new jobs created in Canada since September 1984, more than a million—or 80 per cent—were created by SMEs. Most new SMEs are created in three main economic sectors: services, retail trade and construction," *Les Affaires*, 17 September 1988, p. 15. It is estimated that by 1988 there were approximately 900,000 businesses with one paid employee apart from the owner, an increase of approximately 50 per cent since 1978. See Ministry of Industry, Science and Technology, *Small Business in Canada, Growing to Meet Tomorrow*, op. cit., p. 4.

49 The Cirque's founder and manager is Guy Laliberté, a 30-year-old professional firebreather. He succeeded, with his partners, in setting up a new form of attraction. The show, performed by a group of young professional acrobats, musicians, clowns and so on, captivates audiences all over the world by its simplicity and charm. It attracts people and makes money. In 1988, its profits were $2.5 million, out of an estimated gross revenue of $15 million. From L. Aisenberg, "Fourth Annual Successors Awards - The Spirit of Success," *Canadian Business*, Vol. 62, No. 9, September 1989, pp. 96-97.

50 See M. Turnbull, "Start-ups - Now why didn't I think of that? - A womb with a view," *Canadian Business*, Vol. 61, No. 10, October 1988, p. 17-18.

51 M. Ritts, "Trends - Places in the heart," *Canadian Business*, Vol. 62, No. 3, March 1989, p. 19.

52 *Ibid.*, p. 20.

53 A larger proportion of consumers look at factors other than price. Small retail firms will benefit from this trend if they are able to offer differentiated products and services. The results of a survey among customers in food stores provides clear proof. See D.S. Litvack, "Opportunities and Suggested Strategies for Small Food Retailers," *Journal of Small Business and Entrepreneurship*, Vol. 3, No. 4, Spring 1986, p. 44-55; other authors see new possibilities for SMEs in current changes in consumption. See, for example, P.A. Julien and B. Morel, *La belle entreprise, La revanche des PME en France et au Québec*, Montréal, Les Éditions Boréal Express, 1986, 237 p.

54 C. Dupont, "Les PMI face aux 'megatrends'," *Revue française de gestion*, No. 55, January-February 1986, p. 97.

55 J.C. Thibodeau, P.A. Julien and J. Chicha, "Les PME au Québec face à la tourmente économique de 1975 à 1982," in P.A. Julien, J. Chicha and A. Joyal, *La PME dans un monde en mutation*, Sillery, Les Presses de l'Université du Québec, 1986, p. 195-204.

56 T. Van Heesh, "Structural Change and Small and Medium-Sized Business," in P.A. Julien, J. Chicha and A. Joyal, *ibid.*, p. 128, 133.

57 P. Joffre, "Le rôle de la taille ne doit pas être surestimé," *Revue française de gestion*, No. 55, January-February 1986, p. 70.

58 L. Creton, "Internationalisation: L'avance technologique ne suffit pas," *ibid.*, p. 93.

59 P. Joffre, "Le rôle de la taille ne doit pas être surestimé," *ibid.*, p. 70. Our translation.

60 K.G. Hardy, "Key Success Factors for Small/Medium Sized Canadian Manufacturers Doing Business in the United States," working document no. 86-10, London, National Centre for Management Research and Development, University of Western Ontario, 1986, 10 p.

61 Drawn from B. Morel and P.A. Julien, "L'avenir de la PME," in P.A. Julien, J. Chicha and A. Joyal, *op. cit.*, p. 439. Our translation.

62 Empirical studies specify the various other factors necessary for a successful SME. See, for example, A.G. Cloutier, *Profil sélectif d'entrepreneurs exploitant des entreprises à succès au Québec*, Master's project in business studies, Québec, Faculty of Administrative Science, 1973; A.B. Ibrahim and J.R. Goodwin, "Toward Excellence in Small Business: an Empirical Study of Successful Small Business," in P.A. Julien, J. Chicha and A. Joyal, *La PME dans un monde en mutation*,

Presses de l'Université du Québec, Sillery, 1986, p. 223-230. Various other reports on the same subject are quoted elsewhere in this book.

CHAPTER 3

THE CENTRAL FIGURE AT THE HEART OF THE ENTERPRISE

SMEs are often just one person's business. A new venture is simply the implementation of an idea generated by its founder, whose permanent occupation is the daily management of operations. The man and the firm are intimately linked and cannot be examined separately. To understand the person, we must first look at the nature of his job and his working environment. To understand the firm, we have to take into account the ambitions of the person running it. The Canadian small business owner-manager and his enterprise are discussed on the following pages.

Meeting a small business owner-manager is usually interesting, and reveals his many-sided personality and wide-ranging experience. A typical owner-manager is always involved in lots of different things. If he did not launch the firm he is running, he has usually launched others or been involved in doing so. He is the principal owner of his firm, and has shaped it in his own image. The more entrepreneurial he is, the more he is on the lookout for new business opportunities, start-ups and revivals. At the same time, he is the vision maker for his firm as well as being in charge of its day-to-day management.

It is not always easy to draw the line between entrepreneur and manager. The same person often plays both roles—or tries to. An entrepreneur creates his firm; a manager looks after its operations. Launching a business means having to fill other roles later, and ideally an entrepreneur should know what they are. However, small business owner-managers are often called "entrepreneurs," both in the literature and in everyday language. Publications dealing with Canadian small business owner-managers fall into two categories. The first type sets out the characteristics and experience of typical owner-managers; in other words, the general portrait that usually comes to mind. The other type describes particular individuals. In this chapter, I have chosen to present some general profiles of Canadian businessmen and their firms, followed by four more specific, or newer, profiles, and finally a description of what it takes to be an entrepreneur and a manager.

CANADIAN SME OWNER-MANAGERS: GENERAL PROFILES

Observations by researchers and onlookers throughout Canada have grouped small business owner-managers into three categories: inventors and craftsmen, promoters and general managers. Inventors have developed an original product, while craftsmen have made the most of their technical abilities. Promoters use their selling skills to market goods and services, and finally, general managers operate their SMEs like commercial enterprises.[1] Each approach requires particular aptitudes. Many businessmen and women move from one approach to another during their careers, and only rarely do they stay exclusively in one category.[2] The person who seems to do everything in the SMEs we visit on a daily basis is very probably the owner and chief executive. He may well be its creator, too.

The Owner-Manager: A Committed Owner

The central figure at the heart of a small firm is typically a person of action who likes a challenge. He is very attached to his firm and seems more like an entrepreneur than a modern manager. He may, in turn, act as financial manager, technical manager or commercial manager.

The following examples, drawn from research carried out in the 1970s, illustrate many of the characteristics commonly found in small business owner-managers in the past. In Quebec in 1970, the typical furniture industry owner-manager would be around 50 years old and have headed his firm for the last 15 years or so. He would be deeply attached to his family and his work. He would accept change generally, and would have demonstrated a marked competitive spirit. He had been in full-time education for about 12 years, but had no specialized qualifications. Many had fathers who had also ran firms, and some had gained management experience elsewhere before becoming owners. A few had gone back to school or university for management training.[3]

The shoe manufacturing industry also provided some interesting examples. The chief executives studied were, without exception, men. Most of them had either bought or inherited their firm, and had been working there for some time. A few had launched or been involved in launching other ventures. Almost all spent more than 50 hours a week on business-related matters, and were convinced that hard work was the path to success.

In the plastics industry, also studied during the 1970s, the firms were slightly younger. The chief executives, while in the same age group as their furniture industry counterparts, generally had a higher level of technical training. A large proportion had founded their own firms and had been involved in launching others.[4]

A more recent study of a hundred or so small business owner-managers in four Quebec manufacturing sectors revealed some similarities and some differences with respect to their 1970s predecessors. More than 50 per cent had parents who were already in business. They had been in full-time education for more than 15 years, and their average age was 45. Almost half had founded the business they were currently running, and a similar number had launched at least one other venture. Nearly all spent more than 45 hours a week on business matters.[5] On the whole, however, they did not differ substantially from the groups previously studied.

As far as successful women chief executives are concerned, Belcourt has identified many similarities with generally accepted profiles.

> Female entrepreneurs are highly similar to male entre-
> preneurs when environmental conditions are examined.
> Both groups tended to be first-born into families where
> the father was self-employed. Most entrepreneurs come
> from the middle class, etc.[6]

On the other hand, "women do not play off their role as mothers against their role as owner-managers" despite the fact that "managing a business and a home at the same time is very difficult."[7]

Small business owner-managers have their own special way of working. Since they are often the main or sole owner, they are usually the ones to make important final organizational decisions. According to Peterson,

- They must continually face the problem of survival of their enterprise and of their investment.

- Their objectives are to create wealth for their own retirement and for their family.

- They have strong community ties, because they are permanent residents and take an active role in community affairs because their success depends on the success of the community in which they live.

- The business is really an extension of the owner's personality and therefore fulfils not only monetary needs but also meets an individual's social and ego requirements.

- In sum, owner-managers make the key business decisions for which they also take the financial risk.[8]

As far as financial practices are concerned, small business people have their own set of attitudes. For example, they do not like outside investors, and generally prefer active shareholders who can use their skills, abilities and ideas to help the firm, who are ready to share the responsibility and the work and who are prepared to buy up to 49 per cent of the stock.[9] A group of Canadian small business owner-managers were asked about their preferred source of extra funds: 70 per cent opted for existing shareholders.[10] However, research done by Gasse indicates that a higher proportion of younger firms were founded by their owner-managers in collaboration with other people than is the case among older firms. More owner-managers of younger firms would be willing to sell their firm's stock to passive partners.[11] Perhaps this signifies a gradual change in attitudes towards external financing. However, both groups agreed that it is not worth going public.

A further insight into present-day owner-managers is provided by a piece of research on a group of very small successful firms in a variety of sectors.[12] The typical successful owner-manager is 40 years old, has a college-level education and spends around 50 hours a week in his organization. His success is mainly due to a set of entrepreneurial values such as intuition, the need for autonomy, a taste for risk, and so on. His managerial skills are evident in his choice of orientation for the firm, the simplicity of the operational structure he creates, the efficient management of his working capital, etc. This typical profile seems to guarantee success in managing small firms.

These descriptions highlight many aspects of SME owner-managers. But, by concentrating only on the characteristics and attitudes of the central figure, they leave aside the firm itself. The following general description of a particular group of establishments—not chosen at random, but composed of SMEs in the manufacturing sector that managed to ride out the early 1980s crisis years—completes our portrait of the typical owner-manager and his firm.

- The firm operates in one of the following sectors: food and drink, transport equipment, clothing, leather, metal products.

- It has been in existence for less than 10 years and the present chief executive has been in place between six and nine years. The firm was launched following a market survey or because the owner had acquired professional experience with another firm.

- It has more than 50 employees, and a fairly large proportion of the workforce is female. The employees are either not unionized or have their own independent union. In 1982, the average wage was around $15,000.

- In terms of production technology, the owner-manager considers that his firm is ahead of or on a level with the competition.

- The firm buys very little on the local market and sells mainly in Montreal or elsewhere in Quebec or Canada.

- At first, its debt level was high, but it has since managed to repay a large part.

- Its medium-term objective is increased productivity through technological improvements. It is also aiming to increase the volume of its production and sales.[13]

The person and the firm form a single unit. The male SME owner-manager also remains father for his family and the female owner-manager still takes care of the household. They are aware that they have a role to play in their community. We already know, and research confirms, that they are highly committed people in all aspects of their lives.

The Owner-Manager: Often a Founder

Many small business owner-managers founded their own firms. As we have seen, nearly half of those studied had launched the firm they were running at the time of interview. They are the true entrepreneurs in the classical sense of the word. They have created and set up something new: a commercial enterprise.[14] Often, not really satisfied with their job or lifestyle, they decided to change direction and work for themselves. They have identified and taken advantage of a gap in the market and have combined their skills and resources to get their business moving. Some say the entrepreneur is first and foremost an escapee,[15] while others emphasize his desire for self-achievement[16] or independence.[17] But clearly, the main thing is that he has taken the risk of putting thought into action.

Family environment is an important factor in bringing out entrepreneurial skills: one out of two Canadians who have set up their own firms come from a family where the father was self-employed.[18] They launched their businesses when they were between 30 and 35 years old, because they wanted to be their own boss, earn more money or explore new ideas.[19] Those who launch technically oriented ventures have generally received some form of post-secondary education. They commit themselves unreservedly after acquiring the relevant know-how and experience in two or three different jobs.[20] However, they had little management knowledge before going into business.[21] Whatever field he chooses, an effective creator's main strengths are indestructible courage and enthusiasm. He is always deeply committed to his firm.[22] In many cases he has received moral and sometimes financial support from his family and friends. He wants to innovate and is stimulated by a challenge, and he is not afraid of market instability or competition. His previous experience is in production rather than administration. Younger owner-managers are likely to know where to go to get information and who to ask for professional planning and organizational help.[23] Those who are attracted by the service sector sometimes have special characteristics. They are sole owners and often set up small-scale operations at home. They often have a university education, choose a sector in which they have some experience and manage to finance the start-up with their own savings. They keep up-to-date with recent developments in the field through frequent contact with colleagues. However, as is the case with many other entrepreneurs, they are aware of their lack of management knowledge.[24]

Canadian entrepreneurs are not simply "escapees," though. Many are creators who were well prepared, had always thought of going into business and who could profit from the chance to do so when it arose.[25]

Small business owner-managers are often called "entrepreneurs." In this book, only the person who founds a new venture earns the title. A founder is distinguished from the others by the act of creation. The chief executive of an entrepreneurial firm is distinguished by his innovations and plans for the future. He also has unique skills.[26] In this context, creative spirit and leadership both depend on one vital ingredient: entrepreneurship.

Every small business owner-manager is deeply attached to his firm. It is his life. He is also very aware of his responsibilities towards his own people, and fulfils several roles at once. A lot of owner-managers have already launched a business, in many cases the firm they are currently running. In this respect they are often real entrepreneurs. Owner-manager or entrepreneur, the difference is not always clear in practice.

CANADIAN SME OWNER-MANAGERS: PARTICULAR PROFILES

Most SME owner-managers are highly committed to their organization and their milieu. Many could claim the title "entrepreneur." They resemble each other in many ways too, to various degrees, but particular groups are distinguished by some important characteristics. Female entrepreneurs have their own personality, young creators reflect the new generation, and so on. The four profiles that follow, each with its own characteristics, deserve a closer look.

Female Entrepreneurs: Owner-Managers or Associates

The role played by certain groups in Canadian firms, both as owners or managers, is emerging more clearly. The contribution made by women as entrepreneurs or as associates at the head of small or medium-sized firms is a striking example. The percentage of women owning firms compared with men more than doubled in the period between 1969 and 1979: from 16 per cent to 36 per cent.[27] From 1970 to 1981, the number of unincorporated firms in Canada owned by women increased from 53,000 to 142,000, a 2.7-fold increase within the group.[28] The Canadian Federation of Independent Businesses estimates that almost two-thirds of the new ventures launched in Canada in 1984 were launched by women.[29] In British Columbia, for instance, the number of female entrepreneurs increased by 119 per cent between 1975 and 1984; the increase for the male population was 51 per cent.[30] More recently, Statistics Canada reported a growth rate of 20 per cent for firms owned by women during the period 1981 to 1986, compared with 8 per cent for firms in general in the same period. There is a large number of female owners in service and trade sectors but not in forestry, construction or transportation; they are surprisingly well represented in mining and manufacturing.[31] The number of women working with their husbands in small family firms has recently been put at more than 500,000.[32] Female entrepreneurs and wives working in family businesses have their own particular characteristics.

The Female Entrepreneur and her Firm

It used to be thought that women who ran businesses had inherited them from their parents or husbands. However, research now shows that many of them were responsible for launching their firms.[33] In fact, the majority come from families with a business background, as is the case generally speaking for male entrepreneurs.[34] Women are usually aged between 30 and 40 when they start up in business. Many have a college or university-level education, and have held full or part-time jobs for several years. However, they have often had less opportunity than men to acquire management experience before going into business on their own.[35] They go into business for the challenge, for more financial independence and greater individual autonomy. As was the case for Suzanne Leclair, the chairperson of Fourgon Transit, many women had thought about launching a business for some time before actually doing so. They had to take care of their family and get acquainted with the business world before finally being able to achieve their ambition.[36]

Women who launch their own ventures generally use their own savings. Their level of debt during start-up years is often relatively low, and many of them keep their job with another firm during those years.[37] In addition to the sectors traditionally reserved for women, they also go into construction, parts manufacturing, car sales, accountancy, brokerage and so on. Sherry Ruteck was 21 when she took over Trans-Mutual Truck Lines Ltd. after the sudden death of her father. Her Calgary bank manager kept telling her that she should have a dress shop. Instead, she succeeded in switching business from bulk commodities to more profitable flat-deck trailer loads, as well as expanding her firm's territory. She now sits on the board of the Alberta Trucking Association. Sought after as a guest speaker at meetings and trucking conferences, Ruteck says that she is now considering diversification. She has looked at everything from welding shops to cleaning services—but not at dress shops.[38]

Nevertheless, the tertiary sector seems to be the most popular.[39] Female entrepreneurs can be found in organizations of all sizes, but they seem particularly attached to small firms. Female sole owners seem to be more common in small firms, too.[40] They face the same challenge as men in day-to-day operations, but seem to have more difficulty in their relations with lending institutions. It irks them that they are usually less well-integrated in the formal and informal business networks, where they could obtain useful information and form valuable contacts for their firms. In a second piece of research carried out on the same group, White discovered that 47 per cent of firms run by women were still in business three years later, while only 25 per cent of those run by men survived the period between 1979 and 1981. Female owner-managers of successful firms had spent between six and 10 months preparing their project, had sought appropriate expert advice and had, in many cases, followed business management training courses.[41] Female entrepreneurs will perhaps, in the future, provide us with more convincing proof that it is possible for small firms to develop if only their owner-managers bother to prepare themselves properly.

Wives in Family Firms

No one can deny the vital role played by some wives in the success of the family business. We have all at some time known a mother, a relative or "the boss's wife" in a neighbourhood firm who was closely associated with her husband's business. The active role they play has largely been ignored in the past. As wives, they could benefit from the family patrimony but had few real rights. During the last few years, however, some steps have been taken to remedy the situation. A study carried out by the Association féminine d'éducation et d'action sociale (AFEAS) on 1,000 wives working in family firms in Quebec revealed some elements that were common to all these "silent partners" in many SMEs.[42] They have usually been married for some time, are in their forties and have adolescent children who take up less of their time. They act mainly as accounts clerks, saleswomen, secretaries or receptionists. Sometimes they do manual jobs or are in charge of actual management. They often act as intermediaries between their husband (the owner) and customers or suppliers, and their advice is usually sought on subjects that are important for the business. The relationship between the spouses in the business reflects their relationship in their personal and family life. However, the wife is rarely involved in negotiations with banks or in discussions with accountants or lawyers on current business matters.

A large majority of women are not paid as such for their contribution to the family business. This means that they have very little financial autonomy and places them in a precarious position. In addition, since their status is that of unpaid employee, they are not eligible for any of the social benefits normally available to people who work for someone else. Both their job and their financial security depend on the stability of the couple. If they split up, it is by no means sure that the wife will receive adequate compensation for the years she spent working in her husband's business. And if the firm goes bankrupt, she—like her husband—will probably see the fruits of her labour disappear forever.

Today, fiscal laws allow the husband to deduct the salary paid to his wife as a business expense—which is certainly a step forward. The regular activities of the Association of Wives in Family Businesses (Association des femmes collaboratrices) provide an impetus for couples in business throughout Canada to discuss the situation. The association is also campaigning for legal recognition of two distinct statuses with specific privileges.[43] Perhaps we can look forward to a time when someone will suggest ways of facilitating and fostering real business relationships between men and women who look after their firm together.

Young People in Business: Founders or Inheritors

Today, in a context where jobs are difficult to come by, many young people, full of ideas and wanting desperately to do something, choose entrepreneurship. Some of them have realized that the best way to get a job is to create it themselves—an encouraging attitude. While the phenomenon is far from new, it has taken on remarkable proportions in recent years. Other young people have decided to go into the family business. The increased value placed by modern society on family firms has made decisions like these easier.

Young entrepreneurs are usually over 30 years of age, although the average age is tending to decrease. They usually have a solid formation in a technical field or in business management, and have acquired some experience in big or medium-sized firms. Young people who launch ventures usually do so in collaboration with others, thus accepting the fact that a variety of skills are needed to take care of production, sales, finance and administration.

Richard Bourbeau is fairly representative of the young people who have set up business on their own.[44] He was 26 when he founded Venmar. As a recently qualified MBA, he was employed to organize the sale of a special loft ventilator. He finally decided to go into business manufacturing a turbine to replace the imported one used in the product. He employed a tinsmith and, with the help of his brother-in-law, who was a welder, began to produce his turbine. The five shareholders each borrowed $5,000 to cover initial operations. The oil crisis came along at just the right time and encouraged people to insulate their houses. Richard Bourbeau perfected increasingly sophisticated ventilation systems and went on to innovate by selling them in kit form. In 1985, aged 34, he already employed 60 people, held 65 per cent of the Canadian market and was preparing to move into the American market, which he finally did in 1987. He says that he launched his business "not for the money, but for the satisfaction of building something." His biggest difficulties were not financing, but personnel management and general coordination of activities.

Or we can take the case of two young people, in their early 20s. They were still students when they decided to sell their cars, get their savings together and buy a small workshop producing ceramic ovens for craftsmen.[45] They ran their new firm between courses, working long hours and most weekends. They applied for every grant available and borrowed everything they could at first. Their firm, Pyradia, has been based in Longueuil since 1979. And, while its founders were confident in their idea, they spared no effort in their quest for success.

Many other similar stories appear regularly in the newspapers. In July 1984, *Maclean's* Magazine presented five firms that had recently been launched by young people, and that were already on the road to success.[46] Three graduates from Simon Fraser University set up Compu Software, a retail software firm. They had noticed that most computer retailers sold only computers, leaving their customers to go elsewhere to buy programs on disk. Two years later, they had opened three or four outlets in the Vancouver area, and their organization is growing so fast now that they admit they do not know what it is worth. Others, like Alena Aberani and Karen Obermaler, from Halifax, owned a very small commerce. They began by distributing publicity leaflets from time to time, moving on to personalized promotion services. Both only 19 years old, they charged $12 an hour to do street publicity for businesses. All these young people had identified a need they could satisfy and, relying on their own resourcefulness, they launched their ventures.

Jacques Sicotte is chairman of Petro-Sun, a firm that, in 1987, had a turnover of $24 million. In 1976, with his brother and a friend, he founded—in his basement—a small firm specializing in heat reconversion systems. He had had enough of the big firm he worked for, even though it had let him experiment with some of his ideas. He launched a venture that is now flourishing and, thanks to today's energy-conscious society, he estimates that his sales will have reached $100 million by 1990.[47]

An entrepreneurial family background usually cultivates the taste for business. It often generates creators, or provides people to carry on the family firm. While graduates from outside the family may find it very difficult to become part of the team, a young family member can bring new and promising impetus to the firm. A growing number of young people are showing interest in their family's business. The phenomenon is not confined to Canada, but can be seen across North America. The small family business provides many of them with the chance to prove themselves. There have been periods where the economic situation has justified this choice, but that is not the case presently. Today's society values entrepreneurial skills, and the role and potential of many family firms are better understood. It must also be remembered that more young people nowadays have something positive to offer their parents' business, having acquired training or experience elsewhere to add to their knowledge of the family firm. Perhaps, too, the modern generation of owner-managers is more open-minded than previous generations. People have learned to discuss business problems and orientations more, and even to share the profits. Owner-managers are better educated than before, in most cases more aware of the pitfalls that can plague parent-child relationships and are anxious to play a more conciliatory role. In this way, they can facilitate their son or daughter's accession to a position of responsibility within the family clan.[48]

According to Pierre Hugron, who has met many families who run businesses, know-how is transferred in a very different way from ownership. Know-how is handed over gradually, over many years and through a variety of situations, whereas ownership often changes hands only when the father or mother dies.[49] The new central figure at the heart of the enterprise can give of his best only when he is sure that influential family members have confidence in him, or when he has control over ownership of the firm. Real entrepreneurs like to have plenty of elbow room and not be cramped by other family members. They also like to feel they are playing an important part in running the firm they have joined.[50] Whether they created or inherited the firm, they have often given up the advantages of another career to do so, and are thus all the more keen to succeed.

These days, management faculties and schools throughout Canada are producing a lot of managers. Personally, I hope that some of them at least will choose the small business path. Courses focusing on SMEs are offered by a growing number of university faculties, and should encourage young people in that direction.[51] In Quebec alone, more than 10,000 management degrees were awarded in 1983. That means a lot of people on the job market— but these people are better equipped than before. They could provide an extraordinary reservoir of future small business owner-managers. But it is up to the young people themselves to put their skills to work in SMEs.

Many programs have been created to foster initiatives by young people interested in joining the small firm adventure. The following examples illustrate the kind of support given by the Quebec government:

- The PRO-PME program aims to help Quebec's manufacturing SMEs employ young graduates in strategic positions such as accounting, administration, finance and marketing. It provides grants of up to 50 per cent of the salary paid by the firm during the first year of employment of college leavers or university graduates.

- The New Entrepreneurs program is available to anyone who has obtained a professional college or university qualification during the last five years, or who is under 30. It offers a guarantee on two thirds of borrowed capital up to $25,000 used to launch a venture or buy part of an existing business in the manufacturing field. The government takes care of all interest payments on the loan for the first year, and half of them for the following two years.

Young people who launch ventures show beyond any doubt that they have entrepreneurial skills. They like what they do and take risks with enthusiasm. Many of them quickly find themselves at the head of dynamic medium-sized firms; they gradually acquire the ability to work as part of a team and to ask for advice from specialists who can help them. To succeed, they invest a great deal of time and determination in their work. Those who go into the family firm also face a considerable challenge: they must prove their entrepreneurial skills. If they want autonomy and decision-making power, they must also build up their credibility and prestige. They are expected to improve the business and maintain family relationships at the same time. Often, the rest of the family looks to them to become the symbol of their collective success. Sometimes firmness is needed to resolve family matters. Globally speaking, their social role is to make sure that the businesses they run can successfully outlive the founding generation.

Owner-Managers of Technological Firms: Engineers or Managers

A firm's activities are generally based on its founder's particular skills and know-how. People with technological or scientific training often turn to firms specialized in high technology fields. These owner-managers have their own special profile. They start businesses generally known as technology-based, technology-intensive, technology-oriented or high-tech firms. Businesses like these concentrate on research and development or on exploiting state-of-the-art technical knowledge.[52] Many are specialized in the manufacturing of high-technology instruments or equipment.

In the Quebec area, many young entrepreneurs have launched their own high-tech firms. For example, in 1979 Michel Lapointe founded DAP Électronique, a firm that manufactures portable micro-computers and automobile products. He had worked for 11 years as an electronics technician, and had become R&D manager in another firm. Today, his entire operation is concentrated in that field. The firm meets its own needs, fulfils contracts for other companies and even contracts out where necessary.[53] Both Gentec, a firm producing high-power lasers, and Bomem, a firm specialized in spectrometric equipment, are also examples of high technology firms launched by young people in the Quebec area.

Many entrepreneurs worked in big firms before starting their own business. Organizations like Computing Devices Limited,

Bell Northern Research and Northern Telecom have all trained specialists who have since flown the nest. Often, they left because a certain kind of work was discontinued; Mitel is an example of this. But other entrepreneurs had always dreamed of launching their own ventures, and gradually got organized to exploit a promising gap in the market. Firms such as Spar Aerospace, Canadian Astronautics, Lumonics and Gandalf Technologies were all founded by entrepreneurs, and have contributed largely to the development of "Silicon Valley North" near Ottawa.[54] They all started out small and in many cases grew very quickly, as is often the case with firms that exploit an innovative idea with a strong immediate demand. However, many Canadian high technology firms never exceed a turnover of $2 million or $3 million. In 1983, the high-tech sector in Canada accounted for 4.2 per cent of employment in all manufacturing industries. Firms were mainly small and young; 60 per cent had fewer than 50 employees and 54 per cent had been established after 1972.[55] These SMEs play an important role in the development and manufacturing of state-of-the-art technological products in Canada. Nevertheless, we are often reminded that the high-technology sector in Canada has a lot of ground to make up compared to the international situation. If we are to make a real breakthrough, we should count not only on our inventors, but also on our entrepreneurs.

Fairly accurate data already exist on technical entrepreneurs. Out of a sample of 100 studied in 1971, almost one third of those who had launched their own ventures were born outside Canada. More than 50 per cent came from families where the father was self-employed. A similar proportion had a university education, mainly in the sciences or engineering. Many had also launched other ventures apart from the one they were running at the time of interview. Their average age at their first venture start-up—usually done in collaboration with other people—was 33. For the majority, the field of activity of their own firm was closely related to their training or last job.[56]

However, many of these owner-managers were poorly prepared for their administrative responsibilities. Peter Macaulay is a typical example. After a period with Control Data in Ottawa, he worked in the information processing centre at Dalhousie University. In 1975, he began to do some consulting for personal customers, and regularly used Peter Gregson to carry out his work.

Gregson worked for the Department of National Defence and had good experience in designing software for research purposes. In 1977, convinced that they would benefit from pooling their skills—computer science and systems analysis in one case, electrical engineering in the other—they decided to form Micronet, a small firm specialized in manufacturing electronic energy controls.[57] Their first contract, in 1978, brought in $5,000. The following year, they achieved a turnover of $100,000. Between 1980 and 1983, in collaboration with an American firm, they carried out a project worth $600,000. In 1982, their turnover was $2 million, and they expected to reach the $5 million mark in the not-too-distant future. However, the fast growth of their Halifax-based firm brought with it some problems for the owner-managers. It was never easy for them to communicate their personal philosophy to their employees, who did not always want to work the same long hours as their bosses. It always seemed impossible to sort out current administrative problems quickly. Budgeting for revenues and expenditures was always an unpleasant task. They had to learn the rudiments of all these aspects on the job. According to a report on the firm's activities in 1982, many new products were being manufactured, new contracts were being negotiated and the future seemed full of possibilities, but the owner-managers were aware that they would have to completely rethink the organization of their own activities.

High-tech firms exist throughout the country. The following profile of a group of such firms in British Columbia gives an insight into the development of SMEs in the West:

- typically, they manufacture electrical components or develop software;

- they have been in business for at least five years and are located on a single site;

- they have between 10 and 20 non-unionized employees;

- they sell their products mainly to industrial firms in British Columbia or the United States;

- they are managed by engineers who finance them with their own personal funds;

- they often encounter problems in obtaining supplies of specialized technical parts and have trouble with government bureaucracy;

- their ideas for new products are often based on an analysis of needs expressed by customers.[58]

High-technology SMEs almost always have their own scientific and technical expertise. Unfortunately, they are generally much less well-off in terms of management skills. The 1971 sample underlined the lack of management preparation among people launching technological firms, and the same phenomenon can be seen in more recent generations. A Pan-Canadian study has shown that the owner-managers of technological firms are generally weak in finance and marketing—both vital areas if a young firm is to develop.[59] In some cases, lending institutions have even insisted that the chief executives be replaced before agreeing to invest in subsequently profitable projects.

Litvak and Maule reconstituted the history of 47 of the firms making up their 1971 sample, and discovered that only 20 could be said to be successful in 1980. The owner-managers of these firms had worked differently.

All 47 firms managed to enter the second phase of their evolution, i.e., the early growth stage, but it was here that many of the failures took place, frequently attributable to the marketing myopia exhibited by the initial founders, and the financial consequences that followed (. . .) The situation is quite different for many of the successful survivors whose management group includes some professionals with accounting, financial, managerial and manufacturing expertise. Attempts at introducing planning is evident, particularly in firms which have "gone public" and whose sensitivity to money markets is obvious (. . .) The small-medium sized, and threshold firms showed themselves to be heavily involved in international business (. . .) The growth industries in which they competed helped them to reinforce their competitive strength in the area of marketing applications, thus reducing the need to compete largely on price.[60]

The lack of venture capital, so often criticized by those young, developing, dynamic firms, no longer seems to be a problem for successful firms.[61] As more than one financial expert would say, Canada does not lack funds, it lacks good projects. If they want to obtain funding, owner-managers must be able to show that their innovations have potential and that they understand the rules of financial markets, as well as earning the confidence of their investors. Other firms' histories illustrate the need to go beyond the limits of the Canadian market to succeed in manufacturing high-technology products; they need an international clientele.[62] A firm's competitiveness is based not only on its technological innovation skills, but also on its ability to manage innovation. A study by Doutriaux and Simyar on the start-up and growth characteristics of 73 high-tech firms located in various parts of Canada certainly supports this contention. When success is measured in terms of annual sales or total employment, the following start-up factors provide a comparative advantage to young firms: the amount of start-up capital, marketing and financial experience, similarity of the technology with the technology of a previous employer, and public sector sales in the first year. But the capacity to manage gradually becomes the most crucial factor. These researchers have found that the comparative advantage tends to fade away after three or four years, because presumably by that time other firms have hired the required managerial expertise.[63] Effective management, marketing, financing and personnel management are essential for innovative firms to succeed. In financial circles and international markets, high-tech entrepreneurs must develop into a different kind of engineer: their main skill should be putting together real teams to support them in all aspects of management.

The Centre de recherche industrielle du Québec (CRIQ) plays a vital role for many Quebec SMEs by helping them develop and improve their products and processes. The Centre d'innovation industrielle de Montréal (CIIM) provides valuable help to owner-managers wanting to develop and improve their products and processes. The main task of the Research Centre for Management of New Technology (REMAT) is to help Ontario SMEs implement new technologies.[64] Harwill Technologies International in Ottawa has joined forces with the government to speed up technology transfers to Canadian small and medium-sized firms. For its part, the Saskatchewan Research Council now puts CAD/CAM techniques within the reach of the province's small manufacturers.[65]

All these organizations have understood that economic and social progress requires more than the mere existence of advanced technologies; research on new needs and the creation of organizations able to satisfy them are also essential factors.[66] Some universities have taken the initiative by offering specialized courses in technological innovation and entrepreneurship.[67] By doing so, they have recognized the need for both technical and human skills in the management of innovative firms.

Owner-Managers of Alternative Enterprises: Cooperators or Entrepreneurial Animators

The need to work with others has resulted in various cooperative, community and collective formulas. The most common factor in all these initiatives is a questioning of traditional business. Those involved have chosen a new way forward. While earning the title "SME" because of their size, some firms are different because they are based on specific ideologies. Their owner-managers, often young, are sometimes known as the new entrepreneurs. Without going into detail over the differences between the various categories, the following description, together with some portraits of the firms themselves and the people in charge of them, aims to bring out the broad lines of a modern phenomenon and the values underlying it.

The cooperative movement has existed for some years in Canada. The Fermiers-Unis, credit unions, Caisses populaires, the Antigonish Movement and so on, have all played an important social and economic role in various communities. The founders, who are both leaders and managers of local groups, share many of the characteristics of small business owner-managers, and yet have their own personality. They are collective entrepreneurs who want their actions to satisfy both collective needs and their own personal needs at the same time. As organizers, they have the qualities of leadership required to generate militancy and bring together the resources needed for the project. They usually left their family environment fairly young, and often dropped out of university. As managers, they are generally younger than their SME counterparts, and maintain closer links with the community, often being very active in local associations and clubs. They work long hours, especially on projects that arouse their enthusiasm, and do not bother too much with the long-term aspects, making quick decisions that will bring immediate concrete results. Administrative demands are often perceived by them as being constraints, and they experience difficulty with the transitions required by the evolution of their cooperative, which is, to all intents and purposes, a small firm.[68]

During the last 10 years, many countries have seen the emergence of large numbers of new cooperatives and associations. This phenomenon is undoubtedly connected with the historic cooperative movement, and is fed by the trend towards self-management, the ecological wave and new humanitarian values. Although the people involved in this kind of collective project often represent a form of counter-culture, the projects themselves are nevertheless socially acceptable to a certain extent thanks to the neo-liberalism that has led to criticism of state intervention and enhancement of individual initiative.[69] Many names exist for these interest groups; the best known are community enterprises, the social economy, the third sector and cooperatives.[70] Their presence and their role in our society are both becoming increasingly evident.

> New community economic development ventures (...) are springing up across Canada as the traditional methods of generating jobs fail. They include:
>
> - Community development corporations.
> - Worker-owned businesses in which management, workers and outside shareholders have equity.
> - Workers' cooperatives.
> - New wave cooperatives, operating outside the mainstream of the movement.
> - Local Economic Development Assistance corporations established by the Canada Employment and Immigration Commission.
> - Development associations.
> - Regional development councils.[71]

In Quebec, some such firms were launched by movements contesting the closing of villages, such as the JAL cooperative, often quoted as an example.[72] Other initiatives have relaunched firms in difficulty or set up new organizations to exploit natural resources such as forests, to market craft products or to offer cultural and social services.

Most of these organizations reveal one or more of the following characteristics, increasingly accepted as distinguishing alternative enterprises from the rest:

- a method of operating based on collective management;

- a desire to make the enterprise pay, although the objective is not to maximize profits;

- the satisfaction of the real needs of the surrounding population;

- the involvement of people who are often marginal in society.[73]

Some young firms were started by people who wanted to create their own jobs and make money, but who also wanted to respect values based on collective ownership and responsibility and on operational equality. Pierre Guillemette provides an example. In 1982, with some friends, he started a small cooperative business. Almost all those involved had just completed their training in either electrical engineering, economics or management. Guillemette had been working for some years on plans for a musical synthesizer. The employment situation was difficult and bank accounts were empty, but the founders all determined to create their own jobs. They wanted to explore new avenues and do something unique and original. They chose the cooperative formula because it corresponded most closely to their idea of an enterprise. In particular, from a humane point of view, they preferred to establish equality-based relationships between themselves rather than a boss-employee structure. According to the general manager, André Côté, each person contributed his own particular experience, ideas and personality; the more conservative tempered the more extravagant, and a healthy balance was maintained.[74]

Every big city in Canada and the rest of the world has its own "new wave" district, and nowadays even the smaller towns have their share of little café-bookshops, alternative restaurants, natural food stores and recycling and processing workshops.

Alice Klein and Michael Hollett decided to launch a magazine that would be different from the others. Their review NOW is published in Toronto.

> The paper features comprehensive, "what's-on" listings and entertainment reviews, along with a news section that explores everything from the city's homeless to Canadian aid to the Nicaraguan contras (...) NOW addresses the notion of the complete person (...) (They) decided that the best way to ensure that they could write about what mattered to them was to translate their idealism into viable business.[75]

NOW has an annual turnover of $2 million and employed 40 people in 1986.

Not all alternative enterprises have adopted the cooperative structure. Based on a variety of interests and dreams of all kinds, many have taken highly original—and sometimes hybrid—forms of association or enterprise. Some, related to both cooperatives and SMEs, are hard to classify in the usual categories.[76] Those that aim to produce revenues are often explicitly called collective or alternative enterprises. Their owner-managers, the alternative entrepreneurs, come from a variety of backgrounds, both artisan and commercial.[77]

Although care is needed when using the "alternative" label, experience in Quebec seems to reveal two types of alternative entrepreneurs.

> The first category is made up of young university graduates ... who could, in some cases, have found a job in the public or private sector. They preferred instead to create their own jobs in fields that corresponded to their skills and hopes, while at the same time establishing a working framework free from hierarchical structure where job rotation and an equal share of the revenues are practised as far as possible. Their firms are said to have a much more marked social finality than traditional firms (...)
>
> The second category regroups young people with little academic training, those on social security, the phys-

ically handicapped or women wanting to go back to work. For them, in their more or less marginal positions, their jobs represent specific values and objectives. This type of initiative is considered to be part of the alternative movement because of the type of organization adopted.[78]

We can thus see that alternative enterprises are best distinguished from traditional firms by the values and attitudes of the people working in them. In an alternative enterprise, the "why work" is the important factor, followed by the "how"—the way it is done. The kind of working climate found there is difficult to find elsewhere. Power relationships are of a particular kind. "Of course, leaders emerge, but their power depends on legitimacy that is negotiated by those involved rather than on legal fiction or capital holdings."[79]

Versatility is also a common factor. Those involved move from one responsibility to another and from one job to another within the same firm, which perhaps encourages experimentation. This may well be the reason why individuals from different backgrounds and with different skills, but who share similar aspirations, get together to fulfil their ambitions.

However, their enterprises are often highly vulnerable. At the outset, credibility and credit are hard to come by; and later, it is usually difficult to recruit and keep people with essential skills. Enterprises based on temporary interests are clearly the first to disappear. In others, where differing values cause frequent confrontations, the collective project may break up into fruitless adventures.

In some community organizations,

> Finding managers for such ventures is difficult. They have to handle a high degree of ambiguity, balancing demands of community and self-interest, of profit generation and equitable sharing, of self-reliance and the need for mutually beneficial links to others, of decreasing dependency and stimulating cooperation.[80]

Small collective interest firms have to survive all the usual crises affecting young SMEs, and while "some will effectively become cooperatives (...) others will be recovered and turned into private firms; (and) as is the case for SMEs in general, many will face bankruptcy."[81]

Others will continue in their hybrid form to foster the achievement of ideals and, perhaps, to grow rather more than was originally expected. In any case, they will all have been real schools of auto-entrepreneurship.

It seems impossible to classify rigorously the various kinds of collective interest organizations. A large group represents the pooling of energies to satisfy community needs. Another group can be compared to SMEs, in that those involved want to create their own jobs. Only their operating style—which, in many ways, perhaps resembles that of some family firms—distinguishes them from traditional small firms. In any case, if collective interests are to have priority, the leader of an alternative group must, at the same time, be a cooperator, an entrepreneur and a group leader.

ENTREPRENEURS OR MANAGERS: DIFFERENT SKILLS ARE NEEDED

Many people are naturally entrepreneurially minded. They can spot opportunities and usually manage to get the resources together to carry out the project. But not all of them earn the right to call themselves entrepreneurs: they never create a business. In today's language, it is easy to call a small business owner-manager "entrepreneur." However, there are precise conditions to be satisfied to earn this title.

Individuals with Distinct Roles

A person who plays a significant role in an SME can be situated according to two basic aspects: ownership and management. The following diagram shows the possible roles:

		Ownership of the firm	
		YES	NO
Management of the firm	YES	Owner-manager	Manager
	NO	Investor	Retiree

The situation of an individual with respect to these variables allows him to be classified as an owner-manager or investor, chief executive or retiree. Here, we are concerned with the role of owner-manager.

While a manager contributes his know-how as an employee without having a stake in the ownership other than a purely symbolic holding, an owner-manager is different. He is usually defined as

> The individual who holds a large proportion of the firm's capital stock and who takes part actively in the decisions affecting the firm's orientation and its daily problems.[82]

Many SME chief executives fit this profile.

A firm may exist through the efforts of one or the other of the people described above. Each of them can say he took part in its creation, and thus each is an entrepreneur in his own way, perhaps to a degree that it might not be wise to try to determine. It is usually enough to ask if an individual played a part in founding an enterprise or not, as the following diagram shows:

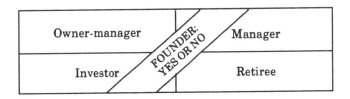

At one extreme, it could be said that they all played a part at the time the firm was created. In practice, however, we usually acknowledge the entrepreneurial skills of the person who, as the owner-manager, assumed the risks of start-up. Since he creates his own firm, he risks more than the others.

> An owner-manager who is considered to be a real entrepreneur because he founds the firm, is emotionally and financially committed to that firm (. . .) He tends to identify himself completely with his firm; often he will say "I am the firm."[83]

It may well be that the title of entrepreneur so sought after these days should be reserved for people like him.[84]

Requirements for Entrepreneurs and Managers

Creating a business presents its own particular challenge, and running one also demands certain qualities that change as the situation develops.[85] The skills required to lead the firm through its development also vary according to the stage reached.

We can simplify matters by saying that a small firm must pass through three main stages during its life. It may be in the start-up phase, the growth phase or the relative maturity phase. Table 10 shows the main challenges met at each stage and the qualities and styles needed to meet those challenges.

Table 10
**Main Challenges at each
Stage in the Life Cycle**

Stage	Main Challenges	Particular Qualities Needed	Management/ Decision style Needed for Management
Start-up	Launch the product on the market	Creator Salesman Inclined to risk	Do everything Decide alone Intuition
Growth	Increase: - in sales - in size	Organizer Interest in systems	Delegate tasks Consult colleagues Share decisions
Maturity	Stabilization of sales General profitability	Controller Preference for order	Assess results Let others decide Analyze

Starting a business is one thing, and running it afterwards is another. At first, the entrepreneur can do almost everything himself, and can innovate as much as he likes. When he is owner-manager of a growing SME, he has to entrust certain jobs to others; he becomes an organizer and has to rely on the skills of his collaborators to decide and act. Once at the head of a more mature small firm, he has to delegate even more. He becomes a source of inspiration for the others, and must also know how to use modern control and analysis methods. In other words, he is a manager.

Can the founder possibly have all these skills at once? And can he remain effective at the head of a developing firm? The various examples given above show that it is very difficult. To launch a venture, you need a vision of the future, the will to realize your ambition and the ability to take risks. To be a good manager, you need to be able to get others to collaborate with you and also, at certain times, be able to protect what has been achieved and consolidate your organization.

The roles of entrepreneur and manager are almost inherently incompatible.[86] Many owner-managers always remain entrepreneurs. Some turn into run-of-the-mill managers in firms going nowhere. Others, after careful reflection, discover leadership skills, put them to work and find themselves at the head of dynamic teams able to keep up a constant rate of progress.

NOTES

1 R.M. Knight observed these three types in various pieces of research. See R.M. Knight, "Entrepreneurship in Canada," *Journal of Small Business Canada*, Vol. 1, No. 1, Summer 1983, p. 9-15.

2 A survey of 360 Canadian small business owner-managers shows that a large number of them had created their firm, sold it and founded another afterwards. See P. Thompson, "Characteristics of the Small Entrepreneur in Canada," *Journal of Small Business and Entrepreneurship*, Vol. 4, No. 3, Winter 1986-87, p. 8.

3 G. d'Amboise, "Personal Characteristics, Organizational Practices and Managerial Effectiveness: A Comparative Study of French-and-English Speaking Chief Executives in Quebec," doctoral thesis, Los Angeles, University of California, 1974, p. 88-104.

4 Y. Gasse, *Entrepreneurial Characteristics and Practices, a Study of the Dynamics of Small Business Organizations and Their Effectiveness in Different Environments*, Ottawa, Ministry of Industry and Commerce, Department of Science and Technology, 1977, p. 108-126.

5 G. d'Amboise, Y. Gasse and M. Bernard, "Difficultés managériales et facteurs de succès perçus par les propriétaires-dirigeants de PME: une étude comparative France-Québec," special document no. 84-111, Re-

search Laboratory, Faculty of Administrative Sciences, Université Laval, 1984, p. 40-48.

6   M. Belcourt, "Sociological Factors Associated with Female Entrepreneurship," *Journal of Small Business and Entrepreneurship*, Vol. 4, No. 3, Winter 1986-87, p. 29.

7   H. Lee-Gosselin and J. Grisé, "Les femmes propriétaires-dirigeantes de la région de Québec (03): mythes et réalités," special document no. 87-110, Research Laboratory, Faculty of Administrative Sciences, Université Laval, 1987, p. 4. Our translation.

8   R. Peterson, *Small Business: Building a Balanced Economy*, Erin, Press Porcépic Ltd., 1977, p. 65.

9   Y. Gasse, "Attitudes et prédispositions des propriétaires-dirigeants et entrepreneurs canadiens envers les bailleurs de fonds externes," special document no. 84-122, Research Laboratory, Faculty of Administrative Sciences, Université Laval, 1984, p. 79.

10   J.V. Poapst, *Small Business Financing and Non Bank Financial Institutions*, Toronto, Facsym Research Limited, 1981, p. 56.

11   The young firms were less than seven years old. See Y. Gasse, *op. cit.*, p. 28, 66.

12   The researchers studied 74 firms having less than 15 employees and with sales under $2 million, drawn from the wholesale and retail, service and manufacturing sectors in the Montreal area. See A.B. Ibrahim and J.R. Goodwin, "Toward Excellence in Small Business: an Empirical Study of Successful Small Business," *Comptes rendus - Colloque international sur la PME en devenir dans un monde en mutation*, Trois-Rivières, 3-5 October 1984, p. 157-165.

13   This portrait is drawn from a study carried out in 1981 by Jean-Claude Thibodeau and Pierre A. Julien on 225 manufacturing firms with less than 200 employees and having operations in several areas in Quebec. See A. Fortin, "Résultats d'une étude dans quatre régions - Les PME manufacturières: une assise importante au développement régional," *Le Journal du travail*, Vol. VI, No. 9, November 1984, p. 3.

14   This observation reminds us of the primary role of the entrepreneur. See Y. Gasse, "L'entrepreneur moderne: attributs et fonctions," *Revue internationale de gestion*, Vol. 7, No. 4, November 1982, p. 4, and J.M. Toulouse, *L'entrepreneurship au Québec*, Montréal, Les Presses H.E.C.-fides, 1979, p. 3.

15   R.M. Knight, *op. cit.*, p. 13-14.

16   See J. Chamard, V.M. Catano and C. Howell, "Entrepreneurial Motivation: Some Evidence to Contradict McLelland," *Journal of Small Business Canada*, Vol. 1, No. 1, Summer 1983, p. 18-23.

17   A sample of Canadian business founders studied by the following researchers appeared to be more highly motivated by a need for

independence and control of their destiny than by any other factor: R. Blais, R. Blatt, J.D. Kyle, A.J. Szonyi, "Motivations underlying Canadian entrepreneurship in a cross-cultural and cross-occupational perspective," *Journal of Small Business and Entrepreneurship*, Vol. 6, No. 3, Spring 1989, p. 7-21; Belcourt found many similarities in motivations of male and female entrepreneurs. She also identified the theme of independence as the strongest motivator of the group of successful female entrepreneurs which she studied. M. Belcourt, "The family incubator model of female entrepreneurship," *Journal of Small Business and Entrepreneurship*, Vol. 5, No. 3, Winter 1987-88, p. 34-44.

18 H. Lee-Gosselin and J. Grisé, *op. cit.*, p. 9.

19 See J.M. Toulouse, *op. cit.*, p. 47-61.

20 See, for example, P. Thompson, *op. cit.*, p. 8.

21 I.A. Litvak and C.J. Maule, "Profiles of Technical Entrepreneurs," *Business Quarterly*, Vol. 39, No. 2, Summer 1974, p. 40-49.

22 See especially the main factors determining success according to a group of self-employed people: N.L. Colwill, B. Suek and J. Haynes-Klassen, "A Study of Self-Employed Manitobans," *Journal of Small Business Canada*, Vol. 2, No. 1, Summer 1984, p. 26-30.

23 Perreault and Dell'Aniello identified common characteristics among a group of successful entrepreneurs. See Y.G. Perreault and P. Dell'Aniello, *Histoires d'entrepreneurs québécois: un chemin qui mène à la réussite*, Montréal, Programme formation de l'homme d'affaires PME inc., 1983, p. 50-52.

24 A directory of new firm registrations held by the Ministry of Industry, Commerce and Technology in Ontario reveals a large percentage of service firms whose profile could be traced. See R. Blatt, "Survey of Small Business Registrants, 1984," Toronto, Government of Ontario, Ministry of Industry, Commerce and Technology, 1985, p. 5 (unpublished text).

25 Some conceptions of entrepreneurship are discussed in a comparative study carried out by Chamard *et al.* between Nova Scotian entrepreneurs and others from the Beauce area of Quebec. See J. Chamard *et al.*, *op. cit.*, p. 18-23.

26 Close ties are confirmed between the personality of the leaders and the entrepreneurial acts carried out in simply-configured firms by D. Miller and P.H. Friesen, in *Organizations - a Quantum View*, Englewood Cliffs, Prentice Hall Inc., 1984, p. 176-201.

27 According to a study carried out by Revenue Canada quoted in J.T. Cook, "Women: The Best Entrepreneurs," *Canadian Business*, Vol. 55, No. 6, June 1982, p. 73.

28 G. La Roche and G. Welbourne, "Les femmes au travail: Place aux femmes d'affaires!," *Commerce Canada*, September 1984, p. 6.

29 R. Black, "Women Showing They're Better Entrepreneurs," *The Financial Post*, 23 February 1985, p. 57.

30 According to a study by the Canadian Advisory Council on the Status of Women, *Les Affaires*, 5 March 1988, p. 24.

31 See R.M. Knight, "Business growth and job creation in Canada, 1978-1986," *Journal of Small Business and Entrepreneurship*, Vol. 6, No. 1, Fall 1988, p. 31.

32 R. Rowan, "Mes amours . . . mes affaires," *Le Devoir*, 3 June 1985, p. 3.

33 In a study carried out in Ontario for the Small Business Secretariat, two-thirds of the 275 female owners had founded their firm. In Stevenson's study in the Atlantic provinces, 70 per cent of the 183 women respondents had done so. See J.T. Cook, *op. cit.*, p.68 and L. Stevenson, "The Role of Government in Woman-Owned Business in Canada," proceedings of the third Canadian conference of the International Council for Small Business - Canada, Toronto, 23-25 May 1984, p. 124.

34 According to studies by Stevenson and Lavoie on female entrepreneurship. See L. Stevenson, *op. cit.*, p.124 and D. Lavoie, "Les années 80 et l'entrepreneurship au féminin," proceedings of the third Canadian conference, International Council for Small Business - Canada, Toronto, 23-25 May 1984, p. 64.

35 See the work of L. Stevenson, *op. cit.*, p. 121-128, D. Lavoie, *op. cit.*, p. 60-67, H. Lee-Gosselin and H. Grisé, *op. cit.*, p. 7.

36 "Even when I was little, I wanted my firm," she said in an interview. G. Paquin, "Suzanne Leclair, présidente de Fourgon Transit," *Le Magazine PME*, Vol. 3, No. 10, December 1987-January 1988, p. 7-9.

37 Ministère de l'Industrie et du Commerce, "Le cheminement socio-économique de la propriétaire-dirigeante d'entreprise au Québec," Study Report, Direction de la promotion de l'entrepreneurship, Québec, 1988, p. 3 and 7 (unpublished text).

38 As reported by R. Bett in "Fourth Annual Successors Awards - The Spirit of Success," *Canadian Business*, Vol. 62, No. 9, September 1989, p. 88.

39 In a Canadian sample of 1,364 firms run by women, 73 per cent were in commerce and services. See J. White, "The Rise of Female Capitalism - Women as Entrepreneurs," *Business Quarterly*, Vol. 49, No. 1, Spring 1984, p. 135. In Belcourt's study, 65 per cent of respondents were in sectors other than manufacturing. See M. Belcourt, *op. cit.*, p. 25.

40 A preliminary inventory of women likely to be owner-managers of firms in Region 03 in Quebec shows that 92 per cent of them worked in

the tertiary sector. See H. Lee-Gosselin and J. Grisé, "Profil des femmes propriétaires-dirigeantes d'entreprises manufacturières de la région de Québec (Région 03)," special document no. 85-104, Research Laboratory, Faculty of Administrative Sciences, Université Laval, 1985, p. 3. The same researchers also found that the size of the firms sampled was inversely proportional to the percentage of ownership of the women owner-managers (p. 57). For a more global portrait, see H. Lee-Gosselin and J. Grisé, "Les femmes propriétaires-dirigeantes de la région de Québec (03): mythes et réalités," special document no. 87-110, Research Laboratory, Faculty of Administrative Sciences, Université Laval, 1987, 34 p.

[41] J. White, *op. cit.*, p. 134.

[42] Study by AFEAS quoted in C. Lord, "Votre conjoint travaille pour vous," *Revue Commerce*, Vol. 85, No. 6, June 1983, p. 64-67. Some other considerations arose from conversations with people who had themselves experienced the situation.

[43] See A. Rowan, *op. cit.*, p. 3.

[44] This example is presented by Véronique Robert in *Entreprise*, Vol. 1, No. 3, March 1985, p. 5-7.

[45] See the case of Michel Hémond and Mario Bouthillier in D. Pérusse, "Des chefs d'entreprise nouvelle vague," *Sélection du Reader's Digest*, 1985, p. 115-122.

[46] The text from the magazine is reproduced in W.E. Jennings, *Entrepreneurship: A Primer for Canadians*, Toronto, Canadian Foundation for Economic Education, 1985, p. 17.

[47] H. Wilson, "Successors - Jacques Sicotte: An Alternate Current in the Energy Business," *Canadian Business*, Vol. 60, No. 8, August 1987, p. 51.

[48] However, the son or daughter must have shown a clear interest in the firm's business. Joining the firm beforehand is very important if the young person wants to be asked to take over later. See J. Naud, *La relève et la succession dans les PME familiales québécoises*, Québec, Institute for Research on Public Policy, Small Business Program, Université Laval, 1986, p. 59.

[49] See V. Robert, *op. cit.*, p. 9.

[50] See M. MacIsaac, "Keeping Family (and Business) Together," *The Financial Post Special Report - Small Business*, 23 February 1985, p. S8.

[51] Courses on entrepreneurship and small business management form part of the regular programs at almost all Quebec's universities. More specific programs have been developed by some Canadian universities. For example, the University of Calgary has developed a multidisciplinary program that fosters collaboration of students in the start-up and development of new ventures in their environment. See W.E.

McMullan, W.A. Long and J.B. Graham, "University Innovation Centres and the Entrepreneurship Knowledge Gap," *Journal of Small Business Canada*, Vol. 2, No. 4, Spring 1985, p. 3-16.

52 These firms can usually be distinguished by their technologically advanced products. The same designations are also used for firms that use up-to-date production techniques.

53 For other examples, see D. Méthot, "Dossier - Recherche et Développement," *Entreprise*, Vol. 1, No. 1, October 1984, p. 6-9, and M. Lambert, "Québec mise sur sa haute technologie," *Entreprise*, Vol. 1, No. 5, p. 12-13.

54 These examples are discussed in an analysis by Professor A. Barnhill of the University of Lethbridge, entitled *Small Business Entrepreneurship and the Growth of High Technology in Canada*, presented at the 30th world conference, International Council for Small Business, 16-19 June 1985.

55 F. Amesse, P. Lamy, "Le secteur des hautes technologies au Canada: une poussée récente de petites firmes à la recherche de la croissance," *Canadian Journal of Administrative Sciences*, Vol. 6, No. 1, March 1989, p. 6.

56 I.A. Litvak and C.J. Maule, *op. cit.*, p. 40-49.

57 A very interesting description of Micronet's activities is presented in case form in a report by the Canadian Program for Studies on Technical Innovations. See M. Martin and P. Rosson, *Four Cases on the Management of Technological Innovation and Entrepreneurship*, Ottawa, Regional Industrial Expansion, Industrial Innovation Office, 1982, 28 p.

58 D.K. Chowdhury and R.W. Vandermark, "High Technology Companies in B.C. - A Marketing and Management Profile," document presented at the 30th world conference of the International Council for Small Business, Montreal, 16-19 June 1985, p. 270-285.

59 R.M. Knight, "Entrepreneurship and Innovation in Smaller High Technology Firms in Canada," document presented at the 30th world conference of the International Council for Small business, Montreal, 16-19 June 1985, p. 198-226. Marketing deficiencies in these firms are also emphasized in D.A. Boag and H. Munro, "Analysis of Marketing Activities in High-Technology Manufacturing Companies," *Journal of Small Business and Entrepreneurship*, Vol. 4, No. 2, Fall 1986, p. 48-56.

60 I.A. Litvak and C.J. Maule, *Entrepreneurial Success or Failure - Ten Years Later - A Study of 47 Technologically Oriented Enterprises*, Ottawa, Ministry of Regional Industrial Expansion, Industrial Innovation Office, 1980, p. 71-73.

61 For a discussion of this subject, see R.M. Knight, *op. cit.*, p.198-226 and T. Ortt and P. Sloan, "Some New Perspectives on Threshold

Companies," *Journal of Small Business*, Vol. 1, No. 4, Spring 1984, p. 31-38.

62 See, for example, I.A. Litvak and C.J. Maule, *Canadian Entrepreneurship and Innovation - Six Case Studies*, Ottawa, Ministry of Regional Industrial Expansion, Industrial Innovation Office, 1982, 67 p.

63 See J. Doutriaux and F. Simyar, "Duration of the comparative advantage accruing from some start-up factors in high-tech entrepreneurial firms," Working Paper 87-21. For a further analysis see also J. Doutriaux, H.C. Tweddle, "High Tech Start-Ups and Marketing, the Canadian Case," Working Paper 89-8, Faculty of Administration, University of Ottawa.

64 See H. Noori, "Insight," communiqué, Research Centre for Management of New Technology, Wilfrid Laurier University, Waterloo, Vol. 3, No. 1, Fall 1987, p. 1.

65 See "Harwill Technologies International - Table Ronde," p. 2 and "Saskatchewan Research Council - Adapter la technologie pour combler les besoins des petits fabricants," p. 12, *L'Innovation*, supplement to *Commerce Canada*, Winter 1986.

66 For an appropriate discussion of technological innovation models, see R. Miller, "L'émergence des firmes de haute technologie," *Gestion, revue internationale de gestion*, Vol. 8, No. 4, November 1983, p. 38-47.

67 In particular, courses at the University of Montreal, the University of Waterloo and Dalhousie University in Halifax.

68 For a fairly detailed comparison, see R. Giasson, *Les PME coopératives et les PME à capital-actions: différences et similarités*, reflective document, Office de planification et de développement du Québec, 1981, p. 48-58.

69 An analysis of the phenomenon appears in J. Defourny, "Les nouvelles coopératives: quelles racines, quel avenir?," *Revue des études coopératives*, no. 208/5, 3rd trimester 1982, p. 77-81.

70 H. Bherer, "Nouveaux entrepreneurs ou nouveaux coopérateurs," *Le Devoir*, 21 April 1983, p. 11-13.

71 Drawn from J. Lotz, "Community Entrepreneurs," *Policy Options Politiques*, Vol. 5, No. 2, March 1984, p. 40.

72 See M. Kronstrom, "Le JAL pour la survie de l'arrière-pays," *Développement Québec*, Vol. 7, No. 6, October 1980, p. 17.

73 See A. Joyal, "Le rôle du tiers-secteur dans le développement économique et régional," Document LAP-84-85, Laboratoire en économie et gestion des systèmes de petites dimensions, Université du Québec à Trois-Rivières, 1984, p. 13.

74 See A. Létourneau, "Tout pour la musique," *Entreprise*, Vol. 1, No. 3, March 1985, p. 14.

75 C. Brouse, "Successors - Alice Klein and Michael Hollett: Toronto's Alternative Press Gang," *Canadian Business*, Vol. 60, No. 8, August 1987, p. 61.

76 A study carried out in some regions of Quebec revealed certain aspects of this reality in mutation. See A. Joyal, "La dynamique du secteur des services et le développement régional: la contribution du tiers-secteur marchand," Document LAP-84-08, Laboratoire en économie et gestion des systèmes de petites dimensions, Université du Québec à Trois-Rivières, 1984, p. 14-20.

77 Some analysts recognize four kinds of "new entrepreneurs" in France: workers, social workers, technological cooperators and alternative entrepreneurs. This latter group, the most heterogeneous, is involved in traditional activities (e.g., joinery, restoration) and competes directly in the market without counting on grants. See J. Chancel and P.E. Tixier, "Le désir d'entreprendre," *Autrement*, 20 September 1979, p. 10-11.

78 A. Joyal, *op. cit.*, p. 5-6. Our translation.

79 H. Bherer, *op. cit.*, p. 11-13. Our translation.

80 J. Lotz, *op. cit.*, p. 42.

81 H. Bherer, *op. cit.*, p. 13. Our translation.

82 G. d'Amboise and Y. Gasse, "Défis prioritaires pour propriétaires-dirigeants de PME: similarités et différences," working document no. 82-113, Québec, Faculty of Administrative Sciences, Université Laval, 1982, p. 2. Our translation.

83 Y. Gasse, "L'entrepreneurship: une stratégie de recherche et d'intervention pour le développement," *Revue de gestion des petites et moyennes organisations P.M.O.*, Vol. 1, No. 5, 1985, p. 13. Our translation

84 The definitional dilemma is ever-persisting in the literature on entrepreneurship. See A.M. Cohen, "Entrepreneur and entrepreneurship - the definition dilemma," National Centre for Management Research and Development, School of Business Administration, The University of Western Ontario, Working Paper Series No. NC89-08. The present discussion does not attempt to solve the conceptual issue; the choice proposed appears nevertheless very practical. It helps identify a specific actor and certainly leads to less semantic confusion.

85 Incubators, increasingly popular in facilitating the start-up of young firms, have a further role to play. Their founders should make venture creators aware very early of the managerial demands at other stages in the life of their business. See the following texts that deal with incubators: R.M. Knight, "A study of incubation centers in Ontario," Working Paper, National Centre for Management Research and Development, University of Western Ontario, November 1988, 18 p.; J. Robidoux, "The incubator approach to new business creation in Quebec - an overview," Entrepreneurship into the 90s, National

Centre for Management Research and Development, The University of Western Ontario, June 1989, p. 17-20.

86 Some other texts have inspired these comments: A.C. Cooper, "Strategic Management: New Ventures and Small Business," *Long Range Planning*, Vol. 14, No. 5, October 1981, p. 39-45; C.W. Hofer and R. Charan, "The Transition to Professional Management: Mission Impossible?," *American Journal of Small Business*, Vol. IX, No. 1, Summer 1984, p. 1-11; J.M. Toulouse, "A propos d'entrepreneurship," *Entrepreneurship-Innovation*, special number, June 1985, p. 15-16; R. Kao, "Entrepreneurial Decision-Making Behaviour Compared with Corporate Managers in Business Management," *Journal of Small Business and Entrepreneurship*, Vol. IV, No. 3, Winter 1986-1987, p. 12-21; J. Lorrain and L. Dussault, "Management Behaviors and Types of Entrepreneurs: The Case of Manufacturing Business in the Survival and Establishment Stage," *The Spirit of Entrepreneurship*, R.G. Wyckham *et al.*, dir., 32nd Annual Conference, International Council for Small Business, June 1987, p. 77-93.

CHAPTER 4

MAIN ADVANTAGES AND PARTICULAR PROBLEMS OF SMEs

SMEs are popular these days. In many people's minds, smaller organizations are generally better able to respond to their environment's individual and social needs. They also have other qualities that give them an advantage over bigger organizations. But they are also widely believed to encounter specific difficulties too. This chapter focuses on these two aspects of the reality of Canadian SMEs.

Many SME operations are favoured by particular environmental conditions, and their effectiveness results from certain distinct skills. In this chapter, these typical characteristics are described on the basis of some classic works on the subject, and particular points are illustrated by more recent observations made in a Canadian context.

The second part of the chapter sets out the main problems regularly encountered by Canadian SMEs. These difficulties were identified in an exhaustive review of a number of diagnoses of firms throughout the country.

Some guidelines that may help SMEs choose their orientation are also put forward. These suggestions are meant to contribute to the thinking of individual owner-managers. They should first make him aware of his firm's limits and then enable him to better identify the real opportunities open to his organization.

SMEs: NECESSARY AND ATTRACTIVE ORGANIZATIONS

Today, we tend to attribute all kinds of qualities to smaller organizations, and generally speaking they enjoy a level of popularity envied by many bigger businesses. During the last 10 years, SMEs have moved from almost total neglect to a position of privilege in the public eye. We have learned to recognize the essential role they play in their environment. They are seen as a way of realizing personal ambitions, and their distinct operational qualities are highly valued.

A Necessary Economic and Social Role

Throughout the world, renewed interest is being shown in smaller units—and Canada is no exception.

For many years, government-related structures, in full expansion, were the source of much economic activity and jobs throughout the country. However, in recent times, with policies of rationalization and restricted budgets, this is no longer the case. In addition, the role of the big firms that were traditionally responsible for a large part of Canada's trade and jobs has changed. Big businesses have become much more automated, and no longer create jobs.[1] They are less and less suited to innovation too.[2]

According to many economists, the methods used to regulate the economy over the last decades are no longer feasible today. These methods were based on systematic growth and ever-increasing productivity to encourage mass consumption, and required state intervention through fiscal and budgetary policies to balance supply and demand. Today, on the one hand, growth and productivity are slowing down; and on the other hand, consumers are increasingly critical of mass-produced goods. With production undergoing profound restructuring and with high unemployment, the State can no longer maintain growth, since growth of incoming funds is slowing steadily and demands made by social needs are increasing steadily. Something else needs to be done.

As Pierre-André Julien said,

Fortunately, the situation is evolving. In particular, thousands of entrepreneurs, in increasingly fragmented markets, imagine new forms of production and goods and services are constantly renewed, creating change and taking advantage of it. We know that the small businesses have been in full expansion for fifteen years, causing the reversal of the secular trend for concentration (which we saw before the 1970s), not only with respect to employment, but also to the added value share. (...) It is true at the same time the large firms merge even more often (...) But these multiple takeovers most often are only tricks which change nothing in an industrial structure rapidly evolving.

In short, with accelerated change by mutation, the entrepreneur will have to be increasingly present. Economic theory cannot stay any longer unconcerned about this phenomenon.[3]

Even traditional small and medium-sized firms are better equipped than big firms to face a period of economic recession. Julien's research on the Mauricie-Bois Francs area of Quebec between 1975 and 1982 reveals the superior performance of the small and medium-sized firms studied.[4] The flexibility of smaller businesses would explain their increased "resistance" to environmental turbulence. In some cases their relative profitability also better prepared them to survive this difficult period.

Their employees, too, are better educated and more open in their criticism of the suffocating bureaucratization of larger bodies. Many of them are increasingly critical of the hierarchical organization of decision-making power and the impersonal relations in big firms. All social classes today are seeking a better quality of life—an indirect consequence of the higher overall level of education—which necessarily implies an improvement in working styles as well as lifestyles. The working style they are looking for is one that allows personal qualities to be expressed and the opportunity for direct access to management, colleagues, suppliers and customers.[5]

The SME phenomenon forms part of the process of questioning certain economic and social values. "Small is beautiful": this famous saying can be referred not only to the beauty of things on a human scale, but also to the fact that "smallness" is necessary, attractive and more possible today than ever before.[6] Clearly, what is being rejected is overexpansion on a gigantic scale, exploitation, inhumanity. The scope of the entrepreneurial movement reflects a certain social questioning. "A small or medium-sized firm that is born and that lasts is not simply a smaller reproduction of a big firm. It represents a questioning of the industrial society of the 1960s and proposes a new social model."[7]

Only recently, economists and statisticians have had to recognize the significant presence of small and medium-sized firms in the economies of many countries. The contribution of such firms has been clearly shown in Canada; we need only remind ourselves of a few revealing statistics. In 1986, Canadian SMEs transacted business worth $460 billion and provided jobs for 5 million people.[8] From 1978 to 1987, firms with less than 500 employees created 1,200,000 net new jobs throughout the country.[9] In addition, 45 per cent of the net increase in the number of jobs resulted from the creation of new firms during the period 1974 to 1982.[10] The same may well hold true for more recent years.

The Canadian Federation of Independent Business, in research carried out in Canada within the framework of an international study, presented three interesting conclusions and highlighted the innovative role of SMEs.

> It has shown firstly that the small business sector is a major source of new economic activity. Nearly seven out of every ten Canadian firms included in the survey had been founded by the respondent.
>
> Secondly, the paper highlights major innovative characteristics of small business. They were shown to take frequent advantage of new market opportunities: about three in ten respondents reported significant changes since 1980 in their range of customers. In addition, over a quarter had carried out innovations to make use of new methods of production, promotion and distribution, while as many as two-thirds of all Canadian firms included in the survey indicated that they were actively searching for information on technological changes for use in some area of their business.
>
> Finally, the contribution of small business to their local economies is a significant feature of their activities. The Canadian firms surveyed tended to deal with a relatively large network of fairly local customers. Further, they played a major role in local net job creation in the early 1980s, with over half of the small

businesses surveyed reporting net growth in numbers employed between January 1980, or start-up date in the case of younger firms, and January 1983.[11]

Once again, this lends support to the idea that small and medium-sized firms are vitally important in today's society. They play an essential economic role through a variety of often innovative activities instigated by them. They also play a central social role through their involvement in the daily life of local communities. SMEs can satisfy a number of needs that are not always met by big business. By their presence, they also act as a buffer against possible abuse by big firms, in that they break up quasi-monopolistic situations.

SMEs are firms that belong to their milieu. They were mostly created to satisfy the needs of a local or regional community, and depend on a particular population for their survival and growth. They must therefore remain alert to the particular demands and social values of that population. Often, they give priority to products and services from local bodies when looking for suppliers, and are privileged places of work for people living in the area. When the firm is successful, the community is the first to benefit. Small and medium-sized firms are largely responsible for the dynamics of the economic and social tissue in many of our regions; Canada's vast territory clearly requires this particular skill. Their owner-managers inspire many different activities and often form the backbone of municipal and community organizations. Many owner-managers of Canadian SMEs recognize that they have certain social responsibilities apart from making a profit.[12] Some researchers have suggested that small firms tend to be more sensitive to social concerns than big firms.[13] They provide our future economic leaders with valuable experience, and foster the development of an entrepreneurial attitude favourable to new initiatives.

Setting up a small firm usually requires relatively limited initial funding, which means that older people can choose entrepreneurship as a way of returning to economic life when bigger firms want nothing more to do with them. In the same way, setting up a firm is a way for younger people to enter the economic world by creating their own jobs. The examples described previously show that it is possible for them to do this, provided they have the necessary determination and skills.[14]

A Possible Way of Fulfilling Hopes

Many of us have dreamed of creating our own business. Some of us have translated this dream into action, and in these cases the adventure has, almost without exception, begun with a small-scale, or very small-scale, operation. SMEs are so-called precisely because their activities are relatively limited. The level of initial requirements and the importance of daily activities depend on individual capacities; it is always possible to stay small. If the firm grows, so much the better; the owner-manager will have had the time to develop, too.

Chief executives of big firms find all kinds of motivating factors in their work. For example, they are usually interested in advantages such as job security, a good salary, social benefits, a career, the possibility of power, prestige and so on. People who choose to work in small and medium-sized firms are obviously not indifferent to this kind of thing, but the majority of them are also driven by a pressing desire for independence. The fact of having greater personal autonomy has often drawn them to smaller firms. SME owner-managers prefer their freedom of action to hierarchical formalities and orders from superiors. Some situations are clearly more propitious for making a personal choice; and those who find themselves at the head of a small firm, whether by choice or by force of circumstances, are usually happy with their lot.

Owning a business fulfils the need of many individuals today. As well as allowing independence and autonomy, SMEs can also, among other things,

- provide a solution to an employee's work-related frustrations. Since he cannot take advantage of his ideas and initiatives in his job, he turns his thoughts towards creating his own job framework;

- provide the chance to master events. Running a firm allows a person to direct events, rather than be directed by them;

- provide a way of achieving self-fulfilment. The difficulty of fulfilling their needs within other organizations often pushes individuals to take risks elsewhere and enjoy the satisfaction of succeeding;

- provide a way of identifying with the work you do. To a certain extent, owner-managers shape their firms in their own image.

For colleagues and employees, SMEs can also correspond to deeply-held personal values. Some people discover the possibility of satisfying the following needs, among others:

- affective needs such as the need to belong, the need to participate and the need to form solid links with other people. The proximity of people in SMEs fosters community of feelings and objectives;
- the need to take on responsibility. The small size of SMEs allows everyone more opportunity to play a recognized role and to feel useful;
- the need to be recognized and to feel important. In small firms, everyone can be in touch with decision centres; they can sometimes influence choices. Everyone can identify more with the firm and feel as though they really count.[15]

Launching your own business, either alone or with other people, is an attempt to satisfy needs like these. Many young Quebec and European entrepreneurs who met in December 1985 to share their experiences as founding owner-managers of small firms confirmed it. This is how some of them explained their choice.

There were many reasons for getting involved in a venture project. The first was the desire to create my own job. But there was also my wish to tackle a sizable challenge, to have my own firm and to fulfil a dream (. . .)

For me, there was only one factor that inspired me: the need to go forward. I had lots of ideas, I wanted to innovate and persevere, and the creation of the business was only the normal extension of the aim I had fixed for myself: to get away from the beaten track and do something for myself (. . .)

We were very aware of our own potential and we wanted above all to concentrate on it and develop it for ourselves, rather than leaving it in the hands of a state body or a big firm. Although we were all very different personality-wise, we all shared a common, and very important, characteristic: the taste for risk and challenge. Also, our different university backgrounds became a driving force in the decision to create something using our own means. We were attracted by innovation, risk, the rarity of the product and the difficulty of designing it.[16]

This is in no way meant to be an in-depth analysis of entrepreneurial motivations that have already been discussed elsewhere in this book. It is merely an additional reminder that entrepreneurial initiatives like these are encouraged by the way SMEs operate.

Investing all their energies in their own business is also, for some owner-managers, a way of achieving financial success. Playing a part in their own firm's profitability, working for themselves and making money, building up a fortune for themselves and their families, are all factors that may contribute to their decision to put their dreams into action. In fact, many have achieved personal financial success through building their own firm.

The most striking feature, however, is often the level of satisfaction experienced by people running their own businesses. The comments made on the subject by a group of independent workers confirms this.

They considered themselves to be in control of their work and personal life and felt a great deal of satisfaction. In spite of the frustrations from long hours and multiple demands, they were rewarded by having independence, flexibility and a sense of accomplishment. Few of them would have it any other way.[17]

They had found work they liked—as is often the case for owner-managers of small firms.

Distinct Operating Characteristics

It is a recognized fact that small and medium-sized firms have some characteristics that give them an operational advantage. Relations with the environment are often easier than in big firms, and their internal operating characteristics are often more attractive.

The proximity of the customer means that the firm can acquire an intuitive appreciation of his needs. In addition, frequent contacts with a regular clientele help develop a feeling of loyalty towards the firm. This privileged relationship is often strengthened by the efforts made by many SMEs to supply a specialized product tailor-made to meet the customer's requirements, and to provide a reliable after-sales service. Many small manufacturers and tradesmen of all kinds have perfected the personal touch that big firms can never provide. Top performers are typically specialized firms. The proximity of the customer also means that the firm hears about new openings much more quickly. For example, how many firms have begun to produce a new product or improved piece of equipment simply because a loyal client specifically asked for it? SMEs can produce in small quantities; they are not always forced to submit to the demands of mass production. Even a relatively small contract can be profitable for a small organization.

Small firms are particularly quick to react to requests from their environment. The interaction between market and production is quick and direct. It is astonishing how speedily a small firm can come up with a tailor-made service or concrete solutions to new problems. Whereas in a big firm, moving away from standardized production can be a long process, in a small firm it may take only a few days. Lighter commitments mean that SMEs can seize opportunities that present themselves, especially in markets that change quickly. They can also generally follow up new trends identified in a market or try to thwart a competitive strategy. The same goes for new legislation or new directives from various bodies. The problems that may arise in cases like these are all too often caused by the weight of the fiscal load imposed by new demands.

Droughts and price downturns greatly affected big farm equipment manufacturers in the early 1980s. For smaller Prairie firms, it was a new opportunity. The following analysis illustrates an important advantage of being relatively small:

> While overall Canadian farm equipment revenues dropped by as much as 40 per cent during the 1980s,

sales of such western makers as Saskatoon's Flexicoil Ltd. and Morris Industries Ltd. of Yorkton, Sask., increased by 25 per cent.

In part, the growth of local manufacturing has come because of the tough times. Most of the Prairie firms are what farmers call "shortlines." Instead of producing the entire range of agricultural equipment as their so-called "mainline" competitors such as John Deere Ltd. do, most shortlines construct only a few products. And while sales of some high-ticket items such as tractors and combines declined precipitously in the 1980s, those of others hardly missed a beat. Particularly strong performers were the tillage and seeding equipment in which many Prairie shortlines specialize. Saddled with high overheads and tractor and combine lines that simply wouldn't move, the mainlines fell with a thud. For the shortlines, this fall was an opportunity. Significant gains in market share came their way when once loyal mainline equipment dealers and farmers began to question the wisdom of brand loyalty.

From their traditional strengths of building niche-filling equipment that is better adapted to prairie conditions, many small manufacturers have moved on to making mainline equipment that is just plain better. The Prairie companies seem to be a little ahead of the game. Their machinery is designed here and it's often better suited to (the Prairies) kind of farming."[18]

Their smaller size offers SMEs the possibility of a simpler, more flexible structure—and that means they can adapt more easily than big firms that are often too hierarchical and hampered by bureaucracy.[19] Centralized yet uncomplicated decision-making mechanisms make immediate action possible. In a larger organization, you would often have to draw up a service note, make an appointment and wait. In a small firm, you simply need to get in touch with the owner or small management group, and you know very quickly what to expect.

In an SME, everyone knows each other. Employees are in daily contact with each other; management is generally on a first-names basis with everyone. In fact, communications cannot be impersonal. Everyone has the chance to get to know everyone else better: management through employees' problems, employees through management's ambitions and concerns. Since information circulates better than in a big firm, the employees are more aware of the need to be personally effective. Everyone benefits from a vision of the firm as a whole, and can better imagine the consequences of his own actions and the results of his contribution. There is a good chance that this kind of working milieu is perceived as being more humane, and consequently people are more motivated to spend their time and energy there.[20]

Many small firms are reputed to have lower operating costs than their larger counterparts. This better performance can sometimes be explained by the employees' concern for effectiveness, versatility, lower indirect costs and so on. R&D activities seem to be more effective and less costly relatively speaking in smaller firms. In the service sector especially, efficiency and small size go hand in hand.[21]

Magna International, today a large firm, is a typical example of faith in the distinctive skills of small organizations. It based its development on entrepreneurial resources and decentralized operating units. Each unit is run independently by a general manager and is associated with the group for financing, transactions, exchanges and various services. The general manager is also a shareholder and receives a share of the profits. No unit may exceed the 100-employee mark; units that do so are broken down to form new, smaller units. This formula joins group strength and professional management to the flexibility and team spirit of a smaller unit, and could serve as an example for other similar initiatives.[22]

A visit to any successful SME will reveal the very particular spirit to be found there. SMEs foster the development of an attitude that breeds initiative and encourages action. Enlightened management, teamwork and a general concern for good quality work are all factors that contribute to their dynamism. They are often essential ingredients for success and can all be put to good use in small firms.

We can say, then, that small firms have distinctive capacities. Their results in terms of certain activities are better than those achieved by big business. To sum up, in concrete terms they should allow the demands of the job to be better satisfied in particular situations, such as:

- when experimenting with a new idea, a new product or a new type of firm;
- when the owner's personal commitment weighs heavily in the sale of a product or service;
- when the target market is mainly local;
- when the business is specialized in the sale of perishable goods;
- when aiming at a specific, limited market segment;
- when the industry is characterized by a wide variety of product styles or customer tastes;
- when it is essential to maintain close relations with employees to achieve harmonious operations.[23]

If, in addition, the firm can find a market segment that has been left aside or badly served by big business, if it can put together the skills needed to assure a competent and thoughtful service, if it is ready to devote plenty of time and energy to its business, then it has all the basic prerequisites for success.

SPECIFIC PROBLEMS OF SMALLER FIRMS

Small firms, by their very nature, have characteristics that mean they can become highly effective. Quick decision making, simple structures and flexible operations, for example, have led to success for many SMEs. Their smaller size, however, exposes them to certain difficulties that bigger firms avoid. For example, they carry less weight in a world where the strongest set the rules of the game; they lack resources because of their limited funds; and they have weaknesses at the managerial level. All these factors expose them to a variety of problems. Despite their vitality, they are generally more vulnerable to business risks than bigger firms, and some problems are accentuated by the size factor.

A great deal has been written on the difficulties and problems of small firms. The texts begin with a model of the ideal firm and go on to provide an exhaustive list of the actual and potential problems to be encountered. In the pages that follow, I will be discussing the specific problems of Canadian SMEs. I have been able to identify these problems fairly accurately using both the work done by other researchers in a Canadian context and my own personal observations. An analysis of these problems may help owner-managers overcome them.

Frequent Vulnerability to Events

Despite the fact that they are usually well able to adapt, SMEs are nevertheless fairly weak and vulnerable to a variety of threats. They operate in an environment that has not always been tailor-made for them. Economic, industrial and political structures are more suited to the large organizations or institutions that defined them. The limited powers of smaller organizations do not usually give them much say in what goes on, and their limited resources offer little protection against difficult situations.

The clientele of a SME is generally geographically limited and restricted to a well-defined market segment. Such firms usually avoid direct competition with bigger businesses by choosing interstices in economies or markets that have been neglected. However, if a big firm decides to enter that market, small firms are sometimes threatened. A price war, for example, that could easily be envisaged by a giant firm could quickly use up a small firm's entire resources. Small firms are also easy victims of piracy through imitations of their original products; they are generally poorly equipped to control this kind of thing and to counter stronger organizations that steal their products. Unfortunately, they also serve as a training ground for specialized workers who then move on to bigger firms, where they find better job security and more attractive financial compensation. SMEs lose many of their best employees this way.

Since they are traditionally less well-organized to defend their interests, SME owner-managers do not place much faith in their lobbying powers with government. New standards in terms of health and safety at work and new working regulations imposed on some industries do not always take account of the capacity and methods of smaller organizations. The consequences are often proportionally more serious for smaller firms than bigger ones. How many small firms have disappeared because of exaggerated standards that brought financial difficulties and discouraged owner-managers?

The ultimate responsibility for the firm's operations almost always rests on one person's shoulders. Sometimes the owner-manager shares the task of looking after his firm with a few close colleagues. He lacks time; he cannot always be as vigilant as circumstances demand. His absence, whatever the reason, may well prove fatal for his firm. Everything depends on him, nothing works if he is not there. All this is perhaps symptomatic of a lack of managerial skill that is unfortunately all too common in small and medium-sized firms. It can be seen through poor management, a day-to-day approach that inevitably keeps the firm in a weak position with respect to its environment.

During the 1981-82 recession, many SMEs were forced to close down. An estimated 10,000 small firms with annual revenues of less than $2 million went under in 1982, and many others simply ceased to exist.[24] Very high interest rates had a proportionally greater impact on SME operations, often representing a larger part of their expenses. However, these additional demands on their financial resources were more a catalyst than the main cause in many cases of bankruptcy. Deeper-rooted problems already existed, and the recession only accentuated them. Many SMEs were unable to meet the new demands, and it was too late to change.

In his study of the characteristics of bankrupt firms, Lalonde explains the difficulties caused for many by a lack of managerial knowledge on the part of the owner-managers and, more importantly, by their lack of vision for the future; for them, the future boiled down to an average of two months.[25] Knight compared a sample of bankrupt SMEs with a sample of survivors. Those that had ceased trading had done so when they were young, while they were relatively small. His inquiry confirms that such firms experience continual problems in terms of working capital, have inadequate accounting systems and are often run by owner-managers who are incompetent managerially.[26] Ibrahim and Ellis support this latter point.[27] All this reinforces the hypothesis that the position of SMEs, already vulnerable because of their lack of resources, is further weakened by a lack of foresight on the part of the owner-managers, who are alone and overwhelmed by the demands of their daily tasks.

In an economically difficult period, many firms, whatever their size, are likely to fail. However, smaller ones are more vulnerable, since for them a single major management error can be fatal. The more fragile the firm, the more it is at the mercy of circumstances; and without reserve resources or an adequate financial structure, it will rarely get a second chance. Despite the legendary ability of small firms to adapt, despite the vitality shown by many of them in difficult situations, this group is at risk far more than bigger, better armed firms.

The pages that follow set out in more detail the problems encountered by Canadian SMEs. They present a summary of a number of studies on the specific difficulties of small and medium-sized firms in Canada, and illustrate more precisely the main day-to-day challenges and concerns faced by SME owner-managers here. The account specifies in turn the problems affecting each major activity centre in the firm, beginning with personnel and moving on to production, financial operations, marketing and general management. Particular attention is paid to the crucial challenges presented today by innovation, both technological and administrative.

Recruiting Qualified Staff

Small and medium-sized firms experience difficulty in finding, training and keeping the employees they need. A survey of its members by the Canadian Federation of Independent Business (CFIB) in 1984 revealed the gravity of the situation.[28] Respondents complained of a real shortage of qualified manpower. An average of 2.3 jobs were unfilled in every firm taking part in the survey; the Federation put the total number at 170,000. Jobs demanding no special skills or training were no problem—there were plenty of candidates. However, finding capable people for office work, sales, management, production or any other professional task proved more difficult. The problem was worse in firms with more advanced production technology. Clearly, there was criticism of the relevance of courses provided by training establishments; and there were even accusations of industrial "kidnapping" on the part of big firms. According to many CFIB members, big firms are unwilling to train their employees; they seem to prefer to attract good employees already trained in small firms by offering higher wages.

> A large number of available positions required on-the-job training and considerable investment. If an employee who had received this training subsequently left the firm for a better-paid job elsewhere, the employer had to start again from scratch.[29]

It was suggested that the government should either force big firms to train their own staff, or do something to help small firms keep their employees.

In Quebec during the last few years, the warning bell has often been sounded. Research showed that in four manufacturing sectors (footwear, sports goods, aerospace equipment and machine tools), the main concern of SME owner-managers was recruiting qualified production personnel.[30] Two subsequent studies by the Quebec Department of Industry and Commerce on the iron and metal industries also revealed serious shortages.[31] SME owner-managers have to face the consequences of this on a daily basis. Michèle Boulé, a co-director of Coccinelle Inc., a children's clothing firm, could not find a qualified seamstress at first; Paul-Henri Fillion of Hoplab had trouble finding argon welders, stainless steel polishers and panel beaters; Jacques Thibault of Pole Air Aviation Inc., a small firm specializing in machining and renovating airplane instruments and accessories, often has to employ master clockmakers.[32] Although at the time there was a surplus of qualified manpower in some traditional professions in Quebec, it is clear that serious shortages existed in fields connected with electronics and computing. Too few young people, for example, were prepared to work in industry, where design and manufacturing are computerized.[33]

Our firms are short of qualified staff, and yet a worrying number of young people are unemployed: a paradoxical situation. Blaming one side or the other does not help at all. It would be in everyone's interest to do something about it, and it is up to everyone to contribute towards finding a solution to these two problems that are unquestionably interdependent. Government bodies must keep an eye on the future to foresee new needs; educational institutions must instil in young people the taste for a job well-done; unions must do their share in getting to the root of the problem by agreeing occasionally to re-examine acquired rights; SME owner-managers also have a role to play by encouraging training and employment. If human resources are a firm's most valuable asset, then SMEs should invest in them. Lay-offs can be avoided by better operations planning; shortages of qualified manpower can be offset by introducing ways of making on-the-job training easier. A deeper analysis of the climate in machine manufacturing firms shows that firms who can maintain their production rate have less difficulty recruiting and keeping specialized workers.[34] To keep up with technology, Rotobec Inc., a firm specialized in the manufacturing and marketing of forestry equipment, puts the emphasis on staff training; in collaboration with the Commission de formation professionnelle du Québec, the firm has invested in training all the staff it will need following expansion.[35] More firms could do the same thing.

Raw Material Supplies

Staff recruitment is a generally recognized problem in SMEs; many owner-managers freely admit it. However, the problem of supplies, although an important one, is much less well-known. Researchers interested in the daily operations of SMEs are also less concerned with this aspect. Nevertheless, an inquiry into administrative difficulties carried out on a group of manufacturing sector SMEs identified this factor as being a constant concern. The scarcity of some commodities, the irregular quality of others, higher prices and, especially, long delivery times, are serious handicaps for some firms.[36] Obtaining raw material supplies is often a real challenge for small firms. In the case of a new venture that needed various products for start-up, Kao discovered an attitude among large suppliers that seems to be a common one in the business world:

> No large material suppliers would supply small quantities to the new firm (...) A special arrangement was made where the new firm must wait until there are orders for the required supplies from other customers (...) Prices charged by large suppliers to the firm were more than the prices they offered to large users.[37]

Big firm representatives sometimes discriminate in this way against small firms. And while practices like these place barriers to entry into certain sectors, as current economic theories explain, they also effectively restrict the smooth operation of daily business for existing small firms.[38] The real scarcity of parts for a product or a temporary, seasonal or cyclic shortage of raw materials can limit the production of an upstream supplier. Artificial shortages have also occasionally been provoked with the aim of accumulating stocks and reselling them at much higher prices. These situations can sometimes explain the difficulty smaller buyers sometimes have in getting supplies. More often, however, the supplier adopts a policy of favouring bigger customers at the expense of those who buy less. A firm that orders in small quantities is clearly a less attractive proposition profit-wise than one who regularly places large orders. The relationship with the supplier is therefore different. A small firm, often captive in its business network, has few alternatives available and cannot negotiate purchase conditions. On a strictly rational basis, the reasoning of big suppliers' representatives is logical. Calculating optimal production runs to maximize profits leads to discrimination against certain customers. As can be seen to some extent in rigorous analyses of situations involving several distinct categories of customers, it is sometimes better to reject low-income customers to allow an optimal rationing policy to be adopted.[39] The resulting conclusions are not usually to the advantage of SMEs.

It is easy to imagine the problems arising from long delays in receiving raw materials that are essential in the manufacturing process of a small firm's main product. The production rate is slowed down or even brought to a standstill; if the delay is prolonged, perhaps employees will have to be laid off; the firm can no longer meet the demands of its own customers, running the risk of losing some—or more if the situation persists or the same thing happens again. The logic of events is clear. However, this scenario is extreme—things are often not as bad as that. Nevertheless, any delay, however short, can disturb production and other activities in a small firm.

It may well be possible for SMEs themselves to protect themselves better against this kind of risk. When a firm's market knowledge is poor, it will have difficulty assessing what it needs to buy. Some SMEs fill their order books during annual trade fairs; others receive orders and contracts, as and when the customers appear. In this case, they have to produce without being able to forecast—that is, without having assessed the quantities needed or placed orders for raw materials or parts. Even if forecasting was attempted, the types and quantities would have to be fixed by guesswork; if ordering was delayed, the suppliers, their own order books full, would not be able to guarantee the quick deliveries needed. On the other hand, an owner-manager who has taken steps to assess his annual market has set realistic objectives and consequently places his main orders early, thus greatly reducing the risk of supply problems. A firm where Kao analyzed the relationship with the suppliers had penetrated its sector with the help of several different but complementary strategies, including the following:

> It differentiates its products from imports in quality and design (...) It is fundamental strategy to employ well-trained and well-mannered salespeople and to concentrate on a target market (...) Most parts are standardized and the production process can easily be automated, once the volume justifies this change (...) The search for better suppliers is a continuing task of the firm. Planning made it possible for the firm to secure needed inventory at better prices from its suppliers.[40]

Better planning results in a more complete overall view of the firm's activities, which can thus be better coordinated, and this in turn facilitates the design of strategies that will eventually lead to success.

During the last few years, some SMEs have wanted to experiment with a new, seemingly effective formula. Several firms joined forces to buy raw materials and supplies. Their joint orders earned more attention from suppliers, and the buying group got both better service and lower prices. The system requires a certain amount of planning on the part of each member: they must all be able to assess fairly accurately the quantities they will need if the system is to be effective.

The following is an example of a successful buying group:

> Gold Leaf Office Products Ltd. is an example of one buying group that has turned out to be a gold mine for its shareholders. It started in 1968 with just three members, all of them in Western Canada. Walter Smith, then president of a

company called Miller Stationers in Edmonton, was its architect; he called up one office supply company he knew of in Vancouver and another in Calgary to suggest they'd benefit from buying together. Months later, all three were equal shareholders in Gold Leaf. Today the group has 11 shareholders across Canada, whose sales total about $180 million a year.

As in most buying groups, the shareholders support an independent office. Besides orchestrating their bulk buying, the four staff at Gold Leaf's office publish catalogues for all 11 members, print the advertising flyers and run a group-wide private brand of supplies, all of a better quality and at a lower cost to the individual firms than they could manage on their own.

Members of Gold Leaf also benefit in less obvious ways. "There's a fair amount of information-sharing that goes on between our member companies," says Michael Overholt, president of both Gold Leaf and Murphy Stationery Co. Ltd. of Vancouver, a member firm. "Our sales managers get together to talk about sales techniques, our computer people to talk about line support systems. We're all in the same business and we have similar problems. So it's important to discuss strategies. We learn from each other."

Gold Leaf owes its success in part to its careful selection of members. Ten of the 11 shareholder-companies have at least a one-third market share in a major Canadian city: this gives the group stability. Secondly, because the members are all in different cities, they're not in direct competition with one another. Finally, Gold Leaf's members are all about the same size, so they all gain far more from the group than they could ever achieve on their own.

In a fiercely competitive, ever-shifting market, the members of Gold Leaf have found the sort of stability that comes from enlightened self-interest. Although it has grown far beyond its beginnings in Edmonton, Gold Leaf has expanded without losing sight of how it came to be in the first place. The only thing that's remained the same, in fact, is the motivation: making sure the independents get their products at the lowest possible prices. And, in the end, that's what buying groups are all about.[41]

The Need for Technological Innovation

Technological innovation can be defined either as the creation of a new product that differs technically from previous products, or as the adoption of a new manufacturing process.[42] For SMEs, as for most other firms, there are two main reasons why innovation is necessary. Especially in today's context, SMEs should be able on the one hand to create new products, offer new services or improve existing products or services, and on the other hand, to adopt and use the most up-to-date tools and equipment.

Small and medium-sized manufacturing firms, especially those that have chosen high-tech sectors, have to continually develop and market new products. Manufacturing SMEs that never need to innovate in some way to penetrate a market or satisfy their regular customers' demands are rare indeed. It is a recognized fact that SMEs have contributed considerably to perfecting new products over the last few years. The R&D activities needed to do this clearly require funding, as do market surveys prior to marketing a new product, but many SMEs succeed despite their relatively limited resources.

> A small company may not have an elaborate lab or R and D personnel, but if there is any creative talent (at a minimum, the owner-manager himself), R and D activities can be based on technologies appropriate to the firm's need. Innovative undertakings can hold significant benefit for the smaller firm without the need for special R and D staff.[43]

A young physicist realized that fluorescent light, while used everywhere, was much disliked. He found a solution. Referring to the scientific principle of total internal reflection (the basis of fibre optics), he created an entirely new method of transmitting light. He called it The Light Pipe. TIR Systems Ltd. of Burnaby, B.C., was launched in 1982. Light Pipes are now installed in more than 150 locations in Canada and the United States. Sales were $1.2 million in 1987. The Light Pipe cuts maintenance costs, reduces heating bills and can even channel natural light into windowless enclosures. But investment in R&D must still continue. According to Lorne Whitehead, the U.B.C. graduate physicist-entrepreneur,

"The engineering costs were astronomical, because with each new sale the product had to be tailored to suit each customer's needs. The new objective is to identify areas in which TIR can produce products or applications that match specific market needs ... A deal signed in October 1987 with the giant Japanese trading corporation C. Itoh, illustrates Whitehead's intention to make this a global technology."[44]

It nevertheless seems that the founder is still doing most of the scientific thinking and research going on in the firm. He even saw to heightening the company's profile by lecturing at international lighting conferences and presenting papers at scientific seminars.

Many SMEs also take advantage of the various new technology assistance programs offered by governments. Some can also sub-contract their research to government bodies or educational institutions. Carterchem Inc., of Montreal, seems to do this successfully, according to its managing director.

We haven't got budgets to pay for Ph.D.s, chemists and all the staff needed for the research we've undertaken (...) We did the preliminary research ourselves to determine the problems to be dealt with and the sectors worth investigating. But the whole research and development process was done at CRIQ, under our constant supervision.[45]

Carterchem employed thirty or so people and had an annual turnover of $7.5 million. During the last few years, it has carried out several important projects in collaboration with the Centre de recherche industrielle du Québec (CRIQ), half of which are financed by the Canadian National Research Council (CNRC). Carterchem has in effect invested only a percentage of the total cost of the work, and yet is now winning new markets and appreciably increasing its productivity as a result. Dynamic SMEs will always find ways of creating and marketing a new product—as many current examples ably demonstrate.[46]

Designing and marketing a new product is quite a challenge for a small firm. Many will not tackle it, content to continue manufacturing products under licence or copying other firms' ideas. Each firm makes its own choice. However, the appearance of new production and management technologies presents a greater, more threatening challenge. Today, product quality, speed and efficiency of production and reasonably priced services all depend largely on improved production and management methods. All SMEs have to face up to the new technological challenge; nobody can afford not to introduce more modern, improved equipment. Very small firms could even gain a comparative advantage by doing so—an advantage that would allow them to reach the modest place they are aiming for in their market. Introducing a new product on the market is never perceived as a problem for a firm, but rather as a stimulating experience that requires effort but that can bring ultimate success. However, improving a production process, reducing costs and changing the way something is done are often seen as problems that need to be solved. For that reason, I have paid more attention to these factors here.

Economic and industrial structures are being destabilized by the rate of technological innovation. Both the shop floor and the office have been affected by changes in the business environment. The technological challenge is both a threat and an opportunity for modern SMEs. Those that want to grow need to take advantage of the most modern equipment; others, just to survive, need to install new production methods as quickly as possible. The operations of too many SMEs are archaic—neither production nor management tools have been changed since the firm was launched. In many cases the investments required are substantial for a small firm. Also, changing habits and learning another way of doing something is never easy, even for SMEs that are typically considered to be more flexible. However, those that have made the effort needed to adapt are usually the most dynamic and the best performers.

> Traditional scale strategy advocates bigger factories with longer runs which produce fewer products at a lower cost per unit. NT capabilities—extreme flexibility, rapid response, greater control, greater consistency, and faster throughput—suggest that the economies of scope argument is a better suited manufacturing strategy for today's competitive environment. Economies of scope exist when efficiencies are wrought by variety not volume, and where the same equipment can produce multiple products more cheaply in combination

than separately. In a marketplace which increasingly favours product customization and quick response to market demands, the emphasis on economies of scope enables the companies to effectively respond to the changes taking place in the market. For Canada, with a small manufacturing base, the notion of economies of scope makes sense as it enables the achievement of "flexibility of response to the fundamental changes in technology and world markets" without the requisite volumes of scale arguments. In short, manufacturing firms in Canada are better able to match costs, provide service and generally, compete internationally by utilizing the NT.[47]

All sectors have to face the technological challenge, although some are threatened more than others. In a study of 22 Quebec industries, Pierre-André Julien defined 13 sectors where firms need to modernize their equipment very quickly. Firms producing machinery, industrial electrical equipment and metals are the main ones to have to modernize and catch up in terms of productivity if they want to avoid an invasion of their market by outside competition—an invasion that may well result in their disappearance.[48]

It seems clear that when tariff barriers between the United States and Canada are significantly lowered, these sectors will be under an even greater threat. Whatever happens, the need to modernize will not just go away.

At present, big firms seem to take up the technological challenge quicker than small ones. The main innovations in recent years, especially in terms of latest technologies, have in fact come from larger organizations that are well-equipped and have ample budgets and considerable R&D units. For small firms, appropriating technology developed elsewhere is already a problem. They are neither sufficiently big nor sufficiently well-equipped production-wise for optimum use of technology, and the more progressive among them have had to uncover their own ways of transferring it and adapting it to their particular conditions, as well as inventing methods that suit their management.[49]

For example, big firms in Canada have paid much attention to production process automation, while only a few small firms are seriously interested. A study carried out in Ontario on small and big manufacturing firms provided interesting results on levels of acceptance of programmable automation:

> From the survey, it becomes apparent that many small firms are aware of the importance of programmable automation (. . .) Large firms are significantly more advanced than small firms when it comes to considering feasibility. Their present level of technology is higher and they have carried out more specific studies on automation. Yet, their concerns mirror those of smaller firms—increasing costs putting pressure on productivity and quality. Both see finances as the major barrier to automation, while the attitude of senior management is seen as the major promoter.[50]

The conclusions here highlight the fact that smaller firms are less advanced in terms of adopting automation, and also bring out the important role played by management. Some theories even propose the idea of firms that are "conservative" or "entrepreneurial." In conservative firms, management considers that innovation is generally costly and often harmful for production activities, whereas in entrepreneurial firms, they see regular, sizable innovations as being essential elements in a good overall strategy.[51] Any form of new technology requires some degree of openness to change. SMEs wanting to achieve a minimum level of technology need top managers who are favourable towards it. According to Gasse, the socio-economic environment can influence an SME owner-manager's decision to innovate.[52] If the enterprise environment is dynamic, if there are "champion" firms to clear the way and if the state provides sufficient incentives, then the adoption of new technologies would become generalized more quickly.

In reality, both external and internal factors have simultaneous effects on the decision to introduce new technologies into the production process in SMEs. Some of these factors were revealed in interviews with owners of small manufacturing businesses in Quebec. Market demands, such as fashion trends, the need to use new equipment and the need for better quality products, all play an important role in the decision to become better equipped. Another strong motivating factor is the need to keep up with competitors who already have more modern installations. The most frequently mentioned internal factors touch on high production costs and problems with product quality. Management often associates these factors with poor productivity and outdated production methods.[53]

The majority of owner-managers recognize the simultaneous influence of internal and external factors in their decision to modernize their manufacturing equipment. However, once the decision is made, purchase and, especially, implementation of the equipment also bring their own share of problems. The two main concerns mentioned by the owner-managers interviewed were connected with the various technical difficulties arising during operation of new machinery and the lack of training among the firm's regular employees. In the first case, the equipment has often not been sufficiently tested before being installed, and in the second case the necessary steps were not taken to train the employees who were to work with it. If the employees are not involved from the outset, or if they are given only superficial, hurried, on-the-job training, there is a high risk of misunderstandings and resistance. This study, like many others, also highlights the need for good preparation of the process as a whole when an SME wants to adopt more sophisticated technology for its manufacturing operations.[54]

Needless to say, the process from beginning to end usually takes much longer than anticipated. SME owner-managers who want to improve their equipment should not be put off by this, but it should serve as a warning to chief executives who are used to making on-the-spot decisions and seeing their projects realized quickly. Other research shows that the average length of time between awareness of the existence of the new technology and purchase is three and a half years. The time needed to install the equipment is seven and a half months, and mastering it takes another six months.[55] It is therefore a process that may well cause considerable upheaval in SMEs, as well as tying up a good part of their resources.

The following case, based on a real situation, highlights the kind of problems all too often met by SMEs undergoing modernization.

A firm's top manager realized he was having trouble keeping his good customers, for whom he had been manufacturing sawmill equipment for some years. He also discovered that his main local competitor had bought a highly efficient machine that meant he could produce more at a lower cost. As he was in danger of losing his market, he decided to look into the possibility of buying a digital lathe. He went to St. Louis in the United States, with the eventual operator, to see how it worked. After analyzing all the advantages and drawbacks, he and his collaborators finally decided to buy it, at a cost of $150,000. He then met with several government representatives to look into the possibility of financial support, but the complex procedures and time involved put management off this option, and it was eventually decided to finance the whole project privately.

Once the machine was installed, the employees had to get used to it, and this too took longer than anticipated. Because conditions were not ideal, the machine ran the risk of breaking down every four days or so. This meant bringing in a technician from St. Louis, not to mention the down-time during which everyone did what they could with the old machinery. All this was reflected in order delivery times. Customers on the whole were patient—but how long would their patience last? Faced with frequent breakdowns, the employees lost confidence in the machine. The operator in charge of it had to achieve the impossible, and became almost indispensable—a heavy burden for him to carry. At the time the case was written up, the company chairman had just called a special executive meeting to look into the problem. Since the lathe was out of action 10 per cent of the time, the investment was far from being a paying proposition, especially as management could no longer count on employee cooperation. Should the firm abandon the idea of modernizing and send the machine back to the suppliers? Michel Dubé was extremely disappointed, and wondered what had caused the project to fail. Had his decision been made too quickly? And yet, small firms must, sooner or later, face up to the fact of modernization. If they abandoned the project then, they would eventually have to start all over again. This is the kind of dilemma faced by many small firms.

Is this kind of situation typical when small firms commit themselves to a project without sufficient planning? The least we can say is that this is the kind of risk you run when a project is not adequately prepared.

Far-sighted SME owners know how to get help from suppliers and how to use manpower and training centre services to train specialized workers. For example, when Textiles Dionne Inc. decided in 1981 to build a new, highly automated factory, management involved the employees in the whole process. The employees themselves installed the machinery, under the supervision of specialists from a consultancy firm and with the help of equipment suppliers. Many of them are now able to repair breakdowns and even make improvements to the machine they operate.[56]

A study conducted in the Kitchener-Waterloo area in Ontario on the implementation of new technology, mainly computer-aided design, computer numerical control and computer-aided manufacturing, revealed some interesting facts.

> Factors most important to the success of these firms were quality, prompt delivery, manufacturing skills and marketing skills.
>
> Changes in numbers of personnel did not occur, but worker training requirements increased as job design was altered to include more technical knowledge, problem-solving, responsibility and accuracy.

According to the authors of the above study, some of the key implications of these results are quite evident.

> Small companies must recognize the need for technology and the opportunities it offers in terms of competitive ability. Management in small companies may be better equipped to analyze their strengths and weaknesses. The companies who met their expectations in technical areas were generally smaller in size than those who did not. Workers may be less resistant. Worker satisfaction was rated higher in smaller companies than in medium to large. The demand for quality with prompt delivery may force small manufacturers to adopt technology.
>
> The "soft" side of management becomes more and more important as new technology takes over. Much time and money must be expended on training to ensure a successful technology implementation. The respondents to the survey rated training of managers and training of production workers highest in areas where support is required. Management is realizing the need and reaching out. The two most useful methods of implementation involved training, both in-house and vendor supplied. Worker training requirements had the largest

increase in the question concerning human dimensions. The workers are also concerned about training as evidenced by the fact that retraining was considered the most central issue.[57]

Computer-based simulation training for employees is certainly worth considering in some cases. Many training organizations advocate it. As a *Financial Post* article said some time ago,

> While computer-based training is already standard procedure in some areas such as flight simulators for pilots and so-called war games played by the military, it is now making headway in business and industrial applications (. . .) How do you train your employees to operate and/or repair new, complex—and extremely expensive—computerized equipment? (. . .) You use computer-based training that simulates the performance of that equipment (. . .) Computer-based simulation lets employees test different conditions and get a walk through the process before the live performance.[58]

This formula is widely used for staff training in big firms and could certainly be adapted and offered to employees in smaller firms. Training organizations will undoubtedly discover a market for it.

The office is changing, too—just take a look at what has happened to your own work environment during the last few years. Rearranged floor space, computerized accountancy and bookkeeping, local electronic communication, quicker word processing and reproduction, and even electronic messenger services are all around us these days. SMEs will have to follow suit, to ensure quick communications, efficient services, staff well-being and their own public image. Small and medium-sized firms are certainly not indifferent to the new possibilities opening up, and the majority of them would like to install computerized office procedures. Even though many are not yet equipped, or only poorly equipped, they are nevertheless showing increased interest, as many studies reveal.[59]

SME owner-managers generally perceive information systems as being expensive but extremely useful in increasing efficiency and productivity. However, many Canadian SME owner-managers unfortunately do not understand the complexity of this new technology particularly well. The financial aspects are seen as being very important.[60] Yet, in general, not enough attention is paid to the human problems that may arise.[61] SME owner-managers do not usually know much about computers, are not always aware of the training needed and do not even think about offering leave or training courses to employees likely to use them. This is probably the main reason for the problems that arise when modern computer equipment is installed in offices.[62]

Innovation, whether in the factory or the office, means changing something. Learning a computer-controlled manufacturing process or producing their first letter on a word processor will make anyone feel insecure. But, when people gradually become more skilled and feel more in control of their work, and especially if their new skills have improved their output, then they are usually ready to invest a great deal of energy and initiative.

SME owner-managers must plan their projects, especially those that require significant changes. After carefully choosing the people they will work with, they should be confident in their ability to adapt and move forward.

Financing

Small firms have fewer resources than large ones. In fact, small firms are by definition limited in terms of assets and resources. It could be said that all their troubles stem from their limited financial resources. If the owner-manager had the money to do this, pay for that, and so on, things would be so much better. Making sure his firm has adequate funding is an owner-manager's constant worry—and some manage better than others. But financial problems also occasionally have non-financial roots.

How many small firms never got off the ground because the people behind them could not raise the necessary funding? Gathering preliminary information, taking the first steps, developing a prototype, building up an inventory—all this takes money, and you aren't even in business yet. You also very quickly need money as working capital and to buy equipment and premises. Firms are launched with ideas, a lot of work and willpower, but it also takes financial resources.

Anyone who has accumulated some financial assets is already in a better position to start up his business. There, too, you have to live within your means. Mostly, people do not have enough personal funds—and that means a first serious confrontation with the real world. An entrepreneur's first concerns are having enough confidence in his project to convince others of its value, inciting them to invest their savings in it and getting contributions from lending institutions. Every venture start-up, of course, has its own story. Many would-be entrepreneurs were able to count on funding from people close to them—"love money" from a relative's nest-egg or a loan from trusting friends. This happens throughout the world.[63] Others found themselves wealthier partners. In a lot of cases, financial institutions, after a close examination, had enough confidence in the project to underwrite it. In Canada, venture capital can be obtained from a wide variety of official sources. Start-up grants, loans of every kind and share capital are all available for projects that meet specific conditions. Obtaining funding depends on making a realistic estimate of the project's financial needs. A guarantee from the outset that the amount needed will be available can often prevent the quick failures unfortunately experienced by many entrepreneurs.

When the first years are successful, financial worries diminish. Products are well-received, customers abound, sales figures increase and the firm makes a profit. Money is no longer a problem, and other projects become possible. If the owner pays income taxes, it means he is making money: or so many entrepreneurs, content with their success, like to think. The firm is buzzing, business is increasing—the outfit is growing. But the amount invested in inventory is also growing, customer accounts involve higher amounts and the weekly payroll is increasingly demanding. Often, new equipment or bigger premises were financed with a temporary cash surplus or a credit line. In the worst cases, profits have not increased proportionally to sales. Market opportunities are more obvious than ever, and growth is possible, but the financial resources needed to buy more raw materials, extend the factory or pay the salaries of new management staff are lacking. Once again, the owner-manager is faced with a money shortage. If he cannot find additional funding, the situation becomes critical. The demands created by business expansion become a financial crisis. Robidoux calls this kind of situation a liquid assets crisis when it results from a policy of pursuit of exaggerated profits and growth. If a firm has trouble finding funds to finance expansion, only then does he call it a financial crisis.[64]

Intensive financial needs can arise in SMEs when activities multiply or when business is particularly poor. However, not all SMEs live in a state of crisis, even if their financial reserves are almost dry. Some have more foresight than that. All businesses need additional funding at some point in their development. Internal assets generated by the firm's operations may sometimes be enough for the more profitable among them, but the vast majority have to count on external sources, too.

SME owner-managers have different ways of dealing with the difficulties they face when looking for funds. For example, some of them always ask for better conditions when applying for extra credit facilities. Others say that financing as a whole is their major problem.[65] The interviews mentioned earlier with 100 or so owner-managers of Quebec manufacturing SMEs highlighted the existence of problems related to the perception of debit accounts and the lack of funds for specific activities.[66] Other authors from various academic fields have also recognized the real financial problems experienced by small businesses. Some have said that the present financial market structure is inadequate to meet many SME needs.[67] The following analysis is based on the main recent Canadian studies.

Small and medium-sized firms generally have a deficient financial structure. The way they go about financing hinders expansion and makes them very vulnerable during periods when credit is tighter. Statistics show that SMEs do not use self-financing enough; most opt for loans. They are often said to be undercapitalized.[68] Many suffer from

> an unbalanced financial structure and a deficiency at the level of permanent funding (. . . which means) a reduction in their borrowing capacity in the long term and (in the) possibility of undertaking new investments without endangering their current operations.[69]

This fragile structure may also partly explain the disastrous effects of high interest rates in the early 1980s. The cost of interest, disproportionately high compared with overall operating costs, could not be recovered quickly from product sales and brought hard times for SMEs. This, on top of the recession, led to many of them going bankrupt during that period.[70] Even today, far too many SMEs operate at the limit of their financial capacities with no safety margin, which makes them extremely vulnerable. As the owner's capital contribution is often kept to a minimum, financing is largely ensured by external creditors. Many authors contend that small business owners are in fact encouraged to choose this option because credit costs are better treated in terms of taxation than equity funds. The slightest jolt in the financial markets could mean the end for a tragically high number of SMEs.

Small business owner-managers complain about the lack of funding sources, and some analysts criticize the structure of financial markets. To what extent are these opinions justified? Are there enough sources of funding in Canada to finance small firms?

Canadian chartered banks offer a wide range of debt financing possibilities to firms of all sizes, and most have developed specialized credit services for SMEs.[71] The Federal Business Development Bank is very active with small businesses throughout the country. If we take into account the federal and provincial government assistance programs for project funding, equipment purchase, loan guarantees, interest payments and so on,[72] then clearly there is a vast number of short-term and even long-term funding sources.[73] It is not true that debt funding available to SMEs is insufficient. Facsym's 1981 study based on 300 SMEs showed that 74 per cent had always received a positive answer to applications for funds from financial institutions.[74] Many refusals can be explained by poor presentation of the initial application, insufficient equity or an obvious lack of management skills.[75] A study conducted to identify corporate determinants of bank lending decisions to small firms confirms some of these points.

> It was found that three factors influenced the decision to grant (or not to grant) a term loan: firms with a history of market or financial distress, a non-rural location, and non-manufacturing firms are least likely to receive term lending. The age and the size of the firm, as well as the rate of sales growth, were not found to be significant variables.

For new lines of credit, it was found that a history of financial or market difficulties was the single determinant of the lending decision.

The primary determinants of the decision to increase existing lines of credit were the rate of sales growth and the history of distress.[76]

According to the authors,

The importance of the distress variable may also be a proxy for (lack of) management expertise.[77]

Since credit unions have been increasing their involvement in commercial lending especially in Quebec and Saskatchewan, borrowing conditions seem to be changing for some small businesses.

. . . small firms find better financing conditions in provinces where the credit unions have a significant share of the lending market. Increased competition leads to lower collateral requirements for small businesses which are the first concern of small business owners.[78]

While small and medium-sized businesses have many possibilities for regular borrowing, access to venture capital is less obvious—a conclusion that emerged from several surveys.

Whether we call it start-up, development or contingency capital, venture capital is in fact the amount invested in a business where uncertainties cannot be assessed using the criteria of traditional financial institutions.[79] Despite the relatively recent appearance in Canada of this type of financing, there are already a good number of venture capital corporations. In 1983, more than 40 such companies belonged to the Canadian Association of Venture Capital Corporations. Some provinces have set up their own parallel venture capital programs, for example: Nova Scotia's Venture Corporation, P.E.I.'s Venture Corporation, Quebec's Sociétés de développement de l'entreprise québécoise, Ontario's Small Business Development Corporation, Manitoba's Venture Capital Companies, Alberta's Vencap Equities Ltd., and so on.[80] Other organizations have also set up similar programs. Venture capital corporations are now playing an important role in a number of Canadian businesses. They are sometimes criticized for not being "aggressive" enough, especially with small and medium-sized firms. Venture capitalists prefer to fund large or medium-sized firms in high-tech sectors, at the expense of smaller firms, no matter what their field of activity is. Being extremely selective, they do not necessarily provide the services originally hoped for.[81] Knight concluded from his analysis that available venture capital as a whole had increased during recent years, but it had not increased sufficiently for SMEs.

> This confirms the fact that start-up situations and indeed even firms under five years old usually do not receive funding from venture-capital sources (...) It is the smaller firms and those in the more rural areas of Canada which are not currently eligible for venture-capitalist assistance or for assistance from other sources of funds. "There is" need for changes.[82]

A more recent examination of the behaviour of new entrepreneurs in the Ottawa-Carleton area does not reveal any new trends. In fact,

> It was found that the entrepreneurs had raised capital primarily from personal resources, friends, and informal investors. Institutional venture-capital firms, governments and other financial intermediaries did not generally have a role. The entrepreneurs, however, had experienced difficulties in raising adequate risk capital. They had been obliged to commit significant amounts of time to the search for financial resources and frequently had diverted short-term financing to long-term needs.[83]

In some regions, supply of risk capital is even more scarce and expensive. In Newfoundland and Labrador, for instance,

> The fundamental problem with supply is that supplies are limited to a few public and private sources at present. It is a serious problem for a number of reasons. First, there is effectively no competition among suppliers. The experiences of other provinces demonstrate that, to be effective, supply must be generous and the sources, or venture capitalists, must be indigenous to

the respective regions. Secondly, the local venture capital community cannot manage a large number of projects or investments simply because they do not have the resources to do so. Thirdly, there are often incompatibilities between those with capital and those seeking it. The biggest problem in this regard is that firms without experienced management are, understandably, of little interest to the private sector.[84]

Consequently, few SMEs have the chance to use venture capital to finance their operations. Even in a period of growth, they must rely on loans.

Firms that have already reached a certain size can, however, think of going public. Although the stock market is not a traditional source of funds for SMEs, a new trend has been identified in some countries. In Canada, for instance, medium-sized firms with less than $5 million in stock are now increasingly using public money.[85] But this source, attractive though it is, is restricted to entrepreneurs with an excellent performance record and good growth potential. Very few medium-sized firms are dynamic enough to tackle the stock exchange teleprinter.

When a firm is relatively unknown, access to the financial markets is generally delayed by the expenses related to the first stock issue. Costs of the prospectus and the public sale of the shares themselves are proportionally higher than for large firms already registered on the Stock Exchange. Until recently in Canada, few brokerage houses got involved in public financing of medium-sized firms because of the higher risk their securities presented on the secondary market. However, Quebec's experience over the last few years has resulted in changing habits. Owner-managers of progressive SMEs and dynamic brokers wanted to take advantage of assistance programs for the capitalization of developing businesses offered by the provincial government. A grant of up to $400,000 was available to cover the costs of the first stock issue, and this incited brokers and owner-managers alike to put the shares of some already prosperous Quebec SMEs up for public sale. At the same time, the Stock Savings Plan offered small investors significant tax benefits when buying these securities. In May 1985, for instance, 226,000 Quebecers held shares qualifying for the QSSP. At the end of February 1986, they numbered 271,000: an increase of 45,000, or 20 per cent in 10 months.[86]

The Crash of October 1987 turned things upside down. Stock market prices fell and the market value of the shares issued through the QSSP also plunged. Investors became more prudent, and even nervous, despite tax incentives. Several public financing projects had to be ended. The QSSP program attracted far fewer investors in 1987. People were looking for newer, better adapted formulas.[87]

Various incentives have changed attitudes to a certain extent. But have they managed to create new habits for some investors and owner-managers, despite the shock of the stock market collapse? Will people return to the stock market once prices are back to normal? Experience seems to indicate that some changes will be needed in secondary markets to facilitate transactions of junior securities.[88]

To sum up, there is enough money available to fund many small and medium-sized firms, as can be seen by the variety of sources mentioned above. However, it has to be said that not all are equally accessible to ordinary SMEs. Some SMEs are just too small to justify the costs involved in some forms of financing, while others will never be profitable enough. Can prospective investors be blamed for wanting to make a profit? Can we ask people to invest their own savings without any chance of a return—or, to put it bluntly, to make charitable donations?

The fact remains that the structure of too many SMEs is deficient and risky. Many have an abnormally high debt level, and will certainly not be able to grow without an additional investment from the owners or new equity capital from other partners, whether private or public. But owner-managers of SMEs, overly fearful of losing control, are not known for being particularly receptive to the idea of involving other people in their firm's business. Total control allows the managing shareholder to make arbitrary withdrawals without having to account to anyone; outside partners reduce this autonomy and bring with them additional management costs.[89] Many SME owner-managers readily admit that public funding does not interest them. For example, in a Canadian survey, most respondents preferred financing from existing shareholders, chartered banks and trust companies. The survey results indicate that external equity sources are the least-preferred form of financing, due to a perception of external equity-inferiority. This attitude was prevalent across all size groups.[90]

Some of the main reasons mentioned by another group of owner-managers thinking the same way are: a desire to keep the firm's family character, the avowed fear of losing control, the business being too small, irritating administrative aspects and the necessity of disclosing financial information.[91] In many cases, part of this resistance is due simply to poor knowledge of the ways of obtaining external equity or lack of familiarity with the basic principles of financial management.[92]

However, the opinions of most of the small business owner-managers who had recently obtained public funding were encouraging to a certain extent. They considered this kind of funding to be very positive, despite the important changes that resulted.[93]

Undercapitalization and over-indebtedness do not arise only because of conditions for obtaining external institutional financing. Generally speaking, financing conditions for promising SMEs are relatively attractive, taking into account the level of risk involved and the guarantees offered. According to Saint-Pierre and Suret, it is mainly the unprofitable, high-risk SMEs that are actually undercapitalized.[94] The imbalance in the financial structure of many SMEs would seem to come mainly from their lack of pull with investors, from a deliberate choice by the owner-managers themselves and from the owners' reluctance to share ownership and management of their firms. Clearly, too, this kind of attitude has been reinforced by financial assistance policies that provide more incentives for debt financing than stock financing. But despite this, a firm must first demonstrate a reasonable level of profitability before seeking commitment from a serious partner.

There are successful businesses in Canada, sometimes called "threshold firms" or emerging businesses. They have achieved excellent financial results and have demonstrated their capacity to progress. Many of them, however, are hindered in their development by the lack of equity funding sources or by deficiencies in their management team.

> The research "on those firms" suggest a disturbing situation (. . .) lack of a single management skill and an equity gap have serious implications (. . .) Additional equity must be made available (. . .) The tax and regulatory environments for both investors and corporations must be framed with a view to fostering entrepreneurship and promoting investments (. . .) Our studies conclude that the manager must receive assistance from those with both the missing management skills and relevant industry knowledge.[95]

The problem is a complex one. The above recommendations certainly apply to all SMEs seeking success. To grow, SMEs need steady financial resources like those that can be derived from guaranteed financing and adequate equity.

To obtain those funds, SMEs have to earn the confidence of prospective investors: confidence in the open-mindedness and management skills of the team in charge and confidence in its future. It is probably there, more than anywhere else, that the real solution to financial demands is to be found.

Marketing Management: The Need to Export

Many small firms have achieved success through the sales skills of their central figure. This kind of dynamic businessman is very familiar with his environment, maintains close relationships with almost all his customers and knows how to respond to their needs. His friendship is a guarantee of their loyalty. For him, this is enough, since he succeeds; for him, that is what marketing is all about. But even in small firms, marketing can rarely be left in the hands of one person for long. However dynamic he is, a salesman-owner cannot be everywhere at once. The firm is growing, and he has other things to attend to. Customers' wishes evolve, there is competition and new opportunities emerge—but the owner-manager is inclined to think that nothing has changed (his product is the best and his approach is effective). This kind of scenario is typical of many small firms that disappear, along with the people who launched them. It is the fate waiting for SMEs that cannot grow because the idea their owner-managers have about marketing—the key component that is supposed to keep them in touch with their market—is too narrow.

Marketing is offering the right product at the right price to the right people at the right time and in the right place.[96] For some people, marketing takes in all the activities between production and consumption, ranging from the identification of customer needs to customer service and commercial control. Unfortunately, some SMEs have skipped over some steps. Their owner-managers have devoted a lot of time to sales, but too little to studying their markets and planning their marketing activities. For example, a study by Kao reveals that many new ventures are launched without any kind of remotely professional market study.

> Although the marketing texts and courses available at universities and colleges stress formal market research, the interviews revealed that virtually none of the respondents contacted indicated having done formal market research. On the other hand, most entrepreneurs were able to acquire some information informally.[97]

Most respondents said they tried to test the ground and formulate their own idea based on intuitive considerations:

> I got this business idea when I was in Europe (. . .) I asked friends and relatives about their feelings on the product or service I was interested in (. . .) I talked to people in business similar to mine and got a few tips from them.[98]

Another study, this time on the procedure for introducing a new product, surveyed 40 or so small industrial businesses in Ontario and showed that they mainly put emphasis on the technical aspects of the operation. The vast majority of the firms studied surprisingly neglected aspects as important as a general analysis of the market and competition; they did not even worry about assessing the receptiveness of their potential customers to new developing technologies.[99] Retail business is the same. In 1982, for instance, out of a total sample of 40 small stores in Newfoundland, 37 had done no market research in the last five years. Only nine were able to present a written advertising plan for the future.[100]

Small business owner-managers criticize marketing experts and advertising agencies for their high fees and overly theoretical approach that is not sufficiently adapted to small business realities. Many use one of several government programs available; they often deplore the weighty administrative processes and long waiting periods. It has to be said that the SMEs achieving the best performances had often used both consultants and government programs for marketing management. However, the vast majority perceive consultancy services as being unaffordable, or even useless. No matter what formula is used, any firm that wants to progress has to institute a permanent search for information. A drop in turnover or an urgent need to find a new outlet will generally lead to limited information gathering, but it will rarely result in anything more.

Using research in this way does no harm, but nor does it enable an organization to adapt quickly to the constant changes in the market and the regular attacks from fierce competition. Successful SMEs develop innovative plans and strategies for progress, and keep a systematic eye on them to make sure they are still adequate.[101] Serving the customer who knocks at the firm's door quickly becomes routine. But inciting him to come in the first place and being prepared for his arrival presuppose management skills and an adequate vision of the future.

SMEs that offer a high-quality, original product or service and that have succeeded locally can think of tackling a wider market. After the rest of Canada, they can try the United States and—why not?—even go further afield.[102] But to do so, they must be able to meet the demands involved. Exporting is not simply a question of selling excess stock on foreign markets; it requires research and organization. If the firm is too weak, the extra pressure created by exporting will only make its problems worse. Many small firms have failed not because they lacked the necessary resources, but because exporting was not part of an overall, well thought-out plan. Successful firms proceed with care, whereas those that fail are often in too much of a hurry and are badly prepared.[103] All too often, they went ahead without knowing why, haphazardly picking up on opportunities that arose.

Too many firms begin exporting not of their own initiative but because they were contacted by intermediaries or foreign buyers or because government foreign trade promotion services invited them to take part in missions or trips abroad (. . .) Many firms do not deliberately choose their foreign markets, but are chosen by them.[104]

Others, after deciding to export some of their products, choose the wrong distribution network. They will want to be like the others and export directly, even though they are still beginners in the field. And taking on all the work and expenses involved in prospecting and promoting, including debt recovery and sometimes customer service, may just be too heavy a burden for their limited skills and experience. Perhaps they should have used a market intermediary, especially in the case of distant markets, to take care of part or even all their international activities. Intermediaries generally have a good knowledge of the countries in which they are established. But this presupposes that SMEs can get the information they need from appropriate government organizations to be able to assess the quality of the services offered by particular organizations.[105]

SME owner-managers who have had some experience of exporting admit that the main problems they had to face were closely related to marketing. They include lack of market data, communication difficulties with foreign customers and unsuccessful relationships with intermediaries. Higher than anticipated financial costs and economic barriers, whether tariff-related or not, come next.[106] Export profitability is always clearly linked to a full commitment strategy that is well integrated into the general business plan. "Commitment, i.e., resource ratio, is important for export intensity as well as profitability. Export profitability also tends to be linked to the application of domestic distribution strategy to carefully selected foreign markets."[107]

When they are well-coordinated, export activities do not seem to hamper domestic operations. On the contrary,

the findings in this study suggest that exporting particularly to the U.S. does not necessarily pose significant change in terms of domestic activities. In fact, the evidence in this study suggests that exporting not only enhances sales volume but, more important, a firm's profitability. (And these) which market to less developed countries tend to experience higher relative export profitability.[108]

Canadian firms agree increasingly that the domestic market will probably not experience a new rapid-growth phase in the near future. Many of them are looking for new outlets abroad. SMEs that decide to specialize and aim to expand must think about exporting.[109] New tariff conditions with the United States, for example, provide encouragement. Many firms have already taken their first steps there or elsewhere.[110] But many others are still on the starting blocks. Either they do not know how to go about it or where to start, or they are frightened by the high start-up expenses they will have to assume, the fierce competition existing in some markets or the basic administrative requirements of exporting. A small business that is not successful on the domestic market will not be more successful abroad. But if it is already well-managed, it will, with good preparation, be able to tackle new markets with success.

General Management: The Challenge of Innovation

In the preceding pages, several problems specific to Canadian small and medium-sized firms have been revealed and, without being exhaustive, this list underscores the practical difficulties faced in each major organizational department. But Canadian SMEs can also be observed from another, more global perspective: the general management process. If SMEs are analyzed using models devised for big firms, they rarely meet the parameters. Studies on the causes of bankruptcy and other problems in small firms invariably and almost routinely invoke bad management.[111] Generally, all SMEs have some trump cards; and obviously, they all suffer some restrictions resource-wise. It is up to the owner-managers to get the best possible results with the least possible resources. What factors constitute obstacles to success today? The following indications emerge from a variety of studies and observations.

When nine out of 10 sampled firms have no precise knowledge of their market, it means that they lack information.[112] When it is revealed in another group that many managers order raw materials "intuitively," without assessing exactly how much they need, then it means that the lack of information is hindering management in its most elementary state.[113] In his study on bankruptcy, Lalonde noted that most respondents only realized that they had problems after being pressured by their suppliers and bankers.[114] They were, to say the least, very poorly informed on their true business performance. Bearing in mind that many SME managers do not know either the cost price of their products or the results of their last financial period, the natural conclusion is that access to information is a major difficulty in many small and medium-sized firms. For them, obtaining the necessary data on their socio-economic environment or producing enough internal data seems impossible. There are far too many firms like this— and their future is far from being assured.

SME owner-managers have to see to thousands of daily tasks, which means that they often leave aside those that take too much time—including stopping to think about the orientations of the business, taking a good look at the future and specifying objectives. Activities like these are often neglected, or even considered superfluous. Many of the problems encountered by small firms can be explained by a generalized lack of planning. In many cases, hurried staff recruitment and rushing to the bank to cover cheques that have been issued are symptomatic of this kind of deficiency. Various studies confirm the lack of systematic planning methods and low usage rate of elementary tools in many such firms.

This weakness is invariably noted in all research into bankruptcies, and the few studies that exist on long-term or strategic planning in SMEs are also very revealing. For example, in the Quebec furniture industry at the beginning of the 1970s, very little planning was done,[115] and the situation was no better in Newfoundland retail firms in 1982.[116] A 1983 study using a sample of 80 Canadian firms revealed that the vast majority did not use cash budgets in the management of their current operations.[117] Many SME managers have got into the habit of deciding everything themselves and storing things in their heads. If they have a particular vision of their firm's future, they rarely discuss it with others and, above all, they have difficulty stopping a while to commit their ideas to paper and instil some organization into their projects. Every SME owner-manager needs to know where he is going—a firm cannot possibly be successful if no objectives have been set. In a small business, planning does not necessarily involve complex procedures. But time has to be taken to think about the future and apply adapted, relevant and useful decision-making tools. Using tools like these adds rigour to the process and gradually pushes the decision maker towards professional management.[118] The road will always be a hard one for people who have until then managed their firm's business amateurishly. But some succeed.

Lack of external data is a considerable hindrance to any planning effort—but simply starting a planning process might help develop the necessary reflexes for a continual environmental analysis. Anyone wanting to be able to envision the future has to be able to count on good inside information. Knowing the business, its internal data and its performance details is a crucial management factor that many small firms do not achieve. A perceptive chief executive will obtain the critical information he needs to guide daily operations—he sees to it that the established information system will provide it. He also knows that the quality of the information he is able to give his financial colleagues will determine how useful they can be to him. Too many SME owner-managers think that they can simply go by the figures in their bankbook, while others are swamped in useless reports that are routinely produced by accounting staff, often on the advice of incompetent accountants.[119]

I used to be a public accountant, and I soon realized that many small business accounting systems are inadequate, not to say costly. Large amounts are invested in general bookkeeping. Registering the operations and then, if a slight error has been made, starting all the ledger postings over again, can eat away long hours and result in late, sometimes incomplete information. I used to dream of providing my customers—small business owner-managers—with a real information system. Cash registers were already fairly sophisticated—so why not use them as the sole means of registering transactions? Putting the data on to magnetic tape and processing them in an appropriate centre was only a matter of logistics. The aim was to provide the customer with a progress report and a statement of his overall position in as short a time as possible. It would have been perfect. Later, I became a professor and dreamed other dreams for small and medium-sized firms everywhere. And then the computer came along, with all its possibilities: remote processing, batch processing, on-site use of standardized software, whether adapted to the business or designed specifically for it, are just some of the vast number of computerized services that, today, make it easier to prepare and analyze the internal data needed for the healthy management of any business, from the biggest to the smallest.

In Quebec, computer equipment seems to be relatively common in small firms, as some recent surveys show; the presence of the equipment increases with size.[120] In all sectors, computers are most commonly used for accounting purposes. However, in some cases it would have been more urgent to start with other types of applications. Inventory management software is fairly widespread in the trade and manufacturing sectors, while word processing is popular in service SMEs.[121] Other surveys across Canada reveal more or less the same trends.[122] But—and this is important—small business managers need information, not information systems. Information systems are only ways of supplying managers with relevant information and possibilities for using it intelligently.

During 1985, Louis Raymond completed an in-depth study of the computerization process in a group of small firms. Some of the conclusions in his preliminary report provide food for thought.

> Computerized information systems have the potential to contribute much more to the performance of small firms than they do presently. The obstacles to better utilization of information technology in SMEs are not technological (. . . but) organizational and individual, in that the deficiency lies primarily in management and training methods and tools.[123]

According to Raymond, the initial computerization process in SMEs is too often carried out with insufficient analysis, no specific mandate and no timetable. In many cases the result is personal dissatisfaction and a low usage rate. More emphasis on general planning using an improved information system, shortening the implementation time by developing local applications and prototypes, keeping the decision-making process simple and choosing interactive user modes are all essential elements if information systems are to be successful in SMEs. Computers—and especially micro-computers—can mark the beginning of a new era for small firms—on the condition that the owner-manager knows what he wants to do with them. Instead of being fascinated, he has to decide what he can do with a computer, bearing in mind his firm's human resources. The computer is not a cure for all ills, but a powerful tool that has to be mastered. And for many SMEs, it is the beginning of the technological path they will have to take sooner or later.

The structure of Canada's economy is gradually evolving; the relative importance of the sectors is changing: some sectors are disappearing, others are emerging. We are currently changing from a post-industrial society to a knowledge and information society. A growing percentage of new ventures—most of them prosperous—are related to the communication and information industries. The advanced technology that is seen in those ventures requires new forms of work and organization in both small and large firms, and will probably result in a greater need for personalized relationships that will be as demanding as those in the classical hierarchical structure. For small firms, this new megatrend brings with it new possibilities—and new threats. It is no accident that prompt action, customer proximity, flexibility, the spirit of enterprise, motivation and competence have all become priorities once more.[124] Economists would describe them as new significant trends. Of course, they also represent the predominant characteristics of the best SMEs. The future should provide these firms with an opportunity to create for themselves a hitherto unhoped-for place in the market, provided they manage to keep the same human qualities as they grow.

The future will probably require still quicker changes and constant innovation. In this context, will SMEs still be able to offer an environment characterized by cooperation, brotherliness and personal growth? It all depends on the styles of management that will be adopted.

> "High creativity," the key to future success for the most dynamic SMEs, will only be obtained through relations conducive to an open and stimulating atmosphere (. . .) (Chief executives) will need to be able to lead, and also accept to be led where necessary, to direct (. . .), to communicate interest(. . .), to be sensitive to everything(. . .). If information and knowledge are destined to become a new raw material, the raw material that the "change masters" must concentrate on in the future will be the potential, the diversity and the harmony of the human environment.[125]

If he is to be up to the challenge facing him, the small business owner-manager must acknowledge his personal training needs and be ready to fulfil them through specially designed courses. On his own, he would not be able to understand and follow the evolution of new technologies and attitudes. But, once he knows about the most recent developments, once he has learnt the most modern methods, he will be able to adapt those technologies and attitudes to his own firm's context. And he will quickly be able to use the available technologies wisely to help him manage. But he must also be able to go one step further and innovate constantly in his management of the men and women working with him. There is no point trying to imagine tomorrow's ideal management formula. But we can say that, even in small business, management is likely to become more collective. Co-workers, probably more educated that those currently working in small firms, will probably demand full participation in the decision-making process—if not in actual ownership.

They will probably want to work together on developing the management formula that suits them best. The capacity of many of today's SMEs to adapt would certainly be put to the test. The chief executive must learn to share his views, delegate responsibilities; in short, to trust others more. To do that, attitudes will first have to evolve considerably. We should all also learn to have confidence in the true entrepreneurs, who will always be able to adapt.

Until then, some daily facts of life cannot be left aside. Business today requires permanent relationships with the main people and organizations involved in a firm's success. Customers, suppliers, creditors, debtors, public bodies and other owner-managers are as important to a firm's success as those directly involved. They are sources of information and collaboration, as well as sources of business.[126] Business today means going full-steam ahead, which prematurely wears out many otherwise valiant managers. The SME owner-manager, both for his own benefit and the benefit of his people, must be able to conserve his energies, enjoy life and occasionally leave his work aside.[127] To this he can add a concern for the people who will take over from him and whose role will be to make the business progress after he has retired or taken a back seat role. SME owner-managers justifiably want to stay in the driving seat for as long as possible, but many will also discover the pleasure of leaving it to someone else.[128] Why not start thinking about it now?

THE FIRST REQUIREMENTS FOR SUCCESS

Small and medium-sized firms possess undeniable advantages, the most important of which have been amply discussed above. As a group, small businesses play an obvious social and economic role in our country—observations and analyses leave no doubt about it. However, to succeed, SMEs have to overcome their proverbial vulnerability; the preceding chapter sets out in detail the problems and challenges confronting them today. Much of what has already been said may turn out to be crucial for some SMEs, but does not necessarily apply to them all. Success, though, might be based on more generalized factors, and the basic considerations contained in the following pages could well serve as a guide for every SME owner-manager.[129]

For anyone at the head of a small firm, the secret of success is hard work. Long hours are needed. We have all seen small business owner-managers working from morning to night, often seven days a week. Persistence at work usually guarantees success, and is still one of the best recommendations to be made to anyone wanting to launch a business. But most of us probably know an owner-manager somewhere who seems to have everything under control. His firm is flourishing, and yet he does not spend all his time there. He succeeds because he seems to know how to organize. He discredits the theory that you have to put in long hours, because he has discovered another way of doing it. While enthusiasm for work is still a key to success, other skills can be added to it. Today, the small business owner-manager has many management methods and techniques at his disposal, and can call on consultants of all kinds if he thinks it will be useful. But he will still keep to himself the responsibility of knowing his firm inside out, wisely counting on his own strengths and keeping things simple, but sharing his vision of the firm with those around him.

Know Your Strengths and Weaknesses

Self-knowledge is very demanding, but it is the basis upon which every human being grows. The SME owner-manager is in close daily contact with his employees and business partners. He must be able to recognize the situations where he operates more effectively and those he finds more awkward. Nobody finds it easy to accept his weak points, but it is the first condition for improvement. Frank conversations with sincere colleagues can provide an appropriate mirror for this learning process, and can even reveal unsuspected talents and powers. Better self-knowledge is often developed in parallel with a better understanding of the firm's strengths and weaknesses. Both types of learning can be sustained by an improved capacity for observing facts and greater personal assurance.

Every business has its own strengths—if it did not, it would not exist. Even if these strengths are limited, they enable the firm to produce a particular product better than anyone else or to benefit from the loyalty of a particular clientele, and so on. Every business also has its own limits and constraints it must observe, and weaknesses it can correct. The chief executive must take the necessary steps to get a fairly good picture of both strengths and weaknesses, or he runs the risk of making wrong decisions. A navigator must know how to judge conditions at sea, and also what he can ask of his crew; and the same applies to small business leaders.

If the SME owner-manager could develop a certain amount of intuition for external events and maintain a global and more faithful picture of his firm, he would be better placed to judge the situations that arise. Being able to assess your vulnerability or advantages when you have an important choice to make is an enviable skill.

The difficulty of obtaining information that small business owner-managers have always experienced could become a thing of the past for many of them. Computer systems and networks now mean that internal management data can be made available quickly, and they also provide low-cost access to comprehensive external data banks. Every firm has a relatively small number of critical factors whose level can indicate accurately both internal performance and the external conditions likely to affect it.

Vigilant owner-managers should identify the critical information they need and make sure they receive it regularly.

The reduced size of an SME means that the owner-manager can easily keep his finger on the pulse. This gives him a significant advantage over big firm managers. He should not rely on yesterday's information on his firm, but must renew it constantly. If he knows the secret of his success, that is, what makes him the best, then he will, to use strategic language, have discovered his competitive advantage. All he has to do is keep using it and keep improving it.

Playing Your Trump Cards

A good card player knows when to play his trump cards, and always plays them. Small business leaders also have trump cards, and must play them. A small firm's strength often lies in its ability to provide a specialized, adapted, tailor-made product or service, a factor multiplied by the fact that big firms could not, and would not want, to serve these markets. Small firms do it better. Some have developed exceptional skills, and their success is based on the choice of a product-market pair that they exploit perfectly. They enjoy close and frequent contact with a well-chosen and loyal group of customers, are profitable and continue to grow. Some even have the choice between staying small and human or growing. Many could take this kind of strategy and turn it to their advantage. Many others would benefit enormously from specialization. The favourite activities of dynamic SMEs have always been providing unique and personalized products or services and satisfying local needs. Profitable market opportunities arise for some firms through spin-offs generated by big firms and through limited sub-contracting work. Another perfectly good way would be to sell specialized products or services on a foreign market. Product/service differentiation and market segmentation are generally very appropriate strategies for small and medium-sized firms.

The legendary flexibility of small organizations is an increasingly valued skill in today's shifting environment. The present growth in the number of SMEs is clearly connected with the economic and socio-cultural transformations we are currently experiencing. If small firms can adopt mechanisms to monitor the environment and detect emerging changes early enough, they will be in a position to play this as yet another trump card. The SMEs that perform best are not conservative; on the contrary, they are always ready to change things. They count on their natural capacity to adapt, and the speed of their decision-making process and the flexibility of their structure makes it possible for them to consider whatever changes are necessary. However, firms wanting to do the same must integrate new skills into their staff reservoir and open up quickly to new ways of working.

Small firms, with their limited resources, must select their future activities and markets very carefully. They should also get to know the different conditions prevailing in the new contexts, and deliberately set up a learning process, especially when they are involved in foreign markets. They must also learn to criticize so that they can choose among the overabundance of information made available to them today. A capacity for intelligent management is demonstrated through being able to recognize passing trends, premature working techniques and unproven forms of management. A small business leader must know what is valuable for his firm and adapt only as required and when it is likely to help him play his trump cards as effectively as possible.

Keeping Things Simple

It is very easy to complicate things, whatever the subject. A good way is to mix everything up—ideas, people and objects—and keep adding to the mixture without any leading structure. Another way is wanting to provide for everything, aiming for a state of affairs that is too ideal and too perfect. It is much more difficult to keep things simple so they can be understood by everyone.

Growing organizations all run the risk of complicating their operations or even becoming bureaucratic. As they grow, they also risk becoming more rigid and, consequently, less open and less easy to understand. In many cases, firms that started out small and simple end up looking like self-imposed mazes. The founder had to step down in favour of his successors, or the entrepreneur left management of the firm to professionals. The new people were more educated, had more confidence in systems designed for big firms and did not hesitate to impose them on an organization which, until then, was prosperous. The situation would be even worse when these new people were specialists in organization charts and forms and were convinced of the benefits of precise task definitions for specific people. And if, to boot, they considered the hierarchical chain to be sacred, then the firm was likely to find itself with a very heavy overall structure.

We have all at some time enjoyed the quick, courteous and competent services of a small firm that has just started operations. And, perhaps, we have also been surprised a few years later to find a totally different attitude in the same establishment. Business looks good, everything seems to be in order, but the customer has become a number who has to deal with one department rather than another, and so on. And the hitherto loyal customer is now frustrated by conversations with the firm's representatives who have made it clear that policies have changed. And we have all probably seen the same thing happening from the other side of the fence, working for a firm where procedures and executive positions keep multiplying, and where finally nobody can help anybody else and where it is impossible to make a decision. Everyone has his own caricature of increasingly more complex organizational operations; everyone, of course, disapproves—and yet everyone encourages it to happen, whether consciously or not. Small business owner-managers, especially those who want to do the right thing and who want to see their firm grow with assurance, are far from being immune to this kind of risk. The following words of caution should perhaps be added to their list of good management practice:

- remember that the customer is more important than the firm's internal regulations;
- keep the number of administrative positions to a minimum;
- entrust projects to people rather than creating operational positions;
- provide everyone in charge with regular opportunities to discuss their work;
- try to reduce the number of forms;
- (perhaps) put the latest electronic aids to good use.

Small business owner-managers who want to maintain an entrepreneurial attitude in a growing firm will certainly find inspiration in these few points, and will eventually be very glad they were able to keep things simple.

Sharing a Vision

A vision is a view of the kind of future we want to achieve, or a definition of a goal we want to reach. It takes the form of a mental image of a possible future and desirable state for an organization. With his vision, an owner-manager can bridge the gap between his firm's present and its future.

Sharing this vision is communicating it, circulating it among all the members of the organization and making it a guiding principle for everyone. As a constant reminder of a possible future, it is an effective rallying point. Owner-managers who can share their vision also learn to improve it.

It has been said over and again that SME chief executives do not look far enough ahead and carry out their daily tasks with no precise direction in mind. This assertion is not always true—indeed, many owner-managers have a very enlightened vision of their small firm's future. They are often accused of not planning, or of managing without taking tomorrow into account. In fact, very few owner-managers excel in formal planning exercises, but the number who take the time to sketch out coherent plans is increasing. Leaders have also been taken to task—often with reason—for not talking about their projects enough, for keeping everything in their heads and not saying a word to anyone. This might result from an imprecise vision of the future, a fear of compromising themselves, a lack of habit or a lack of confidence in other people.

An SME owner-manager often works in a context where resources are limited and conditions difficult. He wears many hats and does not always have time to do what he would like, taking care of the business at hand and not much else in many cases. But, as an individual, he would like to succeed and therefore has to do more. As a chief executive in charge of other people, he has to look further and guarantee satisfaction and a good living for the people who depend on him. If he wants to ensure the consistency of his firm's activities, he must have a vision for it. If he wants to boost people's energies and provide his co-workers with a reference point, he has to communicate his vision. And if he wants to strengthen it, he must be ready to discuss his own vision and try to understand other people's.

Sharing a vision is always possible in a small firm. Since decisions are often made by a single person, the owner-manager simply has to decide to do so.

NOTES

1 More than 90 per cent of net new jobs created by firms in Canada between 1978 and 1987 were created by firms having fewer than 500 employees. See Appendix L.

2 It should be remembered, for example, that firms with fewer than 1,000 employees in the United States produced 24 times more important innovations per dollar spent in R&D between 1953 and 1973 than firms with 10,000 employees. See G.P. Sweeney, *Les nouveaux entrepreneurs, petites entreprises innovatrices*, Paris, Les Éditions d'organisation, 1982, p. 56. The rate of innovation (number of innovations per million employees) of small American firms was considerably more than for big firms in 1982. See U.S. Small Business Administration, *The State of Small Business: A Report of the President*, Washington, United States Government Printing Office, 1985, p. 128.

3 P.A. Julien, "The entrepreneur and economic theory," *International Small Business Journal*, Vol. 7, No. 3, April-June 1989, p. 33.

4 P.A. Julien, "La dynamique des PME face à la crise structurelle entre 1975 et 1982 dans la région Mauricie-Bois Francs et ailleurs," proceedings of the third Canadian Conference, International Council for Small Business, Canada, Toronto, 23-25 May 1984, p. 41-47.

5 For a more detailed account of the conditions favouring the development of small firms, see especially G.P. Sweeney, *op. cit.*, p. 15-26.

6 See the interesting account of what happened after Schumacher in G. McRobie, *Small is Possible*, New York, Harper and Row Publishers, 1981, 331 p.

7 "Les petites et moyennes entreprises (PME), le nouveau visage de notre économie," *Revue Notre-Dame*, No. 10, November 1979, p. 2. Our translation.

8 See Tables 4 and 6 in Chapter 2.

9 See Appendix L.

10 Minister of Regional Industrial Expansion, *Job Creation in Canada, 1974-1982*, Ottawa, Government of Canada, 1985, p. ii.

11 P. Thompson, "Small Business: Canada's Engine of Economic Change and Growth," *A Decade of Progress*, proceedings of the fourth Canadian Conference, International Council for Small Business, Canada, Calgary, 7-9 May 1986, p. 91-101.

12 The following study reveals that 81 per cent of a sample of businessmen in Sudbury, mainly SME owner-managers, assumed responsibilities vis-a-vis customers, employees and the local community. K. Loucks, "Social Responsibilities of Small Business, A Survey," second World Conference, International Council for Small Business, Halifax, 26-29 June 1983, p. 53.

13 U. Staber and N.V. Schaefer, "Small is Beautiful and Bountiful: Is It Also Socially Responsible?," *Journal of Small Business and Entrepreneurship*, Vol. 3, No. 3, Winter 1985-1986, p. 45-50.

14 Among other documents that inspired these pages, the following were particularly useful: G. d'Amboise, "Perspectives d'avenir pour les PME," special document 82-113, Faculty of Administrative Sciences, Université Laval, 1982; A.G. Fells, "Venture Capital and Small Business," *The Business Quarterly*, Vol. 39, No. 2, Summer 1974, p. 21-31; M. Archer and J. White, *Starting and Managing Your Own Small Business*, Toronto, Financial Post/Macmillan, 1978; P.A. Fortin, "Devenez entrepreneur," *Le Soleil*, (series of 16 articles in collaboration), Québec, 29 December 1985, p. A-8 and A-9.

15 P.A. Fortin, *op. cit.*, p. A-8 and A-9.

16 These are the words (our translation) of three young Quebecers who have succeeded in creating their own businesses with others. They were taking part in the international forum "Les Jeunes entrepreneurs du Québec, de la France et de la Belgique," at Lac Delage from 2-5 December 1985. Taken from Secrétariat à la Jeunesse, *Les Jeunes et l'entrepreneuriat, Monographies des entreprises*, Québec, Gouvernement du Québec, 1986, p. 11, 19, 43.

17 N.L. Colwill *et al.*, "A Study of Self-Employed Manitobans," *Journal of Small Business Canada*, Vol. 2, No. 1, Summer 1984, p. 26-30.

18 From J. Sutherland, "Trends - cultivating business," *Canadian Business*, Vol. 62, No. 3, April 1989, p. 19-20.

19 These observations are supported by a good number of organizational studies. See especially H. Mintzberg, *The Structuring of Organizations, A Synthesis of the Research*, Englewood Cliffs, Prentice-Hall, 1979, p. 233-235.

20 The following texts have also dealt with the distinctive characteristics of small and medium-sized firms: Association pour l'emploi des cadres, *Le gestionnaire de PME*, Paris, APEC, Dossier emploi, 1980, p. 12-13; H.J. Bocker, "Small Business Today - Canada, South Africa and the United States - A Comparison," *Journal of Small*

Business Canada, Vol. 1, No. 1, p. 30-36; J. Perrier, *Petites et moyennes entreprises, moteurs de notre économie*, Berne, Banque populaire suisse, 1984, p. 8-9; R.M. Knight, *Small Business Management in Canada, Text and Cases*, Toronto, McGraw-Hill Ryerson Limited, 1981, p. 12-13; H.B. Pickle and R.L. Abrahamson, *Small Business Management*, 2nd Ed., New York, John Wiley & Sons, 1981, p. 12-17; C.E. Tate *et al.*, *Successful Small Business Management*, 3rd Ed., Plano, Business Publications Inc., 1982, p. 3-7.

21 A.G. Fells, *op. cit.*, p. 22.

22 Magna International has been in business for 30 years. In 1985, the group's sales were almost $700 million, which made it the biggest Canadian automobile parts manufacturer. The group at that time was composed of 90 operating units each employing fewer than 100 people. A number of texts describe this organization's profitable activities, including: G.N. Benninger, "New Technology and the Entrepreneurial Organization," conference text, *Technology Canada Conference, Managing New Technology: Today's Competitive Weapon*, Waterloo, Wilfrid Laurier University, May 21-22 1986; P.A. Fortin and E. Morency, "Enquête pour un Québec plus entrepreneurial réalisée auprès des chefs d'entreprises," research report, Groupement québécois d'entreprises, Québec, January 1986, p. 33-40. Recent business news reveals that Magna is experiencing management problems, reinforcing the importance of constant awareness regardless of company structure.

23 A detailed presentation of these circumstances appears in D. Steinhoff and J.F. Burgess, *Small Business Management Fundamentals*, 4th Ed., New York, McGraw Hill Book Company, 1986, p. 19-22.

24 The Canadian Federation of Independent Businesses put the total number of small business closures in 1982 at 84,000. See "Au Canada, les PME vont de l'avant," *PME Gestion - H.E.C.*, Vol. 5, No. 2, October 1984, p. 3.

25 C. Lalonde, "Caractéristiques et pratiques de management des propriétaires-dirigeants dont l'entreprise a été mise en faillite: une étude en contexte régional au Québec," Doctoral Thesis, Québec, Université Laval, 1985, p. 321.

26 R.M. Knight, "The Determinants of Failure in Canadian Small Business Firms," Annual Conference of the Canadian Association of Administrative Sciences, Saskatoon, 28-30 May 1979, p. 16.

27 "Managerial incompetence and lack of entrepreneurial skills were identified as major causes of small business failure in this empirical research." See A.B. Ibrahim and W. Ellis, "An Empirical Investigation of Causes of Failure in Small Business and Strategies to Reduce It," proceedings of the 4th Canadian conference - A Decade of Progress - International Council for Small Business, Canada, Calgary, 7-9 May 1986, p. 21-29.

28 J. McDonald-Andrew, "Enquête de la FCEI sur la situation des entreprises - Réalités inéluctables," Canadian Federation of Independent Business, Toronto, May 1984, 31 p.

29 *Ibid.*, p. 21. Our translation.

30 G. d'Amboise and Y. Gasse, "Les défis administratifs quotidiens dans les PME québécoises," *Revue Commerce*, May 1982, p. 50-68.

31 Ministère de l'Industrie et du Commerce, *Profil de l'industrie québécoise de la fonderie des métaux-ferreux,* Québec, Gouvernement du Québec, 1985, 176 p; Ministère de l'Industrie et du Commerce, *Profil de l'industrie québécoise de la métallurgie des poudres,* Québec, Gouvernement du Québec, 1985, 188 p.

32 V. Robert, "Main-d'oeuvre qualifiée demandée," *Entreprise*, September 1985, p. 5-9.

33 Ministère de la Main-d'oeuvre et de la Sécurité du revenu, *Surplus et pénuries de main-d'oeuvre au Québec pour 1985*, Québec, Gouvernement du Québec, 1985, 121 p.

34 L. Larrivée, "Le recrutement de main-d'oeuvre de production tel que vécu par les PME manufacturières du secteur de la machinerie," Master's Thesis, Québec, Faculty of Administrative Sciences, Université Laval, 1985, 211 p.

35 P.H. Drouin, "Rotobec mise sur la formation de son personnel," *Le Soleil*, Québec, June 16 1986, p. A-11.

36 G. d'Amboise and Y. Gasse, *op. cit.*, p. 50-68.

37 R.W. Kao, "Entry Barriers and New Venture Strategies," *Journal of Small Business Canada*, Vol. 1, No. 2, Fall 1983, p. 37-42.

38 M. Porter, *Choix stratégique et concurrence - technique d'analyse des secteurs et de la concurrence dans l'industrie*, Paris, Economica, 1982, 426 p.

39 Y. Gerchak, M. Parlar and T.K. Yee, "Optimal Rationing Policies and Production Quantities for Products with Several Demand Classes," *Canadian Journal of Administrative Sciences*, Vol. II, No. 1, June 1985, p. 161-176.

40 R.W. Kao, *op. cit.*, p. 41.

41 From M. Clarke, "Strategies - Pulling Together," *Canadian Business*, Vol. 61, No. 11, November 1988, p. 28.

42 For more details on the concept of innovation, readers can consult: Y. Gasse, "Le processus et les déterminants de l'innovation dans les organisations," special document 83-109, Québec, Research Laboratory, Faculty of Administrative Sciences, Université Laval, 1983; F. Marc, "L'innovation dans les entreprises moyennes et ses difficultés,"

Cahiers de recherches en gestion des entreprises, La gestion de l'innovation, No. XIV, Université de Rennes, March 1982.

43 R.W. Kao, "Research and Development for Small Business," *Journal of Small Business Canada*, Vol. 1, No. 1, Summer 1983, p. 25-30.

44 From K. Banks, "Innovators - Leading Light," *Canadian Business*, Vol. 61, No. 12, December 1988, p. 18.

45 Y. Barcelo, "Carterchem sous-traite sa R&D," *Les Affaires*, July 5 1986, p. 14. Our translation.

46 In his book, Raymond Chaussé sets out the situation of several firms who have successfully launched a new product. This book will be much appreciated by owner-managers of any innovative SMEs. R. Chaussé, *La gestion de l'innovation dans la PME*, Chicoutimi, Gaëtan Morin, 1987, 203 p. Other authors also propose the contingency manufacturing theory for small firms to develop new products. See H. Munro and G.H. McDougall, "New Product Assessment: A Contingency Approach," *The Spirit of Entrepreneurship*, R.G. Wyckham *et al.*, dir., 32nd annual conference, International Council for Small Business, Vancouver, June 1987, p. 255-265.

47 H. Noori, "So why the sudden need for new technology (NT) in Canada?," The Research Centre for Management of New Technology, School of Business and Economics, Wilfrid Laurier University, Waterloo, February 1988 (unpublished paper), p. 7.

48 P.A. Julien and L. Hébert, "Le rythme de pénétration des nouvelles technologies dans les PME manufacturières québécoises," *Journal of Small Business and Entrepreneurship*, Vol. 3, No. 4, Spring 1986, p. 28.

49 Adopting a new technology is a particular problem for small firms. Comparisons with big firms can be read in H. Noori, "Benefits Arising from New Technology Adoption: Small vs. Large Firms," *Journal of Small Business and Entrepreneurship*, Vol. 5, No. 1, Summer 1987, p. 8-16.

50 R.G. Craig and H. Noori, "Recognition and Use of Automation: A comparison of Small and Large Manufacturers," *Journal of Small Business and Entrepreneurship*, vol. 3, No. 1, Summer 1985, p. 43.

51 See D. Miller and P.H. Friesen, "Innovation in Conservative and Entrepreneurial Firms: Two Models of Strategic Momentum," *Strategic Management Journal*, Vol. 3, No. 1, 1982, p. 1-25; G. d'Amboise, "L'utilisation des technologies nouvelles par les PME: un défi de taille," conference presented during the Colloque international sur la petite et moyenne entreprise, Brussels, April 28 1983, Document No. 244, Québec, Research Laboratory, Faculty of Administrative Sciences, Université Laval.

52 Y. Gasse, "L'adoption des nouvelles technologies: un défi majeur pour les PME," *Gestion*, September 1983, p. 27-34, Document

No. 267, Québec, Research Laboratory, Faculty of Administrative Sciences, Université Laval.

53 G. d'Amboise, "The Process of Implementing New Technologies: Some Empirical Results in Small Manufacturing Firms," Technology Canada Conference, Waterloo, The Research Centre for Management of New Technology, Wilfrid Laurier University, May 21-22 1986.

54 See especially R.L. Crawford and L. Lefebvre, "Closing the Low-Tech Gap," Lapedim - Conférence international sur la petite entreprise, Trois-Rivières, October 1984; R. Craig, "Users, Potential Users and Non-Users of New Manufacturing Technology," *Journal of Small Business and Entrepreneurship*, Vol. 4, No. 2, Fall 1986, p. 26-33.

55 J.L. Malouin, M. Oral and J. Rahn, "L'impact des programmes d'aide gouvernementaux sur le développement technologique des entreprises au Québec," unpublished research report, Québec, Faculty of Administrative Sciences, Université Laval, 1982.

56 M.A. Thellier, "Des machines et des hommes à la filature Textiles Dionne," *Productividées*, Vol. 3, No. 5, March-April 1983.

57 REMAT communiqué, "Highlights of Remat Survey," the Research Centre for Management of New Technology, Wilfrid Laurier University, Waterloo, Vol. 4, No. 2, Summer 1989, p. 5-6.

58 R. Lerch, "The Advantages of Simulation Training," *The Financial Post*, September 7 1985, p. C-16.

59 In 400 SMEs in the Montreal area, 75 per cent showed a high level of interest for an office computerization training program, while only a third said they were well-equipped. See S. Messier "Le marché de l'offre et de la demande en formation de bureautique dans la région montréalaise," research report, Montréal, Centre spécialisé en bureautique et gestion de l'information, Collège de Bois-de-Boulogne, May 1985. See also L. Raymond and N. Magnenat-Thalmann, "Information Systems in Small Businesses: Are They Used in Managerial Decisions?," *American Journal of Small Business*, Vol. 6, No. 4, Spring 1982, p. 20-26.

60 But even so, in one study, 80 per cent of the firms had no master plan and had done no cost-benefit analysis. The most notable contrast between the firms with and without master plans was in the difference between expected and real costs of computerization. See L.A. Lefebvre and E. Lefebvre, "Computerization of small firms: a study of the perceptions and expectations of managers," *Journal of Small Business and Entrepreneurship*, Vol. 5, No. 5, Summer 1988, p. 55.

61 A study showed that a positive but somewhat naive attitude towards office automation was apparent in many small firms. See C.A. Higgins, R.H. Irwing, S.M. Rinaldi, "Small Business and Office Automation," *Revue canadienne des sciences de l'administration*, Vol. 2, No. 2, December 1985, p. 374-381.

62 Data gathered in 34 Quebec SMEs led to the following conclusion by Louis Raymond: "The obstacles to greater and better utilization of information technology in SMEs are not technological in nature (but) have much more to do with the firm and the individuals, the main shortfall being in management methods and tools and in training" (our translation), in L. Raymond, *Validité des systèmes d'information dans les PME: Analyse et perspectives*, Québec, Institute for Research on Public Policy, Les Presses de l'Université Laval, 1987, p. 95.

63 It is worth noting that informal investors often play an important role in the start-up of small firms. According to one study, they are usually found in clusters, linked by informal networks of friends and business associates. In Ontario, a matchmaking network known as COIN (Computerized Ontario Investment Network) has been established to help mobilize informal risk capital; in British Columbia, VentureNet helps investors as well as businesses seeking equity capital. See A.L. Riding, D.M. Short, "On the estimation of the investment potential of informal investors: a capture/recapture approach," *Journal of Small Business and Entrepreneurship*, Vol. 5, No. 5, Summer 1988, p. 26-40, and *Investing in Canada*, Vol. 3, No. 1, Summer 1989, p. 6.

64 J. Robidoux, *Les crises administratives dans les PME en croissance*, Chicoutimi, Gaëtan Morin, 1978, p. 35, 77.

65 A national survey among members of the Canadian Federation of Independent Businesses in 1979 revealed that financing was the main worry for 19.5 per cent of the 11,000 members interviewed, compared with 15.6 per cent who identified inflation and 15 per cent who said paperwork and qualified manpower were their main concerns. *Mandate*, CFIB, No. 73, February 1980, p. 1.

66 G. d'Amboise and Y. Gasse, *op. cit.*, p. 50-68.

67 See A. Naciri, "Le financement des petites entreprises: mythe et réalité" (unpublished text), Montréal, 1985; J. Saint-Pierre and J.M. Suret, "La sous-capitalisation des PME: mythe ou réalité," preliminary report (unpublished text), Montréal, Institute for Research on Public Policy, June 1984.

68 The following study on the financial structure of Canadian firms from 1975 to 1977 highlights the excessive debt coefficient of SMEs in comparison with big firms: J.M. Gagnon and B. Papillon, *Risque financier, taux de rendement des entreprises canadiennes et intervention de l'État*, Ottawa, Canadian Economic Council, 1984, 109 p.

69 Ministère de l'Industrie, du Commerce et du Tourisme, "La capitalisation des entreprises," reference document - Forum of March 22 1984, Québec, Gouvernement du Québec, 1984, p. 17. Our translation.

70 During the first trimester of 1982, interest payments in firms with assets of less than $10 million dollars represented 99.4 per cent of their pre-tax profits. In big firms the ratio was 79.1 per cent. The

difference can be attributed to the higher debt level of small firms. See H.P. Rousseau, "Crise de liquidité, sous-capitalisation et faillites d'entreprises au Canada et au Québec," conference of the Association des économistes québécois, September 1982.

71 A study reveals that Canadian SMEs are better off from this point of view than is the case in many other industrialized countries. R. Peterson and J. Shulman, "Entrepreneurs and Bank Lending in Canada," *Journal of Small Business and Entrepreneurship*, Vol. 5, No. 2, Fall 1987, p. 41-45.

72 R. Dupaul, "Le financement de la PME au Québec: la nouvelle prise de conscience provoquera-t-elle un développement équilibré?," *Dossier Finance*, September 2 1985, p. 27-30; See also "Federal Business Development Bank," in *Small Business in Canada, Growing to Meet Tomorrow 1989*, A report by the Entrepreneurship and Small Business Office, Ottawa, 1989, p. 59; *Handbook of Grants and Subsidies - Federal and Provinces*, Canada Research and Publication Center, Montreal, 1986 (regular updating).

73 The availability of loan capital may have led SMEs to accumulate too many debts during the 1970s when interest rates were lower than at the beginning of the 1980s. See National Bank of Canada, *Economic Review*, Vol. 5, No. 4, 4th trimester, 1984, 8 p.

74 Facsym Research Ltd., *Small Business Financing and Non-Bank Financial Institutions*, Vol. 1, text, 1982, 233 p. In addition, 15 per cent of firms had generally obtained the funding they asked for, while only 11 per cent had not received enough.

75 L. Wynant, J. Hatch, M.J. Grant, *Chartered Bank Financing of Small Business in Canada*, London, University of Western Ontario, 1982, p. 215-223.

76 G. Haines, A. Riding, R. Thomas, "Small business loan turndowns by Canadian chartered banks: some empirical findings," *The Entrepreneur and the Challenge of the '90s*, Proceedings of the 34th World Conference of the International Council for Small Business, Quebec, June 21-23 1989, p. 495.

77 *Ibid.*, p. 496.

78 P. Cléroux, "Small business financing conditions: credit unions vs. banks," *The Entrepreneur and the Challenge of the '90s*, Proceedings of the 34th World Conference of the International Council for Small Business, Quebec, June 21-23 1989, p. 85.

79 For further details, see P.A. Pomerleau, "Capital de lancement d'entreprises," p. 70 and J. Saint-Pierre, "Tour d'horizon sur le capital de lancement," p. 12, discussion paper from the conference entitled "Le capital de lancement d'entreprises," Québec, Faculty of Administrative Sciences, Université Laval, April 16 1986.

80 For more information on some of these corporations, consult: A. Gadbois, "Capital de risque - Les expériences canadiennes hors

Québec," p. 107, conference entitled "Le capital de lancement d'entreprises," Québec, Faculty of Administrative Sciences, Université Laval, April 16 1986; R.M. Knight, "The Success of Ontario's SBDC Program," *Journal of Small Business Canada*, Vol. 2, No. 1, Summer 1984, p. 37-41; G. Fells, "Venture Capital in Canada - A Ten Year Review," *Business Quarterly*, Spring 1984, p. 70-77; P.K. Sahu, "Small business and the venture-capital industry in Canada," *Journal of Small Business and Entrepreneurship*, Vol. 5, No. 4, Spring 1988, p. 27-33.

81 According to Grasley's study, many corporations accept only 1 per cent of all applications received. See R.H. Grasley, "Venture Capital for High Technology Companies," Science Council of Canada, 1975, p. 51.

82 R.M. Knight, "An Evaluation of Venture Capital Rejections and Their Subsequent Performance," *Journal of Small Business and Entrepreneurship*, Vol. 3, No. 2, Fall 1985, p. 18-27.

83 A.L. Riding and D.M. Short, "Some Investor and Entrepreneur Perspectives on the Informal Market for Risk Capital," *Journal of Small Business and Entrepreneurship*, Vol. 5, No. 2, Fall 1987, p. 30.

84 Economic Council of Newfoundland and Labrador, "Equity Capital and Economic Development, Newfoundland and Labrador," Economic Council of Canada Project, Ottawa, 1988, p. 52.

85 La Commission québécoise sur la capitalisation des entreprises, *Rapport au Ministre de l'Industrie, du Commerce et du Tourisme*, Québec, June 1984, p. 55.

86 L. Pépin, "Le nombre d'adeptes du REA grimpe de 20 pour cent en 10 mois - Le Québec compte maintenant 497,000 actionnaires," *Les Affaires*, May 31-June 6 1986, p. 2-3.

87 For example, a broker proposed the creation of two different plans to satisfy customer demands. See B. Mooney, "Geoffrion Leclerc propose un nouveau régime pour ranimer le REA," *Les Affaires*, February 20 1988, p. 68-69; see also J.P. Gagné, "La relance du régime d'épargne-actions," *Les Affaires*, April 30 1988, p. 6.

88 Alberta is experiencing the Junior Capital Pool (JCP). It is an innovative financing vehicle for new ventures in search of seed capital. It allows participating companies to gain access to a public stock exchange. See for a description A. Dolan, B. Giffen, "The Alberta Junior Capital Pool: assessing effectiveness as a seed capital instrument," *Journal of Small Business and Entrepreneurship*, Vol. 6, No. 1, Fall 1988, p. 19-28.

89 These comments are based on the agency costs theory discussed by J. Saint-Pierre, "L'offre d'achat, la prime de contrôle et les actionnaires minoritaires," working paper 82-10, Québec, Faculty of Administrative Sciences, Université Laval, 1982; J.M. Suret, "Facteurs explicatifs des structures financières des PME québécoises,"

Conference of the Centre d'études politiques et administratives du Québec (ENAP) and the Laboratoire en économie et gestion des systèmes de petites dimensions (Université du Québec à Trois-Rivières), Québec, May 7 1982, p. 29-45.

90 J. Calof, "Analysis of Small Business Owners' Financial Preferences," *Journal of Small Business and Entrepreneurship*, Vol. 3, No. 3, Winter 1985-1986, p. 39-41.

91 J. Saint-Pierre, "Attitudes des entrepreneurs à l'égard du financement public par capital-actions ordinaires," Conference of the Centre d'études politiques et administratives du Québec (ENAP) and the Laboratoire en économie et gestion des systèmes de petites dimensions (Université du Québec à Trois-Rivières), Québec, May 7 1982, p. 131-137.

92 Y. Gasse, "Attitudes et prédispositions des propriétaires et entrepreneurs canadiens envers les bailleurs de fonds externes," special document 84-122, Québec, Faculty of Administrative Sciences, Université Laval, 1984, p. 71.

93 See the account of a study made in Quebec of a hundred or so SME owner-managers by Jocelyn Desroches, Amed Naciri and Ghislain Théberge. See M. Vallières, "Enquête inédite auprès d'une centaine de dirigeants de PME québécoises cotées en bourse," *Les Affaires*. September 26 1987, p. 2-3. The main changes, assessed as being positive or negative, are shown in Appendix Q.

94 J. Saint-Pierre and J.M. Suret, *Endettement de la PME: État de la situation et rôle de la fiscalité*, Montréal, Institute for Research on Public Policy, 1987, p. 5.

95 I. Ortt and P. Sloan, "Some New Perspectives on Threshold Companies," *Journal of Small Business Canada*, Vol. 1, No. 4, Spring 1984, p. 31-38.

96 E. Dupont and H. Gaulin, "Le marketing: l'engrenage de direction de votre entreprise," *Se lancer en affaires, les étapes pour bien structurer un projet d'entreprise*, Québec, Les Publications du Québec, Gouvernement du Québec, 1986, 450 p.

97 R.W. Kao, "Market Research and Small New Venture Start-Up Strategy," *Journal of Small Business and Entrepreneurship*, Vol. 3, No. 4, Spring 1986, p. 36-40.

98 *Ibid.*

99 G.H. McDougall and H. Munro, "The New Product Process: A Study of Small Industrial Firms," *Journal of Small Business Canada*, Vol. 2, No. 2, Fall 1984, p. 24-29.

100 P.N. O'Dea, G.A. Pynn and H.A. Eaton, "Advertising Management Practices in Small Retail Enterprises: An Exploratory Empirical Examination and Commentary," proceedings of the conference of the

International Council for Small Business - Canada, Halifax, June 26-29 1983, p. 22.

101 Some studies clearly show these relations in small firms. See in particular D. Miller and J.M. Toulouse, "Strategy, Structure, CEO Personality and Performance: An Empirical Study of Small Firms," research report (unpublished) Montreal, École des hautes études commerciales and Faculty of Management, McGill University, 1986, 26 p.

102 Very small Canadian firms tend not to export, for instance. In 1986, only some 3 per cent of manufacturing firms with annual sales below $5 million were exporting. Their exports amounted to 2.4 per cent of the value of their total output and less than 1 per cent of the value of all Canadian manufactured exports that year. See Ministry of Industry, Science and Technology, *Small Business in Canada, Growing to Meet Tomorrow*, A report by the Entrepreneurship and Small Business Office, Ottawa, 1989, p. 7. The various work done by professors Litvak and Maule expose this process in particular for small and medium-sized firms in new technology fields. I.A. Litvak and C.J. Maule, "Canadian Small Business Investment in the U.S.," *Business Quarterly*, Winter 1978, p. 69-79; "Small-Medium-Sized Canadian Firms and Their International Business and R&D Activities," Industrial Innovation Office, Ottawa, Government of Canada, 1984, 58 p.

103 D. Béliveau and J.E. Denis, "Le diagnostic-export de la PME," special document no. 83-104, Québec, Research Laboratory, Faculty of Administrative Sciences, Université Laval, 1983, p. 5.

104 J.E. Denis, "Réussir à l'exportation," *PME Gestion*, Vol. 5, No. 7, March 1985, p. 3, our translation. The same author has also published a book that examines many aspects of the problem. See J.E. Denis, *La PME et l'exportation*, Chicoutimi, Gaëtan Morin, Les Presses HEC, 1984, 115 p.

105 The Ministry of External Affairs distributes free of charge the *CanadExport* bulletin to firms wanting to move into exporting. The bulletin indicates new openings throughout the world, services offered by commercial delegations and the terms and conditions of the many export assistance programs available.

106 See a number of reports on the subject, including: E.J. Kleinschmidt and R.E. Ross, "Export Performance and Foreign Market Information: Relationships for Small High-Technology Firms," *Journal of Small Business Canada*, Vol. 2, No. 2, Fall 1984, p. 8-23; M.R. Brooks and P.J. Rosson, "A Study of Export Behavior of Small and Medium-Sized Manufacturing Firms in Three Canadian Provinces," in M.R. Czinkota and G. Tesar, dir, *Export Management, an International Context*, New York, Praeger, 1982, p. 39-54; P.W. Beamish and H. Munro, "Export Characteristics of Small Canadian Manufacturers," *Journal of Small Business and Entrepreneurship*, Vol. 3, No. 1, Summer 1985, p. 3-36.

107 P.W. Beamish and H. Munro, "The Export Performance of Small and Medium-Sized Canadian Manufacturers," *Canadian Journal of Administrative Sciences*, Vol. 3, No. 1, June 1986, p. 38-39.

108 *Ibid.*

109 Today, many successful experiences are reported. See, for example, C. Choquette and S. Lamontagne, "Expériences à l'exportation de quatre PME québécoises," *Gestion*, Vol. 2, No. 1, February 1986, p. 4-12; P. Beauregard, "Le Québec exportateur - sur la piste de nos globe-trotters," *Revue Commerce*, Vol. 88, No. 3, March 1986, p. 87-101.

110 Hardy defines a number of factors that have helped SMEs achieve success on American markets. They are presented in the section of this book entitled "Paths for Future Success." K.G. Hardy, "Key Success Factors for Small/Medium Sized Canadian Manufacturers Doing Business in the United States," Working Document No. 86-10, London, National Centre for Management Research and Development, University of Western Ontario, 1986, 10 p.

111 In particular, the annual analyses of Dun and Bradstreet always arrive at this conclusion which, to say the least, is not very explicit. See Dun and Bradstreet, *The Canadian Business Failure Record*, Toronto, Dun and Bradstreet, 1984.

112 J.C. Cachon, "L'application des techniques de gestion chez les P.M.O.: cas d'une ville isolée de milieu nordique en rétrospective," *Revue P.M.O.*, Vol. 1, No. 6, 1986, p. 17-19, 51.

113 G. d'Amboise and Y. Gasse, *op. cit.*, p. 50-68.

114 C. Lalonde, "Caractéristiques et pratiques de management des propriétaires-dirigeants dont l'entreprise a été mise en faillite: une étude en contexte régional au Québec," Doctoral Thesis, Québec, Université Laval, 1985, p. 321.

115 G. d'Amboise, "Personal Characteristics, Organizational Practices and Managerial Effectiveness: A Comparative Study of French and English Speaking Chief Executives in Quebec," Doctoral Thesis, Los Angeles, University of California, 1974, p. 106.

116 P.N. O'Dea, G.A. Pynn and H.A. Eaton, "Advertising Management Practices in Small Retail Enterprises," *Journal of Small Business Canada*, Vol. 1, No. 3, Winter 1983-84, p. 14-22.

117 S. Srinivasan and L. Sarrafzadeh, "Cash Flow Management in Small and Medium-Sized Businesses in Canada: A Survey," Working Document no. 84-028, Montreal, Faculty of Commerce and Administration, Concordia University, 1984, 24 p.

118 Some publications by Canadian authors give a good idea of the kind of tools available: R.L. Crawford and I.B. Ibrahim, "A Strategic Planning Model for Small Business," *Journal of Small Business and Entrepreneurship*, Vol. 3, No. 1, p. 45-53; G. d'Amboise, "Strategic

Planning for Small Business: Some Proposed Ways to Go About It," proceedings of meetings in St. Gall 1986, Institut suisse de recherche pour les petites et moyennes entreprises, Lugano, September 22-26 1986, Document No. 87-27, LRSA-FSA; M.A. Ragab, "A Concept of Strategy for Small Business," *Journal of Small Business Canada*, Vol. 1, No. 1, Summer 1983, p. 4-9.

119 Many members of the profession are now aware that traditional financial statements are inadequate. See D. Tremblay, "Des normes comptables trop complexes pour les PME," *Revue P.M.O.*, Vol. 1, No. 4, 1986, p. 32-34.

120 It is estimated that more than half of Quebec's SMEs now have independent computing equipment. It goes without saying that a good proportion of those who do not, hope to install it in the near future.

121 A sample of more than 500 Quebec firms having fewer than 100 employees was used here. See A. Lefebvre, "Le taux d'informatisation de la petite entreprise québécoise," *Gestion, Revue internationale de gestion*, Vol. 11, No. 2, April 1986, p. 27-32.

122 For reference, see F. Farhoomand and G.P. Hrycyk, "The Feasibility of Computers in the Small Business Environment," 30th annual conference, International Council for Small Business, Montreal, June 16-19 1985, p. 181-196.

123 L. Raymond, "La validité des systèmes d'information en PME: analyse et perspectives," research report presented to the Institute for Research on Public Policy, Montréal, 1986, 97 p. Our translation.

124 This is based mainly on the excellent article by C. Dupont, "Les PMI face aux 'megatrends'," *Revue française de gestion*, January-February 1986, p. 96-105.

125 C. Dupont, *op. cit.*, p. 105. Our translation.

126 Enterprise networks are presently fashionable. Inter-SME cooperation is no longer seen as a loss of independence, but rather as a way of achieving a better balance of power in business. See for example J.C. Dauphin, "La croisade des chefs mailleurs," *Revue Commerce*, Vol. 88, No. 5, May 1986, p. 112-120, and G. Archier and H. Sérieyx, *L'entreprise du 3e type*, Paris, Éditions du Seuil, 1984, 214 p.

127 The suggestions and analysis of H. Wallot on this subject are interesting. See H. Wallot, "Les aspects humains de la crise dans la petite entreprise," *Revue P.M.O.*, Vol. 1, No. 4, 1985, p. 12-14. Meetings with 34 owner-managers and their spouses on the subject of reconciling professional and private life reveal that, while not easy, such a reconciliation is possible. See M. Courtois, "Réussir sa vie d'entrepreneur et réussir dans la vie - Guide pour le couple dans un Québec plus entrepreneurial," (unpublished text), Québec, Faculty of Administrative Sciences, Université Laval, 1986, 127 p.

128 Professor Pierre Hugron carried out a study of successions in some Quebec family SMEs. His report reveals the continuous process in some cases. See P. Hugron, *Succession managériale dans les PME familiales au Québec*, interim research report, Québec, Institute for Research on Public Policy, Research Program on Small and Medium-Sized Business, 1987, 68 p.

129 Some of the ideas presented here have already been discussed in the following texts: W. Bennis and B. Nanus, *Leaders: The Strategy for Taking Charge*, New York, Harper & Row, 1985; Groupe Naisbitt, *Conjoncture 1986*, Paris, Interéditions, 1986, 211 p.; C. Dupont, *op. cit.*, p. 97.

CHAPTER 5

UNDERSTANDING SMEs— AND SPREADING THE WORD

All firms make themselves known through their products, their personnel and their various activities. If you visit a small business, you can get a mental picture of it. The first things you observe reveal some of its material and structural aspects; conversations with its executives and shop-floor workers give you a better understanding of how it works. But if you really want to understand its ins and outs, assess its performance or advise its owners, you will need to study it in more depth, and even then, you would only know about a single firm. If you wanted an overall picture of a group of firms to be able to assess the most efficient operating conditions and propose better ways of progressing for the owner-managers and advisers, you would need to observe a larger number. Fortunately, here in Canada, some people have had enough intellectual curiosity to try to dig deeper into the reality of SMEs, and the number of publications on the subject has increased considerably over the last 10 years. However, much remains to be done.

On his own, the small business owner-manager is relatively weak in the hustle and bustle of business life. His resources allow him access to only limited services; he has very little power in the face of political and economic authorities. Small business owner-managers have common needs; some of them have learned that grouping together gives them access to more services and means that their voice is more easily heard. In Canada, organizations exist whose essential aim is to support and promote the interests of the country's small and medium-sized firms.

The first part of this chapter sets out the main research subjects tackled in Canada in the field of small business during the last few years. From this information, what is already done, and what could be done, to better understand our firms is identified. The last part lists some of the organizations supporting and promoting Canadian small and medium-sized business.

A GENERAL SURVEY OF WHAT RESEARCH IS DONE AND NEEDED

The new awareness of the importance of small and medium-sized firms in modern society has led governments, socio-economic organizations and many universities and financial institutions to support research into the particular characteristics of SMEs. The few researchers who, of their own initiative, had already begun to analyze Canadian small business, were encouraged by this upsurge in popularity, and a growing amount of research in the field has been carried out during the last few years. It deals with the small business environment, or with various subjects relating to the enterprise as a whole, or with a particular aspect of the SME unit or its operation. Subjects are often determined by such factors as: how acute the problem raised is at a particular moment—for example, the shortage of qualified production workers in certain sectors; how urgent it is to find original solutions to a common problem—for example, under-capitalization; the need to think up more appropriate ways of tackling management—for example, planning methods; how new the emerging phenomenon is—for example, introducing new technologies into small firms.

The following pages examine the main research themes in the field of small business, especially since the beginning of the 1980s. A systemic viewpoint is used to classify various aspects of the research that has been done; subjects that are less popular or completely neglected are revealed. An attempt is then made to highlight certain relevant themes which, given present-day contexts, seem to demand priority.

The Systemic Viewpoint

The systemic model normally used in organizational analysis seems tailor-made for this type of study. It represents the organization as a whole, in an environment with which it constantly interacts. The job of researchers is to understand the different facets of the life of SMEs. The various research projects can be situated in relation to the model's main components.

Since this reference framework can be used in a variety of ways in organizational analysis, it is perhaps helpful here to set out briefly its basic elements. The model (see Figure 1) represents an enterprise in its environment, that is, as an open, dynamic system pursuing certain objectives. The system is influenced by, and has an influence on, its environment. It draws resources from it and transforms them using human and technological skills, and then provides goods and services to other people and systems in relation with it.

The *environment* of the enterprise can be divided into two parts: the macro-environment and the micro-environment. The word "macro" means wide, general and global; its components include:

- the culture, i.e., values, attitudes, beliefs, types of social interaction, etc.

- the political system, i.e., the political and governmental process, laws and regulations, etc.

- the economic system, i.e., mechanisms for allocating resources and sharing out goods and services, price-setting method, etc.

- the technology, i.e., production techniques, how far technologies have advanced, etc.

- the human skills, i.e., the general level of education, manpower training, etc.

- the consumers, i.e., general tastes, buying power, attitudes, etc.

The word "micro" means direct, particular, relevant. The micro-environment establishes a link between the enterprise and its macro-environment, and includes the following components, among others:

Figure 1
Schematic Representation of an Organization

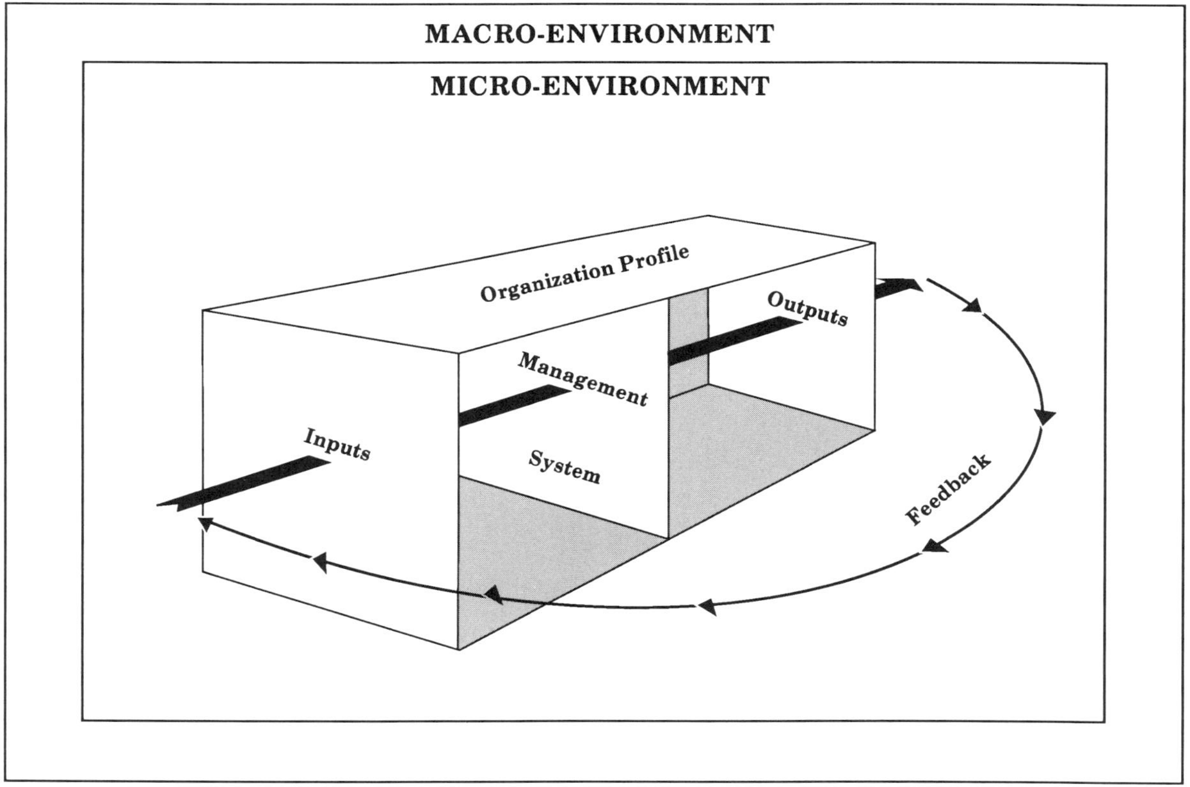

- the local political and commercial environment;

- direct competition;

- raw material and product suppliers;

- clients and users of the products and services;

- banks and other financial institutions;

- professional services.

The firm as such is examined according to three aspects: input, transformation and output.

Input consists of the resources the firm needs to operate: human, material, financial and informational, possibly taking the form of people employed for their skills, goods, equipment and raw material used, money needed to operate or data and knowledge required to do business.

Transformation covers the energy and skills put into operation to create a new product or service. It includes both the technical and human operations resulting in a new commercial value. Clearly, this is where the management system, the basis for an organization's administrative activities, comes in. An important element consists of owner-managers and their characteristics. The term also includes all the facets of the management process: planning, organization and so on. It covers all the management activities carried out in each department of the firm—production, sales, accounting, etc. It goes without saying that researchers in administrative science are particularly interested in studying management systems.

The products and services generated by the firm constitute the model's *output*. However, the word also covers everything that results from the firm's activities, such as employee satisfaction, profits, contribution to the milieu and so on.

The model also includes *feedback*, pinpointing the mistakes made en route, measuring how far objectives have been achieved and signalling the adjustments needed.

This viewpoint is global, allowing one or more firms to be observed, studied and compared. But this kind of framework can also be used to form an idea of the research done on the subject of small and medium-sized firms: research projects can be classified according to one or more elements of the model. The level of research on each subject thus becomes clear, and the subjects which are most often, or rarely, studied can easily be identified. The model is used for this purpose in the pages which follow.

A General Survey of SME Research

The review of the literature focused on research into Canadian small and medium-sized businesses published since 1980. It was intentionally limited to publications which were mainly concerned with SME management, and did not include statistical reports on the number of small firms and their general contribution to the economy. It was carried out using specialized journals, papers presented at small business conferences and documents and research reports published by individual researchers and various research groups or organizations in the field of small and medium-sized business. Although the best-known sources have been examined in detail, this review does not claim to be exhaustive.

Only publications with empirical results were kept for classification purposes. In general, they reported field research or data analysis, as it was felt that this kind of empirical research best represented the real effort made to achieve a better understanding of the world of the SME. The final sample comprised nearly 400 texts, all analyzed and classified according to their main theme. The lack of details in some publications sometimes made interpretation difficult; however, I believe that such difficulties were adequately overcome. The resulting synthesis of research subjects gives a fairly accurate idea of the most revealing work done in the field of Canadian small and medium-sized businesses during the last few years.

Many authors who were particularly concerned with SMEs examined their general environment. As shown in Table 11, 31 per cent of all research deals with this aspect. Research into the macro-environment—making up 60 per cent of this group—focuses more particularly on certain facets of the political, economic and education systems. The role played by government, for example, is regularly examined. The subjects most often dealt with are the influence of government policies, the scope of assistance programs and the effect of laws and regulations, budgets and taxation on various aspects of the life of small firms. Some research into the effects of the Free Trade Agreement is classified here, as is research dealing with small business training programs.

A slightly smaller number of projects focused on themes relating to the more immediate environment—in particular, the financial environment, in other words the various financial institutions, banks and so on. Offers of financing, the position of chartered banks and other credit institutions, methods of finance and forming risk capital were examined. Some studies describe the practice of publicity agencies, others deal with consultancy firms specializing in small or medium-sized business.

Table 11
General Breakdown of Publications on SMEs
by Subjects, from 1980 to 1989

Topic		Number	% of Total
General Environment		121	31
– Macro	72 (60%)		
– Micro	49 (40%)		
Inputs		17	4
Management System		210	54
– Entrepreneurship	46 (22%)		
– General Management	59 (28%)		
– Management of functions	105 (50%)		
Outputs		33	8
Global Profile		11	3
Total		392	100

Researchers do not seem to have concentrated much on the inputs to SMEs as such, and the problem of resources, although important from many points of view, has not been studied in any depth. Research focusing explicitly on input is mainly concerned with the human resources needed to operate small firms, the most popular subjects being job possibilities, the need for specialized manpower and the integration of graduates into SMEs. Some publications have also tried to identify the real contribution made by SMEs to job creation. Some others in the field of financing, although dealing with the search for funds, focus mainly on the external sources themselves, or on internal financial operations, and are therefore not included in this count.

More than half the publications kept for classification concern SME management systems. Researchers have shown interest in various aspects of internal operations. Many studies revolve around the central figure in a small business: the entrepreneur or the owner-manager himself. They try to understand his attitudes, his behavior and his distinctive characteristics. Many authors have tried to paint an impartial portrait of the driving force behind the small firm.

A good number of research reports touch on questions relating to the general management of small and medium-sized firms. Many describe general management difficulties in various types of enterprise, while others analyze the operational strategies or strategies for adapting to change adopted by SMEs, and yet others concentrate on roles and structures. Publications dealing with the global process of computerization in general were also kept for classification. These studies aim to identify needs for computerization, the kind of activities to be computerized and the satisfaction rate among owner-managers as far as computer use is concerned. Many of these activities are related to everyday accounting and production management. It goes without saying that the fairly recent appearance of a number of research projects on this subject in the field of SME corresponds to the arrival of new equipment, better suited to the context of small and medium-sized firms, such as micro-computers.

The most important category of research into internal systems touches on the problems or practices in particular divisions of the enterprise, such as:

- *Production.* Recent technological developments, computerization and robotics, have made this a priority. Some research focuses on the process of innovation and the consequences of introducing new technologies.

- *Financing.* The economic crisis of 1981-1982 and high interest rates made this an important subject. Research is mainly concerned with financing problems, the analysis of the firm's capital structure and the attitudes of entrepreneurs and owner-managers towards the various types of financing available (loans, risk capital, going public).

- *Marketing*. Researchers mainly try to understand how SMEs export their products. Several articles establish types of products, destinations and strategies for entering new international markets.

A smaller number of researchers have concentrated on the results, that is, on the output, of the firms they studied. Some emphasize the performance, the variables associated with success or failure, or the reasons for bankruptcy.

An analysis of subjects studied reveals that in a low percentage of the texts (3 per cent of the sample), the research object is the enterprise as a whole. Some texts, for example, explain the general profile of a particular group of SMEs, such as native firms, high-tech firms, community or alternative enterprises, while others analyze the particular problems of enterprises in certain environments, such as a specific economic region, or in areas far from large centres.

While attempting to complete the process proposed by the reference framework, it became clear that one aspect is not covered at all: the feedback process, which is absent from all the publications examined. Perhaps some of the studies on marketing or accounting systems could have been classified under this heading. However, it seems to be a fact that researchers do not place much importance on explicit studies of the feedback mechanisms used by owner-managers to adapt their firms constantly to their context of operations.

The analysis reveals that management systems are a favourite topic among Canadian small business researchers. Remarkable efforts have been made to understand the personality and management style of the owner-manager. Priority is given to establishing and understanding management methods and the problems encountered in the main divisions of the firm. The general environment is also becoming increasingly popular. However, a closer look at the years 1987 to 1989 reveals a certain shift in emphasis. For instance, the effect of free trade on SME management has triggered a number of empirical publications. Researchers also seem to be much more concerned with evaluating specific educational programs which aim to prepare their students for starting up and managing small firms. The overall proportion of studies on the managerial system seems to be diminishing in relation to the more recent emphasis on the general environment. Although less attention is paid, for instance, to the management of business functions *per se*, attempts to understand the person at the heart of the enterprise are nevertheless growing in number.

However, many other subjects are less common. Do they deserve better treatment? The following pages pursue this line of thought.

New Research Priorities

In 1980, the Federation of Deans, in an attempt to promote research in their management faculties, proposed a series of themes for the coming decade.[1] They were: managing productivity, innovation, international business, social responsibilities, human resources, entrepreneurship, finances and information systems. Clearly, the deans were thinking in terms of all fields of management, and not just those of small firms. However, they were conscious of the real makeup of our business world, and certainly had the Canadian SME in mind—as can be seen by the relevance of all these themes to the reality of small and medium-sized business.

Verbal, organizational or financial encouragement has certainly been responsible for many project choices. For example, many of those subsidized since 1980 by the Social Sciences and Humanities Research Council (SSHRC), focus on concerns previously expressed by the Federation of Deans. However, socioeconomic events have considerable influence on research orientations. Problems become more urgent, more apparent or more important than others depending on the time; for instance, during the economic crisis of 1981-1982, a good deal of research was done on firms' financial problems, assessment of SME capital structure and so on. The high number of bankruptcies during this difficult period could also explain the wave of research on the causes of failures and net job creation by small firms, etc. More recently, a number of studies have appeared on the acceptance level and potential effects among SMEs of the Free Trade Agreement with

the United States. Which of today's phenomena will mark tomorrow's research choices?

The above overview of the research done shows the main
orientations of the last seven or eight years. Less popular or
neglected subjects are also highlighted, and absent topics, such as
those listed below, are no doubt evident to most readers:

- How will the small business owner-manager obtain information from his environment? This question has received very
little attention.

- How does, or could, the SME leader establish fruitful contacts
with his business milieu? No serious study has been done on
small business owner-managers' networks.

- Many SMEs work in collaboration with big firms, and many
sub-contracting and licensed production arrangements exist.
How can SMEs make sure they receive fair treatment in
these circumstances? Other types of agreement should also
be possible. What formulas could be negotiated with big
firms to protect and exploit a good idea or new invention
coming from a small firm with limited resources?

- The difficulties of recruiting qualified manpower and obtaining raw material supplies have been raised, but almost
nothing has been done to check out the plausible solutions
suggested.

- As is the case everywhere, in Canada much work has been
done on the entrepreneur and his characteristics. However,
we still do not have a good enough picture of the set of factors,
circumstances and conditions governing his success. Perhaps
more attention should be paid to the young, successful firm.

- Personnel management in SMEs has been neglected by
researchers. The methods used in big firms must be left
aside, and adapted formulas, more flexible and respecting the
characteristics of different working environments, must be
imagined.

- Computers are here to stay. Enough has been said about
choosing the right equipment. The challenge facing researchers now is how small business owner-managers can really use
it to make decisions.

- International marketing is a favourite topic these days.
Research has highlighted many factors conducive to market
penetration. But how should we go about preparing a small
firm and its executives to pick their way through foreign

markets? The question requires different research initiatives.

- Strategy determination is receiving more and more attention. However, should we not try to associate effective strategies with small firm growth stages? Should we not also pay more attention to assuring the human skills needed to implement the new strategies demanded by each step in the development of an enterprise?

- As the firm progresses from start-up to the cruising phase, its leader must progress from entrepreneur to manager. How can he keep up the same enthusiasm as in the early years? How can he transpose his entrepreneurial spirit into this new management style? How can he go about leaving enough room for those who, in their turn, want to create something? How should he prepare those who will take over from him? How should he promote them to managerial positions? More research is needed on all these questions.

- The small firm as a working environment has not been rigorously assessed. What is the real level of satisfaction? The exact economic and social contribution made by a small firm to its direct environment has rarely been tackled. Specialists in regional development need to do fieldwork to learn more on the subject. In particular, many economists would certainly need to readjust their models.

- The feedback process is only indirectly touched on by researchers. The concern here is similar to that expressed in the first part of this list. More precisely, it is a question of the quality of internal and external information and the effectiveness of the mechanisms producing it. How can the right feedback be obtained at the right time? Small firm owner-managers would appreciate the help of researchers here.

Already, some of the suggestions made here coincide with trends that are more evident today than in previous years. However, thought needs to be given to other, more recent phenomena likely to affect our society in an important way. These new conditions will have a strong influence on the type of behaviour required of many firms, including smaller ones. Researchers interested in the smooth running of SMEs should find food for thought here. The following emerging phenomena may well demand attention:

- World-wide relationships. Easier communications, more link-ups and networks, distant and varying markets, immediate competition, are all increasingly characteristic of business today. How can SMEs survive and profit from these factors, in spite of their limited resources?

- Freer trade. The possibility of freer trade with our powerful neighbour is both an opportunity and a danger for many Canadian small and medium-sized firms. An assessment of the long-term effects of the Free Trade Agreement on our various industrial sectors is urgently needed. How can we help SMEs affected by it to adapt? New opportunities should emerge. How can SME owner-managers discover them early enough? How can Canadian small and medium-sized firms be well-prepared to profit to the full from the situation?

- Intensified relationships with some countries. New cultural and economic links are presently being forged: for instance, between Quebec and France, between British Columbia and Pacific Rim countries, and so on. Owner-managers are already creating fruitful contacts. How can cultures be respected in spite of all the differences?

- The trend towards deregulation and privatization. Are they just passing trends? Or are they cyclic? When we allow private enterprise to take new initiatives, we expect high levels of performance, quality and productivity. How can we make sure the standards of excellence are respected? How can we help SMEs to meet such demands?

- The growing number of women who are owner-managers. How are they really different in their way of running a firm? Will we see new management styles in their firms?

- Venture start-ups by a better-educated young generation. Unemployment is structural: more young people, even with a good education, cannot find jobs—so they launch their own business. How can we prepare more of them to be good managers?

- An aging population. Canada's demographic makeup is changing, with an ever-increasing percentage of old people. The growth in demand for appropriate goods and services is already making itself felt. How can SMEs go about defining these gaps?

- The increasing presence of Neo-Canadians. The regular influx of immigrants is changing the face of our big cities. The new arrivals bring with them new consumer habits and many launch small businesses. It would be interesting to assess their contribution to our economy.

- Ecological concerns. Attitudes are evolving, and stricter measures are in place. Sometimes they act as constraints, but often they also provide new opportunities for small firms. How can we stay on the look-out for these opportunities?

- Even more new technologies. Firms will always have to adapt technologically, and the changes will come even more quickly. Managers and workers must also learn to adapt constantly. How can we avoid dysfunctional upsets in our firms? How can we really make machines serve man in the small firm workshop?

- Future developments in computing. Computers represent an unprecedented potential in terms of production and management. It is worth repeating: researchers must now be at the service of the owner-manager.

An exhaustive list of research needed would have included more subjects, some of which are already underway. The above list contains mainly new issues, new perspectives or new fields; a considerable amount of work certainly needs to be done.[2]

If research is to progress, more concerted efforts will be needed than has been the case up to now. The organizations that develop projects and those that give mandates or grant subsidies must agree on the themes. Energy should be concentrated by choosing more fundamental subjects and fostering the accumulation of knowledge on a few wide themes selected with care. However, many initiatives to achieve agreement must be taken by researchers themselves in the field of small and medium-sized business.

Agreeing on some basic notions is not an easy task. The present situation would be greatly improved, for example, by using the same general definition of SMEs. The parameters suggested in the first chapter of this book may contribute to that objective. Perhaps someone should take responsibility for proposing a bilingual lexicon in the field.

Researchers attached to Departments of Industry and Commerce, who are in a privileged position to collect a large amount of statistical data on companies, have a critical role to play. The research community is counting on them to put together and make available the databases often needed within the framework of research on small and medium-sized firms. Good examples are the recent initiatives by the Quebec and Ontario governments, who published documents on the state of the SME situation, and Statistics Canada, who recently published statistical profiles of small firms.[3] Perhaps other researchers could also be persuaded to share their databases. Much empirical data remains underexploited. In particular, student researchers could do more analysis on them, without breaking confidentiality agreements already made.

The overall picture of SME research gives the impression of being made up of bits taken from various sources, often from several landscapes at once; and some pieces of the puzzle are still missing. An individual characteristic was taken from one source, a behaviour trait from another, a practice from yet another, or a strategy from an unknown context. Is it unrealistic to try to observe all these aspects at once? The reality of the situation is the owner-manager in action in his environment—and it is difficult to conceive this dynamic in separate pieces. This kind of *Gestalt* is worth analyzing and discussing as such. Clearly, the researcher should highlight what he considers to be the most relevant variables and the most relevant relationships according to the units studied. SMEs lend themselves more easily to this type of process than big firms.

Unfortunately, researchers seldom use the same referential frameworks as their colleagues. A better understanding of any phenomenon can be achieved by examining the same variables in different fields and in other groups of enterprises. Comparisons can be made: knowledge is usually advanced by confirmation. This is another way of grouping the energies of those who want to apply a bit more rigour to research on small and medium-sized firms.

Researchers who dare to undertake longitudinal studies on small and medium-sized firms should be encouraged. Statistical studies over several years are in themselves an interesting challenge. More difficult are projects where the management process is observed at regular intervals in various establishments. Equally demanding is an assessment of the changes affecting the configuration of a cohort of SMEs during a given period. However, this type of research is essential for a better grasp of the factors that can influence the important transformations within our enterprises. The turning points in the life of a small firm can be very revealing, but the firm must be followed for several years if the real effects are to be understood. I hope some researchers will find the necessary motivation to undertake such projects—and also obtain the collaboration of small firm owner-managers, for without it the research cannot be completed.

Research on small and medium-sized firms has not yet reached a very advanced stage. It is not easy to combine scientific rigour and short-term pragmatism. Researchers want to achieve a better understanding of the corpus of knowledge, and help it progress; owner-managers agree to collaborate, but only if solutions to their short-term problems can be found. Many subjects need to be examined in more detail; but many new methodologies need to be perfected too. Welcome to those who have the interest, imagination—and courage!—to join the process.

CANADIAN BODIES SUPPORTING AND PROMOTING SMALL AND MEDIUM-SIZED BUSINESS

Any kind of exchange with business people gives us information on their firms. Research helps us get to know SMEs and their owner-managers. Publications, newspaper articles and publicity of all kinds inform the Canadian and foreign public about our small and medium-sized companies. However, some organizations in Canada play a more precise role. They are there to support SME activities, publicize them and promote their special interests.

A number of governmental and para-governmental organizations naturally make important contributions to Canadian small business, but they will not be discussed here. The organizations described below are private. Three of them represent the interests of small and medium-sized business owner-managers; the other two support work on SMEs. They are all relatively well-known, but the part they play is certainly worth underlining.

The Canadian Federation of Independent Business (CFIB)

This non-profit organization was founded at the beginning of the 1970s. Its members take part in formulating its policies and support it financially. It is organized on the same basis as federal counties and groups together members from regions throughout the country. Its two main objectives are:

- to promote and protect a system of free, competitive enterprises in Canada;

- to allow independent businessmen to express their opinions on the laws and statutes governing business and the country.

The Federation's policies are established using a regular ballot system through the publication *Mandate*. Current important national questions of direct concern to small business owner-managers are periodically set out, and members are then invited to give their opinion on present or projected laws, business habits and other relevant subjects. A national summary of the vote is sent to all federal and provincial Members of Parliament, top civil servants and anyone else who may influence policy decisions. Awareness campaigns based on the results of the polls are led with everyone concerned, and certain political action programs are implemented. The Federation also promotes entrepreneurship in colleges and universities.

A membership profile drawn up in 1983 revealed the following characteristics: 86 per cent of member companies employed less than 20 people including the owner-manager; 78 per cent had annual sales of less than $1 million; 52 per cent had been running their firm for 10 years or less.[4] In 1986, the federation had a total of 76,000 members, a large proportion of whom operated commercial or service enterprises. At this time, the federation's leaders were justly proud of the results achieved by a campaign against discriminatory practices towards small firms by banks.[5] In 1989, this figure had grown to 85,000 members.

The Canadian Organization for Small Business (COSB)

This organization, also non-profit, was formed in 1979 to represent the interests of Canadian small firms and independent professionals. Its objectives are as follows:

- promoting a philosophy of independent, competitive and responsible enterprise in Canada;

- helping its members to resolve their individual problems in dealings with government;

- informing governments and elected officials of the concerns of its members and working with them to achieve practical solutions to those problems;

- assisting members in coping with day-to-day problems of management, and where these problems are beyond COSB's scope, putting them in contact with other sources of assistance;

- cooperating closely with other business associations with similar goals and objectives on matters which COSB perceives to be of direct benefit to its members.

The organization's extensive network of contacts with political personalities, civil servants, the media and the academic world means that it can play a leading role in promoting the principles uniting its members: economic freedom, responsible initiative and free speech.

COSB aims to transmit the point of view of the rank-and-file owner-manager to legislators and bureaucrats at all levels of government. It offers a variety of services, including a group insurance plan for interested owner-managers. The organization has a membership of approximately 5,000 people, and is mainly active in Ontario and the Western provinces. Its members are kept in touch with its activities through its bi-monthly newsletter "The Voice of Small Business."

The Groupement Québécois d'Entreprises (GQE)

The Groupement came into being in 1974 "with the aim of grouping together people with the same responsibilities and concerns. Its principal mission is to help small and medium-sized business owner-managers to improve the quality of their management both in human and technical terms."6 Essentially, it aims to help small business leaders feel less isolated, more confident, more creative, more effective, more open and more dynamic.

The Groupement is led by a board made up of 15 company heads elected by the membership as a whole. The board oversees the work of 8 committees formed of industrialists who decide what services to offer members.

Some 500 owner-managers from throughout Quebec are grouped into 50 or so regional small business clubs. Member companies alone employ more than 30,000 people and generate a turnover of several billions of dollars in the Quebec economy. To become a member, candidates must be sponsored by an active, existing member and be accepted by his regional club. The regional clubs meet at least once a month, and members can exchange, share experiences, discover new ideas and help each other. The GQE endeavours to establish links with a number of small business partner bodies, that is, governments, financial and educational establishments and so on. It provides a range of services according to members' needs: contributions to the regional clubs' operations, assistance in setting up boards, support for research and development, marketing and so on, and it also offers a collective insurance plan and various training sessions.

Provincial meetings and conferences are held annually. Members receive a monthly information bulletin and presidents are supplied with personal club management handbooks. The Groupement displays a rare dynamism in the business community, and its prestige ensures that it receives an attentive ear in political and financial circles.

The International Council for Small Business (ICSB)

The ICSB was founded in the United States in the 1950s by a group formed mainly of academics supported by the Ford Foundation. It differs from the organizations described previously by its main objective, which is to advance management practices of existing small business owner-managers and potential entrepreneurs through research, education and open exchange of ideas. Over the years it has become international, with operations in more than 30 countries.

Around 10 years ago, a group of Canadian members, with the support of the Federal Business Development Bank and other institutions, formed ICSB-Canada. Its members come from management consultancy firms, educational and research establishments, government, small business owner-managers' associations and financial institutions.

The council forms a network for exchanging ideas on SMEs, especially management methods. ICSB-Canada organizes national and international conferences allowing many of the people working in the field to meet and talk about the evolution of knowledge on small and medium-sized businesses. For the past few years it has published the *Journal of Small Business and Entrepreneurship*, the only journal covering the whole country dedicated particularly to papers on Canadian small and medium-sized business. The ICSB has played an important role in promoting education and research on Canadian SMEs.

Small and Medium-Sized Business Program—The Institute for Research on Public Policy (IRPP)

Founded in 1972, the Institute for Research on Public Policy is a national organization supported by an endowment fund ensuring its independence and autonomy. Its prime objective is to act as a catalyst within the national community by encouraging informed public debate on major issues of common interest. In 1982, its directorate felt that SME was a subject worthy of attention, and the Small and Medium-Sized Business Research Program was launched at the Faculty of Administrative Sciences, Laval University, Quebec.

The program aims to promote intensive research relevant to Canadian small and medium-sized firms. Its particular objectives are:

- to achieve a better knowledge of SMEs in Quebec and Canada;

- to examine their current problems in more detail;

- to improve management of SMEs while encouraging management education;

- to allow people, institutions and bodies interested in SMEs to work together.

As a major research program, it should also encourage the setting up of a Canadian network of researchers interested in this important sector of the economy and provide guidance for the development of government programs designed to assist small business throughout Canada.

The program is administered by a director who is a professor in the Faculty of Administrative Sciences. A committee made up of business and government representatives supports the director by establishing research priorities and assessing proposed projects. The members of the consultative committee also help improve relations between researchers and business people.

The main subjects covered by research supported by the program are:

- The PME-SME bibliographical file, a computerized file of documents concerning small and medium-sized businesses in Canada;

- The introduction of new technologies into small and medium-sized businesses;

- The level of debt in small and medium-sized businesses: the state of the situation and the role of taxation;

- A profile of small and medium-sized businesses in three native communities in Quebec;

- Small manufacturing firms: 12 Quebec cases;

- The transfer to family-owned small and medium-sized businesses in Quebec;

- The validity of information systems in SMEs: analysis and perspectives;

- Computerization of small and medium-sized businesses;

- Exporting strategies of Canadian small and medium-sized businesses;

- Aid for small business exporting firms: the role of governments and information networks;

- The capacity for technological innovation in small and medium-sized business;

- Small and medium-sized business owners and public stock financing;

- The impact of the Quebec Stock Savings Plan on the financing of small and medium-sized businesses;

- Industrial incubators.

Many of these projects have already resulted in the publication of articles or books under the aegis of the Institute. This book, for example, has been written with its support. A particular aspect of the program is its aim to develop, from research, practical tools to help owner-managers in everyday management of their firms. Guides and software are already being tested with some company heads. Projects are being planned on the following subjects: small service firms, immigrant entrepreneurs, bankers and their relationship with small business owner-managers, cultural aspects of the entrepreneurial process, entrepreneurship as a second career, health and safety at work in small firms.

The program has contributed tremendously to small business research. It has allowed in-depth examination of subjects which would otherwise probably have been left aside; it has also guaranteed circulation and discussion of interesting research results. Its initiative augurs well for the future.

A Clear Sense of Responsibility

Things have changed for Canadian small businesses. Governments now give more credit where it is due. The description of support organizations in the previous pages also shows that others have taken on essential responsibilities.

Today's dynamic owner-managers group together to make their point of view count. They find collaborators who share their values. They meet to structure their energies, with the result that they now exercise more influence over some decisions. Organizations that traditionally were hardly sympathetic towards small business interests seem jealous of the progress made, and their representatives can be seen in ministerial conferences, for example, claiming for all businesses the same things being offered specifically to SMEs. Small business owner-managers need strong organizations to show constantly that their firms are different and that they require special conditions. They have begun to shoulder their responsibilities in this respect.

At the same time, it seems that other, more intellectual bodies are beginning to promote the same cause, but in different ways. Educational and research establishments invest energy and money to improve SME management; few owner-managers dared, or were capable of, doing the same thing. Happily, some organizations are aware of their social responsibilities. Others, described in the previous pages, demonstrate the same sense of responsibility. Their task is, as far as possible, to apply scientific rigour to their research, and to disseminate the results according to university standards. The real job of sharing research results with small business owner-managers is, however, more difficult and more demanding because it comes less naturally to researchers. We need to find a way to communicate our findings in the language of the owner-manager.

NOTES

1 Federation of Deans, *Managing in the 1980s: Choosing Themes for Management Research*. Report, National Conference of the Canadian Federation of Management and Administrative Studies and the Administrative Sciences Association of Canada, Toronto, 1980, 36 p. The International Council for Small Business - Canada (ICSB) had also defined research priorities in the area of small business at the beginning of the 1980s. See: K.E. Loucks, "A Survey on Research on Small Business Management and Entrepreneurship in Canada," unpublished research report, Toronto, International Council for Small Business, 1980.

2 Readers wanting to know more about suggested research on SMEs in other countries should consult the following works: Albach, H. "Contributions of small-business research to small-business policy decisions," *Journal of Small Business and Entrepreneurship*, Vol. 6, No. 3, Spring 1989, p. 22-28; J. Boissevain, "Small Entrepreneurs in Changing Europe: Towards a Research Agenda," Maastricht, European Centre for Work and Society, 1981, 55 p.; "Quelle recherche pour les PME," Deauville Conference Proceedings, Fondation nationale pour l'enseignement de la gestion des entreprises, Paris, 1984, 74 p.; King, King, Rosen, "Small Business Research Topics," research report, International Small Business Council - U.S.A., Milwaukee, University of Wisconsin, 1978; J. Stanworth *et al.*, *Perspectives on a Decade of Small Business Research, Bolton Ten Years On*, Aldershot, England: Gower Publishing Company Ltd., 1982, 199 p.; M.S. Worthman, "A Verified Framework, Research Typologies and Research Prospectuses for the Interface between Entrepreneurship and Small Business," in D.L. Sexton and R.W. Smilor,

The Art and Science of Entrepreneurship, Cambridge, Ballinger Publishing Company, 1986, p. 273-331.

3 See comments by C. Curlook, in "For Starters - Statscan Gets its Facts Together for the Future," *Small Business, The Magazine for Independent Companies*, vol. 6, no. 8, July-August 1987, p. 12.

4 J.A. McDonald, "A Profile of CFIB Membership, 1983," *Journal of Small Business Canada*, vol. 1, no. 2, Autumn 1983, p. 4-13.

5 CFIB, "Notre offensive contre les banques porte fruit," *Mandat*, no. 125, June 1986.

6 "Une invitation personnelle au dirigeant," a publicity leaflet produced for the 10th anniversary of the Groupement, Drummondville, 1984.

CONCLUSION

So there we have it: a fresco of the Canadian SME. It has given us an image of the reality we all have in mind, one that we experience every day of our lives: the small or medium-sized firm. But does the image correspond to what the reader thought it would be? The answer is probably yes, to a large extent. In this book, I have tried to present a summary of what has already been written on the subject. If it adds to the knowledge, pinpoints some elements and helps create a better understanding of our firms and the people who run them, then it has done its job. It may also highlight a few signposts to help direct and manage our SMEs. If these signposts inspire some of our entrepreneurs and owner-managers, so much the better. And if the book contributed in any way to the development of our firms, then my efforts will have been worthwhile.

Small and medium-sized firms exist and, in our minds, they are different from big firms. The term SME is, however, not very specific and sometimes even insufficient to represent the reality. However, it is practical and very widely used. The many definitions mentioned in this book demonstrate the confusion existing in Canada and elsewhere. They all refer to independent firms, but in practice the categories used to identify such firms are not the same. Although, generally speaking, a measure of size is resorted to, the same standards are not always set. Finally, the parameters suggested in the first chapter are different from those generally in use until now in Canada. Undoubtedly, many firms exist that satisfy both criteria at once: that is, less than $20 million in annual sales, and less than 500 employees. Such firms are not big firms—as a visit to one of them would confirm. But the suggested parameters will only be practical if they are generally adopted. In fact, if everyone got into the habit of clearly setting out the parameters he uses in his texts, even that would be progress.

Economic life is always dynamic. The business world is in a state of continuous mutation. The amount of turbulence varies from one period to another and from one sector to another. Uncertainty and risk are part of the business game. Today, all firms, whatever their size, have to face quick changes and often demanding conditions. SMEs are no exception; on the contrary, they are often in a more vulnerable position. However, conditions have been relatively favourable most of the time over the last decade for SMEs in Canada. The present economic situation is less propitious. A general and rapid recovery would again assure survival and growth to most of our firms. Let us hope for it.

Clearly, the most vigilant will be the most successful. Our SMEs are to be found in many different fields—in fact, in almost every sector. They have always been present in the secondary sector, and in recent decades their numbers have grown considerably in the commercial and service sectors. Niches are plentiful. Some, of course, are more favourable than others, more appropriate for the natural strengths of smaller organizations. For example, many SMEs could specialize and offer a product or service that is not available elsewhere, thus covering a market segment they could make their own. SMEs are distinguished by the more personalized relationships they have with all their partners. Those who can position and reposition themselves while still making the most of their strengths in a long-term perspective are the ones that will make progress and grow. Their leaders should keep a close eye on the future.

SMEs are usually run by just one person—or sometimes a small group of people. That person is always very closely tied to his firm, and his personal aspirations will be reflected in its operations. A young person who creates his own job wants to see himself mirrored in what his firm does. An entrepreneur who sinks his savings into a new business does so to realize his life's ambition. An owner-manager who successfully enters the export market takes great pride in his career. The lives of all these people are clearly closely tied to their firm. They have transposed their will to act and their entrepreneurial spirit to their firm. That was why they wanted to create or run a business. When they become managers by force of circumstances, they nevertheless remain entrepreneurs too. Some have lived through the experience of no longer understanding their firm, and no longer controlling it. They were unable to become managers, and quickly found themselves out of their depth. Sometimes the worst happened: they disappeared, or the firm ceased to exist. However, there are many examples of people like them who were able to adapt to the new managerial demands. They never really changed from entrepreneurs to managers, but rather learned new skills. Although still entrepreneurs at heart, they are now able to share tasks and motivate others. Almost all owner-managers could do the same thing, provided they are prepared to change some things.

Small firms have internal strengths that explain their vitality in a business world dominated by big organizations. The accent is on action. The simple structure of SMEs means that quick decisions can be made. Close relations can be maintained with loyal customers. This type of organization belongs to its environment. Many current trends call on the strengths of small firms: individual initiative, taking responsibility, personalized relations, decentralization, independent units, economy of quality, etc., are all inspirational factors in today's management. Our era favours the emergence of SMEs and could also foster a better understanding of how they operate. Nevertheless, small firms are vulnerable. They usually have few resources at their disposal, and a single bad decision could lead to their downfall. Recruiting qualified staff is always a problem for a small business owner-manager. Since the environment continually demands that he has new expertise, he has to think up original ways of attracting the necessary skills into his firm. Many initiatives have been launched to help ease the classic financial difficulties that small firms commonly encounter, and dynamic owner-managers are also willing to associate with new investors. But each small firm has its own particular strength. It may be technological expertise, an advantageous geographical location or a solid financial base. A good owner-manager will, as time goes on, discover his firm's real strengths and the skills of the people around him. He will help others fulfil themselves in his firm. He will have points of reference to help him assess performance, while still keeping things simple. He will also have a vision for his firm, and will be capable of sharing it.

The amount of research on SMEs has increased over the last few years. It has resulted in a better understanding of the place of small firms in our society and, by demonstrating their contribution, has led to a better appreciation of them. Many studies concentrate on the advantages and problems of SMEs, and their general operating conditions now seem fairly well-known. In future, a more global profile will be needed, especially for successful firms. What circumstances and factors set them on the road to success from the start? What ingredients and actions, when combined, guarantee vitality and long life? Researchers have much to think about, models to construct, and must undoubtedly confront their ideas with the real-life experience of the small firms themselves. For research to be effective, more joint thinking is needed. Many bodies have taken the responsibility of spreading the word about SMEs or defending their interests. They bring together groups of small business owner-managers or work in collaboration with them. Their commitment has already brought results, and they play an essential role.

Throughout this book, many studies have been quoted to support the discussion. The authors of those texts clearly did not all use the same definition of small and medium-sized business— as we know, more than one such definition exists. Therefore, a wide variety of firms were covered, even though they can all be described by the terms SME, small business or other variants. The criterion of size does not necessarily lead to a homogeneous set of firms. Even after all the discussion, the concept of SME remains vast and vague. If we use only size criteria, it will never come into focus. The concept covers many other aspects too, and today it is those other aspects that interest us more. Autonomy, vulnerability, proximity of people, affinity with the environment, an action-oriented attitude, and so on, are all significant elements. The kind of firm we usually think of as an SME can vary in size, but is usually smaller rather than bigger. The matter of a definition is far from being resolved, and will certainly never be if we confine our discussion to the question of size. The other aspects, although more difficult, could well be more promising in the long term.

Researchers, while keeping the parameter of relative smallness, could perhaps concentrate on particular sets of firms. They could examine in more detail the conditions for existence and the distinctive behaviour of groups such as family firms, emerging firms, sub-contracting firms, firms in new sectors, more dynamic firms, successful firms and so on. By doing so, they would contribute more directly to advancing knowledge than has been the case in the past. But no matter how relevant the research is, if its results are not known in teaching and business circles, it will be completely useless. Researchers must think up new ways of circulating their work, which should be used much more as a base for discussions with present or future business people.

Many business students, as well as students from other fields such as engineering, dream of being part of a small firm one day. But sooner or later, far too many of them come to the conclusion that they are badly prepared. Clearly, management training should use examples drawn from our own business environment, and programs should foster meetings with heads of firms in action. But the students themselves should learn how to prepare. If they are really interested in small business, if they really have the right attitude to work in an SME, then they should be capable of using their own initiative. During their studies, the more resourceful among them will profit from all possible opportunities to meet businessmen. They can sometimes get holiday jobs in small firms. These are the people who usually succeed in heading their own firm later.

People running small firms will find very few recipes in this book. They will be more interested in some chapters than in the others, and these chapters will give them plenty of food for thought. Some sections will give them practical hints. It is a book that will appeal more to those who have already decided that, for their firm, progress depends on professional management. They will perhaps be more aware of the multitude of slots and possibilities open to them. They will also be glad to read a book that admits that, while rationality has its place in business, their own proverbial intuition is always necessary. New computer technology opens up all kinds of interesting possibilities for improving the management of small and medium-sized firms; SME leaders must, however, choose intelligently and according to their needs.

It would please me greatly if, after reading some pages, small business owner-managers were motivated to take time out to think about the future of their firm.

Originally, this book was intended to be a much less ambitious project. But my interest in the subject often made me pursue my thoughts on particular aspects much further. I learned to understand our SMEs better at the same time—and that, for me, is the most important. Writing this book was a real small business experience. I thought about it constantly and spent a lot of time on it—just like a small business owner-manager does with his firm. The same applied to balancing my professional life with my personal life. Completing the project despite many other demands on my time was my mission. Finally submitting the manuscript was like bringing out a new product. To sum up, the experience increased my respect for the work of a small business owner-manager.

APPENDICES

Appendix A
Quantitative Criteria for Defining SME
Advantages, Disadvantages and Rate of Use

Concrete Measures			*Flux Measures*	
Number of Employees	Quantities Produced	Total Sales	Added Value	Salaries
Advantages • Easiest to obtain • Easy to compare • Brings out the social impact • Not influenced by price fluctuations	**Advantage** • Not influenced by price fluctuations	**Advantages** • Data always exists • Little affected by accounting corrections • Management willing to disclose figures fairly easily • Neutral in terms of proportions of production factors	**Advantages** • Represents participation in production and general economic activity • Easy to compare • Takes account of all production factors	**Advantages** • Usually easy to determine • Easy to compare • Brings out the social impact • Takes account of different qualifications of employees
Disadvantages • Takes account of only one production factor • Not homogeneous • Tends to overvalue small units • Tends to underestimate growth	**Disadvantages** • Limits comparison between firms making same products • Does not take account of product quality	**Disadvantages** • Does not always give a fair idea of production • Only allows comparisons between firms in the same sector • Requires adjustments for inflation	**Disadvantages** • Data difficult to obtain • Concept not well defined • Needs calculation and estimates • Measures firm's activity, not its production capacity • Varies with situation	**Disadvantages** • Represents only one production factor • Tends to underestimate the importance of SME • Sometimes difficult to obtain from managers
Use • Used most in government studies	**Use** • Is almost never used	**Use** • Generally the most used	**Use** • Used very little	**Use** • Used very little

Statements of the Situation		Relative Measures	Measures Based on Structure
Assets	Others: Capital Stock, Owners' equity, Working Capital	Market Shares, Financial Ratios	Number of Hierarchical Levels
Advantage • Easy to obtain **Disadvantages** • Does not always correspond to production capacity • Includes investments not linked to production • Difficult to use in comparisons between firms and sectors • Under-represents role of SMEs **Use** • Used in many Canadian studies esp. on firm growth	**Advantage** • Ensures reasonably fair comparisons between firms **Disadvantage** • Does not really reflect overall size of firm **Use** • Little used, except for financial analyses	**Advantages** • Allows firms to be situated in relation to each other • Gives an idea of performance **Market Share** • Same advantages and disadvantages as variables used to determine it **Financial Ratios** • Difficult to obtain from management • Does not measure firm's size **Use** • Market share is only rarely used to determine scope of activities	**Advantage** • Incorporates some qualitative aspects **Disadvantages** • Differences in levels not always clear • Sometimes impossible to obtain data for all sample • Weak size indicator **Use** • Used in some specialized studies

Source: Many elements in this table were taken from T.H. Nguyen and A. Bellehumeur, "Les mesures de taille d'entreprises canadiennes: une étude théorique et empirique," special document no. 83-115, LRSA - Faculty of Administrative Sciences, Université Laval, 1983.

Appendix B
Size Measures Used to Define SMEs in Some Countries

	United States [1,2]	England [3]	Japan [4]
General Measure	< 500 employees		
Branch Measure • Manufacturing	< 500 employees	< 200 employees	< 300 employees or < 100 million Yen in capital
• Construction	No distinction	< 25 employees	< 300 employees or < 100 million Yen in capital
• Wholesale Trade	No distinction	< £730,000 in annual sales	< 100 employees or < 30 million Yen in capital
• Retail Trade and Services	< 100 employees	< £185,000 in annual sales	< 50 employees or < 10 million Yen in capital

[1] U.S. Small Business Administration, *The State of Small Business: A Report of the President*, Washington, United States Government Printing Office, 1983, p. 28 and 1984, p. 7.
[2] Several recent standards used in administering the SBA programs are given in H.B. Pickle and R.L. Abrahamson, *Small Business Management*, New York, John Wiley & Sons (2nd Ed.), 1981, p. 10.
[3] J. Stanworth *et. al.*, *Perspectives on a Decade of Small Business Research: Bolton Ten Years On*, London, Gower Publishing Company Ltd., 1982, p. 196.
[4] National Finance Corporation, *National Finance Corporation, Its Character and Present State*, Tokyo, National Finance Corporation, 1983, p. 2.

France [5]		Canada [6]	
Small < 100 employees	SME < 500 employees		SME [7] < 500 employees or < $20 million in annual sales
No Official Distinction		Small < 100 employees < 50 employees	No Distinction

5   M. Delattre, "Les PME face aux grandes entreprises," *Économie et Statistique*, No. 148, October 1982, p. 7.

6   Minister of State (Small Business), *Small Business in Canada: Perspectives*, Ottawa, Government of Canada, 1977, p. 5.

7   These categories are used for purposes of statistical analysis by the Small Business Secretariat. See for example Minister of State (Small Business), "Statistical Profile of Small Businesses in Canada - 1983," Ottawa, Government of Canada, 1984, p. 6 (unpublished text).

Appendix C
Number of Businesses and Total Revenues by Industry Group and Revenue Category for All Firms in Canada
Canada, 1986

Industry Group	Small		Medium	Large	Total
N = Businesses R = Revenues $000	10-99	100-1,999	2,000-19,999	20,000 +	
Services					
• N	141,243	71,257	3,499	213	216,212
• R	5,247,985	26,044,813	17,746,408	15,226,596	64,265,802
Retail Trade					
• N	84,381	105,621	11,561	983	202,546
• R	3,686,803	46,523,227	70,113,927	74,335,904	194,659,861
Construction					
• N	94,898	58,794	5,788	310	159,790
• R	3,777,724	23,754,785	32,139,877	14,621,831	74,294,217
Transportation, Com-munication, Utilities					
• N	58,442	24,505	2,090	320	85,357
• R	2,194,325	8,074,795	12,885,324	69,639,317	92,793,761
Wholesale Trade					
• N	18,510	34,985	12,467	1,359	67,321
• R	828,939	20,616,216	78,662,307	110,221,279	210,328,741

Real Estate, Insurance					
• N	35,824	24,945	1,154	75	61,998
• R	1,492,369	8,411,311	5,972,618	4,411,333	20,287,631
Manufacturing					
• N	19,515	28,907	10,744	1,634	60,800
• R	852,045	14,722,155	70,631,923	238,283,864	324,489,987
Forestry					
• N	10,660	4,849	346	22	15,877
• R	406,779	1,718,808	1,544,473	596,452	4,266,512
Mining					
• N	2,818	2,913	765	194	6,690
• R	125,115	1,545,722	5,017,959	29,341,741	36,030,537
Total					
• N	466,291	356,776	48,414	5,110	876,591
• R	18,612,084	151,411,832	294,714,816	556,678,317	1,021,417,049

Source: Statistics Canada, *Small Business in Canada: A Statistical Profile, 1984-1986*, Cat. 61-231, April 1989, Ottawa, pages 47-56.

Notes: The data are derived from tax returns submitted by incorporated and unincorporated businesses to Revenue Canada Income Tax. The tabulations do not present data on business operations reporting less than $10,000 gross income as well as farming operations, fishing operations, professionals and self-employed commission salespeople. Also excluded are banks and other deposit-accepting institutions, credit agencies such as consumer loan companies, sales finance companies, etc., insurance carriers, investment and holding companies and non-profit corporations.

The term "revenue" includes all revenues resulting from the operation of the business entity and investment and other types of income.

Appendix D
Number of Businesses and Employees
by Number of Employees Category
For Each Province in Canada
Canada, 1987

Province	Number of Employees Category				
B: No. of Businesses E: No. of Employees (000s)	<50	50-499	Total SME	500+	Total
Ontario [1]					
B	266,021.0	9,196.0	275,217.0	1,178.0	276,395.0
E	1,200.2	913.6	2,113.8	1,500.0	3,613.8
Quebec [2]					
B	199,656.0	5,938.0	205,594.0	970.0	206,564.0
E	812.2	492.3	1,304.5	690.0	1,994.5
British Columbia					
B	108,214.0	3,421.0	111,635.0	854.0	112,489.0
E	414.6	195.4	610.0	333.0	943.0
Alberta					
B	86,961.0	3,343.0	90,304.0	859.0	91,163.0
E	310.5	182.9	493.4	273.0	766.4
Saskatchewan					
B	39,661.0	1,314.0	40,975.0	583.0	41,558.0
E	113.8	53.9	167.7	75.0	242.7
Manitoba					
B	30,101.0	1,717.0	31,818.0	704.0	32,522.0
E	111.3	71.8	183.1	125.0	308.1
Nova Scotia					
B	24,984.0	1,421.0	26,405.0	621.0	27,026.0
E	92.9	50.7	143.6	87.0	230.6
New Brunswick					
B	21,221.0	1,063.0	22,284.0	545.0	22,829.0
E	71.1	37.7	108.8	62.3	171.1
Newfoundland					
B	15,991.0	621.0	16,612.0	368.0	16,980.0
E	43.9	24.5	68.4	39.8	108.2
Prince Edward Island					
B	5,837.0	231.0	6,068.0	192.0	6,260.0
E	16.5	6.9	23.4	4.6	28.0
Northwest Territories					
B	1,357.0	110.0	1,467.0	68.0	1,535.0
E	7.5	4.0	11.5	3.7	15.2

Yukon					
B	1,110.0	68.0	1,178.0	61.0	1,239.0
E	4.8	2.4	7.2	3.6	10.8
Total					
B	801,114.0	28,443.0	829,557.0	7,003.0	836,560.0
E	3,199.3	2,036.1	5,235.4	3,197.0	8,432.4
Outside Canada					
B	193.0	134.0	327.0	128.0	455.0
E	0.5	1.3	1.8	4.0	5.8
Total					
B	801,307.0	28,577.0	829,884.0	7,131.0	837,015.0
E	3,199.8	2,037.4	5,237.2	3,201.0	8,438.2

Source: *Employment Dynamics, by Industry Division, Canada, Provinces and Territories, 1986-1987.* Small Business and Special Surveys, Statistics Canada (27 June 89, File: 156864), Ottawa, p. 53-762.

Notes: All employees who were issued T4 slips, except those earning less than $500, are included.

Number of businesses corresponds to average labour units (ALUs). ALUs are calculated by dividing annual payroll for each province a business operates in by an appropriate estimate of average annual earnings, derived from Statistics Canada's Labour Division. The ALU concept converts a business's payroll artificially into the amount of labour units this payroll would typically represent if its labour force were paid the average earnings of its industry in that province.

The number of businesses per province add up to more than the totals in Appendix M. A business can be accounted for in more than one province.

1 Based on other criteria, in 1986 there were 304,000 small business owners in Ontario, and most of them—over 90%—had fewer than 20 employees. Eighty-two per cent of all net new jobs in Ontario came from small businesses. In one year over 90,000 new companies were formed in the province. See Ministry of Industry, Trade and Technology, *The State of Small Business*, Annual Report on Small Business in Ontario, Toronto, Ontario Government, 1986, p. 16.

2 In Quebec in 1987 there were almost 158,800 small or medium-sized firms out of a total of 159,800 active firms in all, i.e., 99.3% of the whole. See Ministère de l'Industrie et du Commerce, *Les PME au Québec, état de la situation 1987*, Québec, Gouvernement du Québec, 1987, p. 223-225. In this context, firms in the manufacturing sector with less than 200 employees are classified as SMEs, whereas in the other sectors, the upper limit is 100 employees.

The data for the following groups are excluded: Education, Health and Welfare Services, Religious Organizations, Public Administration.

Appendix E
Number of Employees by Number of Employees Category
for Each Industry Group
Canada, 1987

Industry Group '000s	Number of Employees Category					
	< 50	50-499	Total SME	500 +	Not Class.	Total
Manufacturing	407.4	645.6	1,053.0	1,046.8	1.1	2,100.9
Services	950.4	476.7	1,427.1	426.4		1,853.5
Retail Trade	665.5	260.5	926.0	543.0		1,469.0
Transportation, Communication, Utilities	143.6	122.1	265.7	528.4		794.1
Finance, Real Estate, Insurance	191.2	130.5	321.7	396.2		717.9
Wholesale Trade	304.5	193.9	498.4	115.9		614.3
Construction	353.6	134.6	488.2	40.7		528.9
Mining	33.4	45.8	79.2	113.7		192.9
Farming, Fishing, Hunting	106.6	13.7	120.3	2.9		123.2
	3,156.2	2,023.4	5,179.6	3,214.0	1.1	8,394.7
Not classified	41.9	6.0	47.9	1.0	-5.4	43.5
Total	3,198.1	2,029.4	5,227.5	3,215.0	-4.3	8,438.2

Source: *Employment Dynamics, By Major Industry Group, Canada and Provinces, 1986-1987.* Small Business and Special Surveys, Statistics Canada (27 June 1989, File: 156864), Ottawa, p. 53-104.

Notes: See Appendix D.

Appendix F
Number and Revenues of SMEs by Industry Group
Canada, for 1984 and 1986

Industry Group N: Businesses R: Revenues $000	1984	1986
Services		
N	186,635	215,999
R	36,425,761	49,039,206
Retail Trade		
N	185,744	201,563
R	80,644,923	120,323,957
Construction		
N	140,199	159,480
R	36,657,186	59,672,386
Transportation, Communication, Utilities		
N	77,708	85,037
R	15,799,947	23,154,444
Wholesale Trade		
N	58,503	65,962
R	59,851,311	100,107,462
Real Estate, Insurance		
N	50,818	61,923
R	11,878,736	15,876,298
Manufacturing		
N	53,965	59,166
R	54,528,110	86,206,123
Forestry		
N	12,435	15,855
R	2,504,323	3,670,060
Mining		
N	6,294	6,496
R	5,132,284	6,688,796
Total		
N	772,301	871,481
R	303,422,581	464,738,732

Source: Statistics Canada, *Small Business in Canada: A Statistical Profile, 1984-1986,* Cat. 61-231, April 1989, Ottawa, pages 17-56 (figures for 1984 medium-sized businesses were taken from 1982-1984 cat. 61-231, April 1987, pages 78-87).

Notes: See Appendix C.

Appendix G
Number of Businesses and Total Revenues
for All Businesses in Canada
Percentages for SMEs
Canada, for 1984 and 1986

	1984	1986
Total number of businesses	775,671	876,591
Number of SMEs	772,301	871,481
Percentage of SMEs	99.56%	99.4%
Revenue for all businesses	782,439,589	1,021,417,049
SME revenues	303,422,581	464,738,732
Percentage by SMEs	38.8%	45.5%

Source: Statistics Canada, *Small Business in Canada: A Statistical Profile, 1984-1986*, Cat. 61-231, April 1989, Ottawa, pages 16, 36, 47 (figures for 1984 medium-sized businesses were taken from 1982-1984, Cat. 61-231, April 1987, page 78).

Notes: See Appendix C.

Appendix H
Revenues for All Businesses and SMEs by Industry Group, Percentages for SMEs
Canada, for 1984 and 1986

Industry Group $000	1984			1986		
	Revenues for all businesses	SME Revenues	% SME	Revenues for all businesses	SME Revenues	% SME
Services	48,909,473	36,425,761	74.5%	64,265,802	49,039,206	76.3%
Retail Trade	133,814,728	80,644,923	60.2%	194,659,861	120,323,957	61.8%
Construction	48,642,011	36,657,186	75.3%	74,294,217	59,672,386	80.3%
Transportation Communication Utilities	80,002,826	15,799,947	19.7%	92,793,761	23,154,444	24.9%
Wholesale Trade	141,703,564	59,851,311	42.2%	210,328,741	100,107,462	47.6%
Real Estate Insurance	14,732,510	11,878,736	80.6%	20,287,631	15,876,298	78.2%
Manufacturing	265,898,375	54,528,110	20.5%	324,489,987	86,206,123	26.5%
Forestry	2,837,615	2,504,323	88.2%	4,266,512	3,670,060	86.0%
Mining	45,898,487	5,132,284	11.2%	36,030,537	6,688,796	18.6%
Total	782,439,589	303,422,581	38.8%	1,021,417,049	464,738,732	45.5%

Source: Statistics Canada, *Small Business in Canada: A Statistical Profile, 1984-1986*, Cat. 61-231, April 1989, Ottawa, pages 17-56 (figures for 1984 medium-sized and large businesses were taken from 1982-1984, Cat. 61-231, April 1987, pages 78-87).

Notes: See Appendix C.

Appendix I
Number of SMEs, Number of Employees in SMEs
for Each Province in Canada
Canada, 1978 and 1987

Province	1978		1987	
B: Number of Bus. E: Number of Emp. 000s	Number	%	Number	%
Ontario				
B	194,624.0	34.5	275,217.0	33.2
E	1,479.0	37.7	2,113.8	40.5
Quebec				
B	137,805.0	24.4	205,594.0	24.8
E	1,025.7	26.1	1,304.5	25.0
British Columbia				
B	78,487.0	13.9	111,635.0	13.5
E	453.1	11.6	610.0	11.6
Alberta				
B	58,486.0	10.4	90,304.0	10.9
E	410.6	10.4	493.4	9.4
Saskatchewan				
B	24,673.0	4.3	40,975.0	4.9
E	124.5	3.2	167.7	3.2
Manitoba				
B	23,286.0	4.1	31,818.0	3.8
E	153.6	3.9	183.1	3.5
Nova Scotia				
B	17,900.0	3.1	26,405.0	3.2
E	108.6	2.7	143.6	2.7
New Brunswick				
B	15,609.0	2.7	22,284.0	2.7
E	89.4	2.2	108.8	2.1
Newfoundland				
B	9,510.0	1.7	16.612.0	2.0
E	57.0	1.4	68.4	1.3
Prince Edward Island				
B	3,663.0	0.6	6,068.0	0.7
E	18.6	0.5	23.4	0.4

Northwest Territories				
B	1,034.0	0.2	1,467.0	0.2
E	8.5	0.2	11.5	0.2
Yukon				
B	862.0	0.1	1,178.0	0.1
E	4.7	0.1	7.2	0.1
Total				
B	565,939.0	100.0	829,557.0	100.0
E	3,933.3	100.0	5,235.4	100.0
Outside Canada				
B	274.0		327.0	
E	1.9		1.8	
Total				
B	566,213.0		829,884.0	
E	3,935.2		5,237.2	

Source: *Employment Dynamics, By Major Industry Group, Canada and Provinces,* Small Business and Special Surveys. Statistics Canada, Ottawa. Data for 1978 from report 1978-1987, p. 1-712, Data for 1987 from report 1986-87, p. 53-762 (27 June 1989, File: 156864), Ottawa.

Notes: See Appendix D.

Appendix J
Number of Employees in SMEs
by Industry Group
Canada, for 1978 and 1987

Industry Group ('000s)	1978	1987
Manufacturing	910.4	1,053.0
Services	930.3	1,427.1
Retail Trade	657.5	926.0
Transportation, Communication, Utilities	223.8	265.7
Finance, Real Estate, Insurance	234.9	321.7
Wholesale Trade	422.5	498.4
Construction	385.0	488.2
Mining	55.8	79.2
Farming, Forestry, Fishing, Hunting	76.9	120.3
Total	3,897.1	5,179.6
Not Classified		47.9
		5,227.5
Not Classified	38.1	9.7
Total	3,935.2	5,237.2

Source: *Employment Dynamics, By Major Industry Group, Canada and Provinces.* Small Business and Special Surveys. Ottawa, Statistics Canada. Data for 1978 from report 1978-1979, p. 1-52. Data for 1987 from report 1986-1987, p. 53-104, (27 June 1989, File: 156864).

Notes: See Appendix D.

Appendix K
Total Number of Employees in All Firms by Industry Group, Percentage for SMEs
Canada, for 1978 and 1987

Industry Group	1978			1987		
000s	Total Employees	Employees in SMEs	% SME	Total Employees	Employees in SMEs	% SME
Services	1,216.6	930.3	76.5	1,853.5	1,427.1	77.0
Manufacturing	2,045.2	910.4	44.5	2,100.9	1,053.0	50.1
Retail Trade	1,080.4	657.5	61.0	1,469.0	926.0	63.0
Transportation, Communication, Utilities	872.1	223.8	25.7	794.1	265.7	33.4
Finance, Real Estate, Insurance	564.3	234.9	41.6	717.9	321.7	44.8
Wholesale Trade	509.6	422.5	82.9	614.3	498.4	81.1
Construction	446.9	385.0	86.1	528.9	488.2	92.3
Mining	178.7	55.8	31.2	192.9	79.2	41.0
Farming, Forestry, Fishing, Hunting	85.1	76.9	90.4	123.2	120.3	97.6
	6,998.9	3,897.1	55.7	8,394.7	5,179.6	61.7
Not Classified				43.5	47.9	
				8,438.2	5,227.5	
Not Classified	20.5	38.1		-	9.7	
Total	7,019.4	3,935.2		8,438.2	5,237.2	

Source: See Appendix J.

Notes: See Appendix D.

Appendix L
Changes in Number of Employees
(Excluding Public Administration in General)
for SMEs and Large Firms
Canada, from 1978 to 1987

	Number of Employees (000s)		
	< 500	500 +	Total
Year 1978	3,897.1	3,101.8	6,998.9
Year 1987	5,179.6	3,215.1	8,394.7
Net Change	1,282.5	113.3	1,395.8

Source: See Appendix J.

Appendix M
Total Number and Percentage of Businesses
(Excluding Public Administration in General)
by Category of Number of Employees
Canada, for 1978 and 1987

Number of Employees Category	1978		1987	
	Number of Businesses	%	Number of Businesses	%
< 50	531,258	97.2	787,344	97.7
50-99	8,106	1.5	10,075	1.2
100-499	5,858	1.1	6,943	0.9
Total SME	545,222	99.8	804,362	99.8
500 +	1,308	0.2	1,417	0.2
Total	546,530	100.0	805,779	100.0

Source: *Employment Dynamics, by Major Industry Group, Canada and Provinces*, Small Business and Special Surveys. Statistics Canada, Ottawa. Data for 1978 from report 1978-1987, p. 1, 42-44, 50-52. Data for 1987 from report 1986-1987, p. 53, 94-96, 102-104. (27 June 1989, File: 156864).

Notes: See Appendix D.

It should be noted here that the number of employees determines the category to which the firm belongs. Any reader wanting more detailed information on the meaning of these data can consult the appendices to the official published report.

Appendix N
Types of Strategic Partnerships

Type	Activity
Subcontracting	It usually involves more than just buying supplies from another firm. It usually involves working closely on detailed specifications for a complex product.
Licensing	This included permission to manufacture a product under license, to distribute a product and to include a product, such as a micro chip, in another firm's design.
Joint Venture	These involved the creation of a third firm to manufacture or market a product which had been developed by the entrepreneurial firm and would be marketed by the larger firm. Equity was usually shared by the partners.
Strategic Alliance	This arrangement is essentially a joint venture without the creation of a third firm and no equity is involved.
Consortium	This was usually a group of firms joining together in a buying group to purchase components or equipment, which they mutually share.
Acquisition	This usually involves a larger firm acquiring a smaller firm to obtain entrepreneurial skills and technology, often with a contract for the owner(s) to stay with the acquired firm.

From: R.M. Knight, "Strategic Partnership Alliances for Entrepreneurial Firms," *Entrepreneurship into the '90s,* National Centre for Management Research and Development, The University of Western Ontario, June 1989, p. 28.

This article describes the use of cooperative agreements called Strategic Partnerships or Strategic Alliances by small, innovative firms. These firms often lack the management skills and other resources to successfully commercialize their innovations. Large corporations, on the other hand, often lack the entrepreneurial talents to generate innovations to expand their product lines, using their superior resources, such as funds, established manufacturing facilities, distribution channels and general management skills. Examples of cooperative agreements between such firms are discussed and a typology of such agreements is suggested in the article.

Appendix O
Sources of Information
for Strategic Management

• The vast network of government agencies that distributes strategically valuable information, from Statistics Canada to provincial agencies specialized in credit or financing.

• Industrial organizations and associations where the cost of membership is often well worth the data they collect on markets, contracts, legislation and other subjects.

• Meetings of Chambers of Commerce and Employers' Associations, where spokesmen from various milieus (business, politics, research) sometimes pass on valuable information and where it is easy to establish profitable contacts.

• Enterprise advisers (accountants, lawyers, brokers, bankers) who, thanks to their contact with a wide range of individuals and organizations, can often be a mine of information

• The most valuable sources for SMEs are those nearest to them: suppliers, customers and a usually fairly limited number of public or community institutions, and not forgetting the contact the owner-manager has with his own employees, whose knowledge is sometimes surprising.

From: "Adapting Strategy Models for Small and Medium Sized Enterprises," by R.L. Crawford and W.D. Taylor, Faculty of Commerce and Administration, Concordia University, Montreal, 1985.

Appendix P
Business Intelligence

BOSS

The Business Opportunities Sourcing System is a computerized data bank operated by ISTC in cooperation with participating provincial governments. It contains information on Canadian manufacturing and service companies. Used by Canadian Trade Commissioners abroad, BOSS is also available to domestic users wishing to locate appropriate Canadian suppliers, obtain market intelligence, or identify market opportunities. BOSS now includes more than 25,000 companies and 6,500 active users.

Market Intelligence

The Market Intelligence service provides Canadian business with detailed market information on a product-specific basis. The market information currently focuses on, but is not restricted to, information on imports into Canada. This not only offers information about a significant portion of the Canadian market, it is also an indicator of an internationally competitive product mix. Over the past few years, reports have been expanded to include Canadian and North American markets. The service has moved away from import substitution and toward provision of intelligence that will assist in exploitation of domestic, export, technology transfer, and new manufacturing investment opportunities. Two-thirds of the clientele for this service consist of small business.

Interfirm Comparisons

Interfirm Comparisons support industry's efforts to enhance competitiveness through assessment of the relative performance of firms manufacturing the same type of product or engaged in a similar type of activity. The program helps businesses improve productivity and profitability by providing them with analyses of their strengths and weaknesses in comparison to other firms in the same sector. The majority of the firms involved in this program are small businesses.

Taken from Ministry of Industry, Science and Technology, *Small Business in Canada, Growing to Meet Tomorrow,* A report by the Entrepreneurship and Small Business Office, Ottawa, 1989, p. 64.

Appendix Q
Unpublished Survey of Approximately 100 Chief Executives of Quebec SMEs listed on the Stock Exchange

The six most significant changes in SMEs that have gone public (in order of importance given to each category)

1. Firm's status: "Improvement of the firm's image with suppliers, customers and others."
2. Firm's structure: "Increase in the management function in general."
3. Communications in general: "Increased communication within the firm."
4. Decision-making: "External pressure for short-term profitability."
5. The Chief Executive Officer as an individual: "More personal pride."
6. Labour relations: "The firm's employees feel more strongly that they belong."

The changes experienced that were considered the most positive

- "Improvement of the firm's image with suppliers, customers and others."
- "Easier to obtain external financing."
- "External assessment of the firm through the value of its shares on the stock market."
- "The setting up of a communications or public relations department."
- "More personal pride." (CEO)
- "Greater professional recognition." (CEO)
- "Greater interest in work." (CEO)
- "Higher social status." (CEO)
- "Improved working climate."
- "Increased worker productivity."
- "Drop in employee turnover."

The changes experienced that were considered the most negative

- "Feeling of powerlessness as far as the market value of the firm is concerned on the stock market."
- "Less availability for the family." (CEO)
- "Less availability for employees." (CEO)
- "Higher employee demands for salaries and social benefits."
- "Heavier management load, that is, increased paperwork, reports of all kinds, and so on."

Drawn from: M. Vallières, Compte rendu de l'étude de J. Desroches, A. Naciri, G. Théberge, sur la PME et le financement public au Québec, published in *Les Affaires*, 26 September 1987, p. 2-3 (our translation).

BIBLIOGRAPHY

C.B. MEDIA LTD., *Canadian Business,* Toronto, (Vol. 58, No. 9, September 1985; Vol. 59, No. 7, July 1986; Vol.60, No. 7, July 1987, No. 8, August 1987).

CARRIERE, J.B., "Strategic Vision: An Empirical Study," Presentation at the VIth Annual Conference of the International Council for Small Business – Canada (ICSB), *Entrepreneurship and Small Business: Emerging Trends on the Canadian Scene,* Windsor, Ont., November 1989.

CHAUSSÉ, R., *La gestion de l'innovation dans la PME,* Chicoutimi, Gaëtan Morin, 1987, 203p.

CHOQUETTE, C. and J. BRUNELLE, *Le management de la PME,* St-Jean-sur-Richelieu, Édition Bo-Pré, 1985, 347 p.

CORPORATION PROFESSIONNELLE DES COMPTABLES EN MANAGEMENT, *Guerriers de l'émergence,* Montréal, Québec/Amérique, 1986, 482 p.

D'AMBOISE, G, Y. GASSE and R. DAINOW, *The Smaller Independent Manufacturer: 12 Quebec Case Studies,* Montreal, The Institute for Research on Public Policy, 1986, 201 p.

DESJARDINS, C., *La PME au Québec, situation et problèmes,* Québec, Ministère de l'Industrie et du Commerce, 1977, 69 p.

FILION, L.J., "Vision and Relations: Elements for an Entrepreneurial Metamodel," *International Small Business Journal*, Vol. 9, No. 2, January 1991.

FORTIN, P.A., *Devenez entrepreneur. Pour un Québec plus entrepreneurial.* Québec, Les Presses de l'Université Laval, 1986, 302 p.

FRASER, M., *Québec Inc. Les Québécois prennent d'assaut le monde des affaires*, Montréal, Les Éditions de l'Homme, 1987, 305 p.

FRY, J.N., *Strategic Analysis and Action*, Scarborough, Prentice-Hall Canada Inc., 1986, 329 p.

FUHRMAN, P.H., *Business in the Canadian Environment*, Scarborough, Prentice-Hall Canada Inc., 1982, 550 p.

GAGNON, J.H., *La PME face à la crise financière*, Montréal, Les Éditions Agence d'Arc, 1983, 180 p.

GASSE, Y. et al., *De la transmissibilité des pratiques de management: France-Canada*, Sherbrooke, Faculté d'administration, University of Sherbrooke, 1977, 174 p.

GOULD, A., *The New Entrepreneurs, 80 Canadian Success Stories*, Toronto, McClelland and Stewart-Bantam Ltd., 1986, 387 p.

GRAY, D.A. and D.L. GRAY, *The Complete Canadian Small Business Guide*, McGraw-Hill Ryerson, Toronto, 1988, 561 p.

GROUPEMENT QUÉBÉCOIS D'ENTREPRISES, *Un conseil d'administration au service du chef d'entreprise*, Drummondville, G.Q.E. Inc., 1987, 217 p.

INTERNATIONAL COUNCIL FOR SMALL BUSINESS - CANADA, *Journal of Small Business and Entrepreneurship*, Toronto, Vol. 5, No. 5, Summer 1988.

JULIEN, P.A., J. CHICHA and A. JOYAL, *La PME dans un monde en mutation*, Sillery, Les Presses de l'Université du Québec, 1986, 441 p.

JULIEN, P.A. and B. MOREL, *La belle entreprise, La revanche des PME en France et au Québec*, Montréal, Boréal Express, 1986, 237 p.

KAO, R.W., *Small Business Management: A Strategic Emphasis*, Toronto, Holt, Rinehart and Winston of Canada, 1981, 293 p.

KAO, R.W. and R.M. KNIGHT, *Entrepreneurship and New Venture Management, Readings and Cases*, Scarborough, Prentice-Hall Canada Inc., 1987, 334 p.

KNIGHT, R.M., *Small Business Management in Canada: Text and Cases*, Toronto, McGraw-Hill Ryerson Ltd., 1981, 216 p.

KUBICEK, T. and I. FRASER, *Managing Canadian Business - A Functional Approach*, Scarborough, Prentice-Hall Canada Inc., 1983, 462 p.

LAROCHE, G., *Petites et moyennes entreprises au Québec: organisation, économique, croissance de l'emploi et qualité du travail*, Institut international d'études sociales, Organisation Internationale du Travail, Genève, 1989, 84 p.

LES PRODUCTIONS PME, *Le Magazine PME*, Montréal, Vol. II, No. 7, November 1986; Vol. III, No. 2, March 1987, No. 3, April 1987, No. 5, June 1987.

MINISTERE DE L'INDUSTRIE ET DU COMMERCE, *The State of Small and Medium-Sized Business in Quebec*, Report by the Gouvernement du Québec, 1987, 306 p.

MINISTERE DE L'INDUSTRIE, DU COMMERCE ET DE LA TECHNOLOGIE, *Les PME au Québec*, État de la situation 1988, Québec, Gouvernement du Québec, 1988, 141 p.

MINISTRY OF INDUSTRY, COMMERCE AND TECHNOLOGY, *The State of Small Business*, Annual Report on Small Business in Ontario, Toronto, Ontario Government, 1986, 127 p., 1987, 164 p.

PERREAULT, Y.G. and P. DELL'ANIELLO, *Comment la PME peut survivre aux années 80*, Montréal, Programme formation, Chaire Macdonald, UQAM, 1982, 246 p.

PETERSON, R., *Small Business, Building a Balanced Economy*, Erin, Porcépic Press Ltd., 1977, 192 p.

PETROF, J. et al., *Small Business Management: Concepts and Techniques for Improving Decisions*, Toronto, McGraw-Hill Book Company, 1972, 410 p.

RAYMOND, L., *Validité des systèmes d'information dans les PME, analyse et perspectives*, Québec, Institute for Research on Public Policy, Les Presses de l'Université Laval, 1987, 124 p.

RAYMOND, L., S. RIVARD and F. BERGERON, *L'informatisation dans les PME, douze cas types*, Québec, Institute for Research on Public Policy, Les Presses de l'Université Laval, 1988, 268 p.

ROBIDOUX, J., *Les crises administratives dans les PME en croissance*, Chicoutimi, Gaëtan Morin, 1980, 125 p.

SAINT-PIERRE, J. and J.M. SURET, *Endettement de la PME: état de la situation et rôle de la fiscalité*, Montréal, Institute for Research on Public Policy, 1987, 155 p.

TARRAB, G. and C. SIMARD, *Une gestion au féminin, nouvelles réalités*, Boucherville, Éditions S. Vermette Inc., 1986, 263 p.

TOULOUSE, J.M., *L'entrepreneurship au Québec*, Montréal, H.E.C.-Fides, 1979, 139 p.

UNIVERSITÉ DU QUÉBEC, *Revue de gestion des petites et moyennes organisations, P.M.O.*, Chicoutimi, Département des sciences économiques et administratives, Université du Québec à Chicoutimi, Presses de l'Université du Québec, Vol. 3, No. 2, 1988.